D1543882

THE COOPER UNION   STUDE

THIS BOOK I

Jn 12 '43

APR 1 7 19

JUL 2

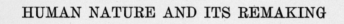

HUMAN NATURE AND ITS REMAKING

HUMAN NATURE AND ITS REMAKING

WILLIAM ERNEST HOCKING
PROFESSOR OF PHILOSOPHY IN HARVARD UNIVERSITY

NEW HAVEN
YALE UNIVERSITY PRESS
LONDON : HUMPHREY MILFORD : OXFORD UNIVERSITY PRESS

B
945
.H6   H
H8   19
       A685H

Copyright, 1918, 1923, by Yale University Press.

First published, May, 1918.
New and Revised Edition, 1923.
New Printing with Additions, August, 1929.
Reprinted, March, 1932.
Reprinted, October, 1934.
Reprinted, March, 1938.

WITHDRAWN FROM
COOPER UNION LIBRARY

All rights reserved. This book may not be reproduced, in whole or in part, in any form (except by reviewers for the public press), without written permission from the publishers.

FEB 15 1943
122269
Morris K. Jesup &
Oswald Ottendorfer
Book Funds

TO
GEORGE HERBERT PALMER
SKILLED INTERPRETER OF
HUMAN NATURE
TEACHER AND FRIEND

PREFACE

SINCE books are no longer supposed, whether by author or public, to contain the final and finished truth, no book need apologize for being unripe. One's hope is, not to close discussion, but to open it. What I have here aimed to do is the work rather of the quarryman with his blasting powder than of the sculptor with his chisel.

Not that the quarry of human nature is a new one. But that we are only beginning to learn the technique of dealing with the larger masses. Few of us, I dare say, are satisfied with the degree of clarity we have reached about the rights of the primitive impulses,—of the instincts of pugnacity, sex, acquisition, etc.,—as compared with the claims of social orders such as we see dissolving before our eyes, or of super-social orders, of art and religion. These and other agencies attempt to transform the original material of human nature; human nature resists the remaking process; the groping effort of mutual adjustment has continued throughout the length of history, has made the chief theme of history; we still seek the broader principles which govern the process, call it what you will,—the process of remaking, of educating, of civilizing, of converting or of saving the human being. Quest of such principles is the object of this present essay.

No doubt, we have always had our authorities ready to spare us the trouble of search, ready to settle *ex cathedra* what human nature is and ought to become. And presumably we have always had a party of revolt against authority, convention, and the like, in the name of what is 'natural,'—a revolt which has commonly been as dogmatic and intuitional as the authority itself.

But the revolt of today is no longer either impressionistic or sporadic. It is psychological, economic, political:—and it is general. The explosive forces of self-assertion which have finally burst their bounds in the political life of Central Europe have their seat in a widespread spiritual rebellion, a critical impatience of 'established' sentiments and respectabilities, a deliberate philosophic rejection not more of Hague Conventions than of other conventions, a drastic judgment of *non-reality* upon the pieties of Christendom.

This rebellion would hardly have become so widespread or so disastrous if it were wholly without ground. It indicates that our moral idealisms like our metaphysical idealisms have been taking their task too complacently. Our Western world has adhered to standards with which it has never supposed its practice to be in accord; but heaving a resigned sigh over the erring tendencies of human nature, it has offered to these standards that 'of course' variety of homage which is the beginning of mental and moral coma. By labelling these standards 'ideals' it has rendered them innocuous while maintaining the profession of deference: an 'ideal' has been taken as something which everybody is expected to honor and nobody is expected to attain.

It is just these ideals that are now violently challenged, and the challenge is salutary. It is precisely the so-called Christian world which, having gone morally to sleep, is now put to a fight for life with the men who persist in reducing their standards to the level of common practice, in reaching their code of behavior from below upward, not from above downward, in keeping their 'ideals' close to the earth or at least in discernible working connection with the earth. Their creed we may name *moral realism;* and the craving for an ingredient of moral realism in our philosophy seems to me a justified hunger of the age. The whole set of realistic upheavals, Nietzscheian, neo-Machiavellian, Syndicalistic, Freudian, and other, crowd forward with doctrines about human nature and its destiny which at least have life in them. Whatever else they contain, unsound or sinister, they contain Thought: and this thought must be met on its own ground. The next step, whether in social philosophy, or in education, or in ethics, requires an understanding between whatever valid elements moral realism may contain and the valid elements of the challenged tradition.

We find our initial common ground with this realism by accepting, for the purposes of the argument, the picture of original human nature as a group of instincts.

With this starting joint, the usual realistic assumption is that human life consists in trying to get what

these instincts want. Mankind's persistent concern
for food, adornment, property, mates, children, political activity, etc., is supposed to be explained by the
fact that his instincts confer value on these objects.
By shaping our 'values,' instinct becomes the shaper
of life. And the first and main business of the science
of living would be to set up an authentic and proportionate list of the instincts proper to man.

Then every social order, every moral or economic
code, every standard of living would be judged by the
satisfaction it could promise to the chorus of innate
hungers and impulses thus revealed.

This view is simple, attractive,—and profoundly untrue to experience. The trouble is that no one can tell
by identifying and naming an instinct what will satisfy
it. Certainly we cannot take the biological function
of an instinct as a sufficient account of what that instinct means to a human being—as if hunger held the
conscious purpose of building the body, or love were
an aim to continue the species. The word 'instinct'
has no magic to annul the obvious truth that satisfaction is a state of *mind,* nor to evade the long labor of
experience in determining what can satisfy a mind.
Conscious life is engaged quite as much in *trying to
find out what* it wants as in trying to get it.

The truth is, *instinct requires interpretation.* We
can set up a usable measure of social justice and the
like only if we can find something like a true interpretation of instinct, or of the will as a whole. Instinct by itself has no claims, because it has no head;

it cannot so much as say what it wants except through
an interpreter.

Our essay becomes, accordingly, an experiment in
interpretation. And there are various agencies which
offer aid in the undertaking. In the person of parent,
pedagog, lawmaker, society stands ready to inform the
individual through its discipline, "This is what you
want,—not that," and to insist on his choosing the
alleged better part. All the usual processes of training or remaking purport to be at the same time works
of interpretation: they profess to bring to light a 'real'
will, as contrasted with an apparent will, and so to
introduce human nature to its own meaning.

But if society (as not a few of our social philosophers believe) is the only or final interpreter of human
nature, human nature is helpless as against society.
Our individualisms, our democracies, with their brave
claims in behalf of the human unit, have no case.
'Socialization' is the last word in human development;
and society is always right.

If we refuse, as we do, to accept this conclusion, the
alternative is to find some way, in independence of
'society,' to an objectively valid interpretation of the
human will. The case of all liberalism, of all reform,
of every criticism and likewise of every defence of any
social régime, must rest in the last analysis upon the
discovery, or the assumption, of such a 'true' interpretation. And my hope in this essay is that we may
chart the way to it, and thus sketch the valid basis of
an individualistic theory of society.

We are not, of course, presuming that mankind has ever, in practice, been without such a standard. For mankind has always had a religion, and it has been one of the historic functions of religion to keep men in mind of the goal of their own wills. And in so far as it has done its work well, religion has in fact set men free from the domination of unjust social and political constraints. The religious consciousness has apprised human nature of its 'rights'—not merely of its claims—and has become the source of whatever is now solid in our democracies.

And even if the social order were perfectly just in its arrangements, freedom would still require the fulfilment of this religious function. For a man is not free unless he is delivered from persistent sidelong anxiety about his immediate effectiveness, from servitude to an incalculable if not whimsical human flux. He is free only if he can mentally direct all his work to a constant and absolute judgment, address his daily labor, if you like, to God, build his houses to God and not to men, write his books to God, in the State serve his God only, love his God in the family, and fight against the (incarnate) devil and the devil alone. Kepler's famous words at the end of his preface to the Weltharmonik are the words of the free man in this sense:

Here I cast the die, and write a book to be read whether by contemporaries or by posterity, I care not. I can wait for readers thousands of years, seeing that God waited six thousand years for someone to contemplate his work.

An age of competition, like our own, unless it is

something else than competitive, cannot be a free age, however democratic in structure, because its chief concerns are lateral. To the competitive elements in our own social order we owe much:—an impersonal estimate of worth in terms of efficiency which we shall not surrender, a taste and technique for severe self-measurement, incredible finesse in the discrimination and mounting of individual talents. But we owe to it also an over-development of the invidious comparative eye, a trend of attention fascinated by the powers, perquisites, and opinions of the immediate neighbors. The eternal standard is obscured: hence we do nothing well; we lack sincerity and simplicity; we are suspicious, disunited, flabby; we do not find ourselves; we are not free. Unless we can recover a working hold on some kind of religious innervation, our democracy will shortly contain little that is worthy to survive.

But it is one of the permanent achievements of our time that we recognize no antagonism between the work of thought and the voice of religious intuition. We must perpetually regain our right to an absolute object through the labor of reflection,—in our own case, the labor of interpretation.

In the preparation of this book, I have accumulated many personal obligations, quite apart from the scientific debts acknowledged at various points in the argument. And beside these, there is an obligation of a less personal character though not less real: that, namely, to the liberal and heartening spirit of the Yale community. Those who heard the lectures on which

these pages were originally based, lectures on the
Nathaniel Taylor foundation given in 1916 before the
School of Religion of Yale University, will hardly
recognize them in their present form. But the incen-
tive is theirs; and if the idea has grown, I trust it is
by way of doing greater justice to the original theme.

W. E. H.

Cambridge, March, 1918.

NOTE TO SECOND EDITION

RESETTING of the type for this book gives a welcome
opportunity to take account of recent discussions of
the place of instinct in human nature, of certain theoretical aspects of the Freudian views, and of Professor
Dewey's notable book on *Human Nature and Conduct*.
The changes made affect chiefly Parts I, II and IV. I
owe to the courtesy of the *Journal of Abnormal Psychology and Social Psychology* permission to reprint
(as Appendix I) an article on the ''Conception of Instinct'' which appeared in 1921.

W. E. H.

Greensboro, August, 1923.

CONTENTS

Sin cannot be causally explained; it is not to be referred
to the 'stronger motive,' nor to the 'curve of learning'; but
the conditions may be described which favor the above-
mentioned blindness, namely, the existence of moral dilemmas. Various dilemmas described. The complete moral
motive combines the ruing of evil with the attraction of
good.

Sin as deed cannot be original. But beside the moral act,
there is a moral status; and if the holy will is a status to be
acquired, it is presumably not inborn; a moral status may
always be regarded as a matter of fact, and as such neither
to be punished nor rewarded; it becomes a corresponding
question of fact whether such status has metaphysical im-
plications. The metaphysical assertion, sin involves finitude
or mortality, a legitimate addition to the moral motive, if
true.

PART IV

EXPERIENCE

Original human nature always a factor in remaking human
nature: ultimately nothing can change a will but itself.
But outer facts must furnish data and incentives: and the
co-operation of outer and inner factors of change is 'experience.' We cannot distinguish between social and individual experience; but we can distinguish between free experience and experience under social constraint.

Experience has (among other tasks) to effect the transformation of general dispositions into individual habits
which interpret these dispositions; the work of intelligence,
curiosity, and play; experience in active form as experimentation.

Pleasure and pain, the universal instruments of experience,
produce different results upon different types of mind; in

the human being, pain leads to discrimination and thought, rather than to blank inhibition. Human experience with any given instinct thus takes the form of a series of hypotheses as to what it wants, constituting a more or less coherent argument, guided chiefly by the 'mental after-image'; this argument might reasonably be called the 'dialectic' of the will.

What pugnacity wants, described in a typical series of hypotheses: destruction, revenge, punishment, cure; this development would probably take place were there no social constraint upon the expression of pugnacity. The basis of individualism in social theory; the will has a bent of its own which is not due to custom.

PART V

SOCIETY

The presumption that social pressure warps human nature; and the counter presumption that conventions have a meaning.

Normally, social interference facilitates, and carries on farther in the same direction, the work of individual experience,—and, for that matter, of organic evolution as a whole; as instances: 'prolonging the vestibule of satisfaction,' as seen in the case of hunger and sex; the widening of the horizon of action together with increasing discrimination or restriction of objects dealt with. Thus, social action is not primarily repressive; but there are three ways in particular in which it becomes so. These are to be dealt with in order.

Most ideals are colored by the selfish wishes of those who promulgate them; but not even the self-interest of society as a whole takes precedence of the interest of its members.

Here is stated an individualistic theory of 'right'; and the *postulate* is deduced with which society must comply if its ideals are to be right ideals. Various social arrangements which help to secure this condition: among others, the natural function of the Recommender; and the conflict of abstract ideals.

When we consider not ideals, but the material basis of all instinct-satisfactions, it is obvious that social life necessarily requires sacrifice, and that the question of the social contract—is society worth the sacrifice?—is not fanciful. The condition under which a social life can be free, or worth its cost, stated in a *second postulate:* it must be possible to subordinate competitive interests to non-competitive interests; this postulate can be complied with only through the existence of the political State: the existence of the State, therefore, is something which men necessarily (hence unanimously) will.

No institutions wholly comply, and perhaps none can wholly comply, with the foregoing demands: it does not at once follow that they should be abolished. It is to be considered that part of the maladaptation, so far as it comes to consciousness, is an incident of progress itself; and that human nature is adapted to maladaptation, provided that it can regard all existing misfit as grist for its will to power. The highest social expression of the will to power is found in the changing of institutions; institutions must be condemned, not if evil exists in them; but if it *persists.* Our *third postulate* is that institutions shall make institutional provision for change, as their unfitness is felt and diagnosed; but since it is the wish of every radical and experimentalist that something be established, he has an inalienable interest in conservation. Hence a *fourth postulate:* conserving force must be proportionate to certainty.

The activity of educating has an instinctive basis and function; it requires social self-consciousness and self-criticism. It is commonly regarded as a sort of social reproduction; but it must provide for growth beyond the type; yet the process of education is such that the type is transmitted;

the first business of education is to bring a will into existence; this can be done only be exposing all instincts to
their appropriate stimuli. Education is, first of all, *exposure;* and this exposure can only be effected by appre-
ciators of the goods in question. The exposure should be
proportionate; various problems considered; education of
thought; of the will to power. Problems of adolescence;
delay in acquisition and in sex-expression; sublimation in
the planning-instinct, and in world-building; education in
originality; the self-elimination of society.

He who would destroy a too conservative social structure
must assure himself (1) whether it has the good will to
change; and, if not, (2) whether he can have faith in its
possible good will. Society has the same two questions to
answer regarding the rebel. There can be no legal right of
rebellion; but this does not decide whether rebellion may
be right.

Punishment consists in making the external status correspond to the internal status. The criminal must be distinguished from the rebel; he must be treated as possible rebel
and as possible citizen. The State has no choice but to
punish; yet punishment, administered by an imperfect
State, contains self-defeating elements; the history of criminal procedure shows the various attempts of society to escape this dilemma; but their chief success, so far, is in
localizing the injury. The restoration of the criminal to
citizenship must be the work of forces not contained in
the State per se; in punishing, as in educating, society depends for its success on agencies beyond its own border.

PART VI

ART AND RELIGION

Can the distinction between the work of society and the
work of religion in remaking human nature be maintained?
The historical differentiation has apparently ended in eliminating the distinct Vox Dei as useless; reasons for doubting this result; and proposal of a method for discriminating the work of society from that of further factors.

objective media; it intends to have the force not of law, but of convincing language,—a freer development of law; beginning as an effort to define, and thus win power over the object of common desire—assuming an ascendency over the minds of the desirers—it finds a secondary satisfaction in creating the image of that object; it thus discovers a field of objects which can be possessed in no other way than by thus reproducing them; these objects are called 'beautiful'; art becomes especially identified with the activity of possessing the beautiful, in which all socially interested activity is suspended; and its specific passion may supersede all social passions; direct and indirect effect of art on the shaping of human instincts: the inadequacy of art.

Religion seems left empty by the removal of law, science, art, etc.; but it still claims a positive content, makes superlative claims for it, and has found devotees who declare its passion supreme over others; we cannot understand this fact if we regard the ascetic as an anomalous and parasitic denier of all social value; it can only be understood through the psychological necessity that all social values, together with those of law and art, be preserved by an alternation between attending to them and turning away from them to their source. Asceticism thus may be, and historically has been, an assertion of the will to power; but it has been a partial and imperfect satisfaction, and must give way to, or be included within, a more concrete type of religion.

PART VII

CHRISTIANITY

The practical injunctions of Christianity are directed toward the feelings, and thus concern the theory of human instinct; but there seems to be a psychological ineptitude in a command to 'love'; hence these injunctions are commonly reinterpreted in terms of behavior; there are reasons, however, for supposing that Christianity may have meant what it says.

the fact, not perceived by Buddhism, that ambition is the
essence of religion; it undertook, as its chief positive appeal to human nature, to swing all energies into the channel
of spreading the 'Kingdom of Heaven,' an interest which,
in personal form, becomes the 'passion for souls,' the most
characteristic product of Christianity; it exists in many
recognizable forms; in this point, the meanings of all the
instincts converge; and there is reason to regard it as the
ultimate transformation of the will to power.

It is precisely in this form of the ideal—that of the will to
save men—that the profoundest objection makes itself felt;
the ideal is fundamentally presumptuous, and becomes increasingly impossible to contemporary moral diffidence and
modest self-consciousness; this fact, however, is an additional reason for regarding it correct as an interpretation
of Christianity; for this was the ground for the hostility
provoked by the doctrine in its early days; and the moral
difficulty of any ideal is hardly a final refutation of it;
what we require of Christianity is that it be responsible for
showing how the ideal is possible.

The 'essence' of any religion is to be found not in its
ethical demand upon human nature, but in its answer to the
question stated: How is it possible? The demands of Christianity create a logical dilemma; the phenomenon of participation, by any given self, in the properties of the object
known, may lead to a solution, provided that the object
known can be an absolute or divine object, having the qualities and powers which the individual cannot claim for himself; the objection to the phrase "the will to power" admitted, and the term rendered finally harmless; the ideal
of 'humility'; but the difficulty still remains that the individual, as imperfect, cannot perceive the divine object.

The logical situation resumed; the idea of salvation from
outside; in what sense obnoxious, and in what sense reasonable; the kind of theology by which Christianity meets
the situation; its large demands on belief; probability in
metaphysics out of place.

Whether the ultimate reality of the world is such as Christianity affirms it to be is a question of fact; and this question cannot be completely settled by philosophical argument; an act of personal discovery or *recognition* is called for. Recognition is a part of the operation of every instinct; as the food-getting instinct recognizes objects which may serve as food, so the total instinct of man will recognize what it needs in the world of metaphysical reality, if what it needs exists there; conversely, metaphysical 'findings' are not indifferent theories, but are matters of life and death for the human instincts; they form part of the circuit of instinctive life; hence the beliefs men have long held are to some extent corroborated by the fact that men have lived by them; but in any actual belief, imagination may mingle with experienced fact in unknown proportions; our beliefs must be perpetually revised by the co-operation of the mystic and the critic; meantime some guide to individual judgment may be had by historical analysis, enquiring what elements of existing beliefs have been essential to those developments of instinct which give our civilization its characteristic qualities. Here follows a rough sketch of such an analysis; it appears that the belief in a quasi-maternal relation of the world to human individuals, a belief partly coincident with the metaphysics of Christianity, has been at the basis of our civilization; and this belief, in turn, might plausibly be explained as merely subjective or pragmatic; objective support for the belief in question, men have supposed themselves to find in the historical process itself, particularly in those *experimental sacrifices* which, though they were deeds of individual men, have seemed to carry an over-individual and authoritative significance. Our argument ends in pointing out the alternatives presented to individual determination; a negation of the characteristic metaphysics of Christianity would not necessarily destroy human happiness: it would discountenance only the highest aspiration, and would render futile only the best of the past.

Cooper Union Library

PART I

ORIENTATION

Argument

WHAT is human nature? What do we want to make of it? What can be made of it? What will satisfy it,—or in other words, what constitutes human happiness?

No animal but man asks questions of this sort about himself. Animals take themselves for granted; they make changes in their physical habitat,—they do not deliberately try to change themselves. The human creature, being highly self-conscious, enjoys himself and criticises himself, tries, eventually, to make himself over.

Animals, no doubt, react to their neighbors and to their obstreperous young, and in so doing alter their habits. It is not at all likely that they are trying to *improve* them; they are dealing with specific situations in a pragmatic manner; the generalities, like habit and character, are taken care of by nature. But the human being sets up a process of 'education.' And he sets up standards, 'ideals,' which apply to everybody including himself, describing not alone what he ought to do but also what he ought to be. He coins his admirations into laws for his own inner man.

Thereby, no doubt, he lays up for himself much unhappiness such as animals are spared. He is strangely capable of thinking out an ideal, or imagining one, which it either wracks him to attain or leaves him wretched and self-accusing to fail of. He may turn to envy the animals that feel no remorse for what they do nor guilt for what they are. His religions, as a rule, have widened the gulf between what he thinks he should be and what he is. It belongs to the nature of an ideal to be difficult, and at the same time inexorable.

But after much experience of failure and moral suffering there is bound to come an era of human courage, a challenge of the authority of ideals, a general repudiation of impossible standards in the name of human nature, a demand for happiness with a clear conscience. This is the battle of the Liberators, as I shall call them; and this battle has been fought and won. It is not our business to continue this conflict, as though we were still debating with the Middle Ages. There are too many knights in the field, whetting up a subjective enthusiasm in the idle game of liberating *free men!* It is our business to consider what the Liberators have *not* done, and to take up the new questions.

For what we now know is that the issue of discipline *versus* human nature is a false issue. That human nature cannot be made happy by repudiating all awkward ideals. That the good life is not found in satisfying *desires,* either one by one, or in combination; it has to be found in satisfying *Selves.* That we cannot live well without the energy and warmth of primitive passion; and that we can get from primitive passion just energy and warmth, never *guidance.* That there is in human nature itself a principle of self-discipline; and that it must find its guidance in the nature of the world we live in. What we require now is a re-survey of human nature, its degree of plasticity, the changeable and relative elements and the elements of absolute permanence in its standards of self-criticism and in its demand for happiness.

For old laws and old ideas of right and wrong in regard to property, warfare, sex, religion, are indeed subject to change. But they do not *all* change: there is a permanent core in them. And, the prophet who harps only on their alterability is a false prophet, and of no use to the present age.

CHAPTER I

AN ART PECULIAR TO MAN

IN understanding the cycle of organic life, reproduction must be taken together with death. Reproduction is most obviously a way of overcoming the
failure implied by individual death,—it is an answer
to death; but death is also an answer to reproduction.
For without the due process of individual death, reproduction must long since have brought all life to an end
by its own excess. In the process of reproduction, then,
nature appears to accept and confirm the biological
failure of the individual as a condition of the success
of the species.

But reproduction is more than a device for continu-
ing the species; it is the main opportunity for new
experiments. However variations may be prepared, it
is in the moments of the transmission of life that they
announce themselves. It is as if life were not satisfied
with the simple success of the species,—as if, feeling
its foothold in the world precarious, it must be forever restless, climbing, multiplying, and fortifying its
shapes. It is fertile in organic inventions, some better
and some worse, some persisting and some vanishing.
The death of the individual is thus also the opportunity for evolution.

When we try to grasp the trend and meaning of this

groping, ramifying process, we commonly picture 'life' as a single impulse, personify it, and regard it as striving for more perfect adaptation to its world. The world is relatively stable: life is endlessly variable. Life *can* change; inorganic nature cannot: if either is to be adjusted to the other, it is life that must adjust itself to the lifeless. In the long run—so we commonly suppose—it is the environment that decides which variations are better and which are worse: better and worse are simply the fitter and the less fit to hold their own in such a world as, once for all, we have.

Few pictures so defective as this have had such wide acceptation. Why should a species already perfectly adapted to its world seek to improve its adaptation? It is not the species that has failed,—it is the individual. If the effort of life is for adaptation, it must be to produce better-adapted individuals. These better individuals also die,—but they die harder, last longer, and accordingly reproduce less and at less cost: so far, the species is less successful, the individual more so.

Further, in this evolution of fitter individuals, the process of evolution itself changes. The experimental variation at the point of reproduction—which we ascribe to 'life' because it forms no discernible part of the conscious intent of the parent organisms—tends to disappear. With a less frequent succession of generations, and fewer offspring in each, opportunities for such change become fewer. But with longer individual lifetime, the possibilities of change in the individual and through individual effort become greater;

and—as the evidence now seems to stand—some of these changes may be transmitted. If so, evolution becomes less a matter of experimentation by life-in-general and more a matter of conscious individual striving.

Finally, whatever life or individuals may be said to strive for, it is not merely to fit an environment. Life strives much more to make the environment fit itself. It is true that the world cannot change itself: but life has the alternative of fitting itself to the world or fitting the world to itself, and, to judge by behavior, it prefers the latter. It is true that physical nature is inexorable and that life is frail, but it is also true that life is endlessly elastic, masterful, and persistent. It finds that it can bring small parts of nature, increasingly large parts of nature, under control, and that nature under control is a servant completely docile, and incapable of rebellion. Hence, wherever we find conscious individuals, there we find efforts to make the world over into forms auspicious for the purposes of those living beings themselves.

Using the word art in the widest sense, as including all conscious efforts to remake the world, we may say that all animal behavior includes some degree of outwardly directed art. While life permits its world to shape it, it promotes thereby the artisanship by which it shapes the world.

There is but one exception, presumably, to the rule that the arts of animals are directed to the environment. The human being does deliberately undertake, while reshaping his outer world, to reshape himself

also. In meeting unsatisfactory conditions,—scarcity
of food, danger, etc.,—the simpler animal does what
it can to change those conditions. The human being does
likewise; but there sometimes occurs to him the additional reflection, "perhaps there should be some change
in myself also." Scarcity of food may become to him
an argument for greater foresight or industry, danger
for more caution. If a beast is threatened, it may either
fight or retreat: if a man is threatened, he may (while
dealing with the facts) become a critic also of his own
fear or anger.

Man thus becomes for himself an object of artful reconstruction, and this is an art peculiar to man. Whatever is done in the world by way of producing better
human individuals, whether for the benefit of the
species or for the ends of individuals themselves, man
is an agent in it: it is done not merely to him but by
him. He has become judge of his own nature and its
possibilities. "Evolution" leaves its work in his hands
—so far as he is concerned.

I do not say that man is the only creature that has a
part in its own making. Every organism may be said
(with due interpretation of terms) to build itself, to
regenerate itself when injured, to recreate itself and,
in striving for its numerous ends, to develop itself—to
grow. It may be, as we were saying, an agent in evolution. But in all likelihood, it is only the human being
that does these things with conscious intention, that
examines and revises his mental as well as his physical
self, and that proceeds according to a preformed idea
of what this self should be. To be human is to be self-

conscious; and to be self-conscious is to bring one's
self into the sphere of art, as an object to be judged,
altered, improved.

Human beings as we find them are accordingly artificial products; and for better or for worse they must
always be such. Nature has made us: social action
and our own efforts must continually remake us. Any
attempt to reject art for "nature" can only result in
an artificial naturalness which is far less genuine and
less pleasing than the natural work of art.

Further, as self-consciousness varies, the amount or
degree of this remaking activity will vary. And self-
consciousness is on the increase. M. Bergson has
strongly argued that consciousness (including self-
consciousness) has no quantity;[1] but I must judge that
among the extremely few respects in which human
history shows unquestionable growth we must include
the degree and range of self-consciousness. Whatever
psychology may be, it is only a self-conscious being
that could have developed such a science. The comparatively recent emergence of this science, and also
the persistent advance of the subjective or introspective element in literature and in all fine art are tokens
of the increasing self-consciousness of the race. And

---

[1] *Les données immédiates de la conscience,* ch. i. Naturally one can
define a situation, such as the relation of being aware of an object, of
which one must say that it either exists or does not exist,—without
variations of degree. Such is Natorp's interpretation of *Bewusstheit,*
not essentially different, I think, from the consciousness of which Bergson's statements are true. But such a situation is palpably an abstraction from the time-filling reality indicated by "consciousness" to which
Bergson himself wishes to call attention.

as a further indication and result of this increase, the art of human reshaping has taken definite character, has left its incidental beginnings far behind, has become an institution, a group of institutions.

Among the earliest of men the shaping of human nature must have been carried on by such sporadic expressions of criticism and admiration as pass perpetually between the members of any human group,—acting then, as they still act upon ourselves, like a million mallets to fashion each member somewhat nearer to the social heart's desire. Wherever a language exists, as a magazine of established meanings, there will be found a repertoire of epithets of praise and blame, at once results and implements of this social process.

Such a vocabulary needs only to exist in order to act as a constant, inescapable force; but the effect of current ideals is redoubled when a coherent agency, such as public religion, assumes in their behalf a deliberate propaganda and lends to them the weight of all time, all space, all wonder, and all fear.

No man can be wholly indifferent to what his fellows wish him to be; but the aggressive and pointed demands of the gods with their unknown capacities for injury and benefit raise the whole matter to a new stage of importance. For many centuries religion was the chief repository of the ripening self-knowledge and self-discipline of the human mind because in the effort to see himself as the gods saw him man became most keenly self-conscious, most alive to what he might make of himself. Now, besides this original agency we have its offshoots, politics, education, legislation, the penal art, as independent institutions for the reshaping of human nature.

The agencies have thus become diverse, and to some extent have lost touch with one another. What the family would like to make of the child, the state of the citizen, the church of the communicant, the fraternity of its fellow, the army of the soldier, the industrial order of the worker, the revellers of their comrade,— these are not all in conspicuous accord: and it is not certain that any of them are in accord with what an individual, who may assume in turn all of these characters, may want to make of himself. Nevertheless, the raw material of human nature is the same in all these contexts. Plastic as it is, it still has a character of its own. Versatile as it is, there must be a degree of consistency in the moulds that are put upon it. Submissive as it seems to be, all its acceptances of standard from outside are tentative; in the long run, the standards by which human nature is to be remade must be *its own*. Obscure as is its presentiment of what it wants to be, that presentiment is its ultimate guide; and the more confused the voices that assume to dictate to it, the more its need of an authentic interpreter.

It is the especial responsibility of philosophy to meet this need. Its obligation is to serve as a critique of all the diverse experimental self-criticism of mankind; it ought to clarify that presentiment of human destiny, and thus give so far as may be a rational voice to human self-consciousness. It is for the philosophical sciences,—psychology, ethics, etc. (certainly not for

psychology alone),—to consider man and what can be
made of him; and thus to make themselves the specific
servants of the art peculiar to man.

CHAPTER II

THE EMERGENCE OF PROBLEMS

FOR all the agencies which are now engaged in remaking mankind, three questions have become vital. What is original human nature? What do we wish to make of it? How far is it possible to make of it what we wish?

I say that these questions have *become* vital, because (though they sound like questions which any wise workman would consider before beginning his work) they are not in any historical sense preliminary questions. It is always our first assumption that we already know both what human nature is and what we wish it to be. Nothing is more spontaneous and assured than the social judgment which finds expression in a word of passing criticism: yet each such judgment ordinarily assumes both these items of knowledge. And it assumes, further, that human nature in the individual criticised could have been, and without more ado can now become, what we would have it. If we convey to our neighbor that he is idle, or selfish, or unfair, and if he perceives our meaning, nothing but wilful failure to use his own powers (so our attitude declares) can account for any further continuance in these ways. Now and always, all spontaneous human intercourse—a nest of un-avowed assumptions—takes for granted the common knowledge and acceptance of standards—at least the fundamental ones—and their attainableness.[1]

It is only as a result of much failure in the effort to remake men that the question of possibility gains a status and a hearing. It is this same experience which suggests that there is such a thing as a 'human nature,' offering a more or less constant resistance to the remaking process. These two questions, of possibility and of original nature, are therefore not independent: we have to consider the human material just because it is this, primarily, which sets a limit to the human art.

It may be regarded, I dare say, as a discovery of religion that there exists a 'natural man' who behaves as a quasi-inevitable drag upon the flights of the spirit. No agency could struggle, as religion has struggled, toward definiteness in its notions of what men ought to be without at the same time winning a large experience of the hindrances to the achievement. It lay in the situation from which the concept of human nature arose that the first picture of the natural man should be disparaging. To say that mankind is by nature bad is, in its origins, only a more sophisticated way of saying that virtue is difficult.

---

[1] One reason why conversation always assumes such knowledge, and such possibility, may be that conversation is itself a momentary assertion, and realization, of an ideal. In conversation the mind of each has laid aside its egoistic boundary, as far as the fact of communication goes, and has so far 'universalized itself.'

A large part of the meaning of our ordinary postulates of knowledge and freedom might with advantage be stated in these terms: You must admit as general principles whatever is implied in your own act of entering into this community of action which we call conversing.

But religion is by no means alone in this experience. Legislation and the social sciences have, with becoming slowness, and each in its own way, reached the conclusion that there is a human material to be reckoned with, having properties akin to inertia, just because each has found its original assumption of transparent rationality and freedom difficult to maintain. Economics, in setting up a typical man whose self-devoted prudence should consistently stand above suspicion, certainly postulated a very moderate degree of virtue even for the sake of the argument; but no science has more thoroughly discarded its error, or more heartily undertaken the task of reckoning with the non-reasoning strands in the human fabric.

Politics, especially the liberal politics of the past two centuries, was inclined to build its faith upon the existence of a reasonable public and a reasonable government. But the disillusioned—not disheartened—liberalism of to-day turns itself heart and soul to psychological enquiry. It perceives that there is a human nature which invites the use of the same principle that Bacon applied to physical nature,—something having laws of its own which must be obediently examined before we can hope to control it. "The Great Society," whether it is to be ruled, or educated, or saved, or simply lived in, has to be taken as a meeting ground of forces to which we would better apply the name instinctive or passional than simply rational. Thus the experience of all social enterprises seems to converge in the common admission that human nature is a problem, because human possibility has proved a problem.

But these problems are not so far identical that the recognition of a 'nature' to be dealt with at once closes the question what can be done with it. On this issue wide differences of judgment are still possible. On one side it may be held that this human nature is unlimitedly plastic,—we can make of it anything within reason; at the other extreme it may be held that it is fundamentally fixed,—we may refine it and polish it but can change none of its essential passions. Let us look more closely at the present condition of this discussion.

CHAPTER III

ON THE POSSIBILITY OF CHANGING HUMAN NATURE

WE are said to have an immediate consciousness of freedom, that is to say, of wide margins of possibility. If this consciousness could be translated into a definite proposition, it would presumably assert not alone "I can *do* (within these wide margins) what I will," but also, "I can *become* what I will."

There have been times when this 'testimony of consciousness' has carried much weight, even to the point of being held decisive; there have been other times when it has forthwith been rejected as more probably than not an illusion on the ground that intuition is the most untrustworthy of all modes of knowledge. At present, there is less disposition to believe that we have within ourselves either a fountain of deception or a fountain of finished truth: we are inclined rather to question what precisely this intuition means, and to seek that meaning in facts of a more objective order, such as the structure of the human being, or his historic doings.

As to structure, human nature is undoubtedly the most plastic part of the living world, the most adaptable, the most educable. Of all animals, it is man in whom heredity counts for least, and conscious building forces for most. Consider that his infancy is longest,

his instincts least fixed, his brain most unfinished at
birth, his powers of habit-making and habit-changing
most marked, his susceptibility to social impressions
keenest,—and it becomes clear that in every way nature,
as a prescriptive power, has provided in him for her
own displacement. Having provided the raw material,
nature now charters man to complete the work and
make of himself what he will. His major instincts and
passions first appear on the scene not as controlling
forces, but as elements of *play,* to be tried in a thousand
modes and contexts and admitted but slowly to the
status of settled habit in forms chosen by the player.
Other creatures nature could largely finish: the human
creature must finish himself.

And as to history, it cannot be said that the results
of man's attempts at self-modelling appear to belie the
liberty thus promised in his constitution. Just as he has
retired his natural integument in favor of an artificial
clothing, capable of expressing endless nuances not
alone of status and wealth, but of temper and taste as
well,—conservatism or venturesomeness, solemnity,
gaiety, profusion, color, dignity, carelessness or whim,
—so his natural mentality appears to have served as a
neutral medium to be fashioned into equally various
modes of character and custom. That is a hazardous
refutation of socialism or of any other proposed revolution which consists in pointing out that its success
would require a change in human nature. Under the
spell of particular ideas monastic communities have
flourished, in comparison with whose demands upon
human nature the change required by socialism—so far

as it calls for purer altruism and not pure economic folly—is trivial. To any one who asserts as a dogma that "Human nature never changes," it is fair to reply, "It is human nature to change itself."

When one reflects to what extent racial and national traits are manners of the mind, fixed by social rather than by physical heredity, while the bodily characters themselves may be due in no small measure to sexual choices at first experimental, then imitative, then habitual, one is not disposed to think lightly of the human capacity for self-modification.

But it is still possible to be skeptical as to the depth and permanence of any changes which are brought about by conscious strain and effort. Admitting the interest of knowing what is possible by way of the curious or heroic, it is still more important to know the level to which all curves tend to return after the fortuitous effort and circumstances are withdrawn. Our immediate consciousness of freedom may prove to have as much and as little significance as our quite similar feeling of physical ability, it may be valid primarily for the moment in which it occurs. I feel just now as if I could leap to any height, and this feeling is not wholly deceptive: I could indeed do so except for the gravity of things in this part of space, which will announce, in the next moment, the level I can reach and where I must come to rest. Similarly, there are few maxims of conduct, and few laws, so contrary to nature that they could not be put into momentary effect by individuals, or by communities. No one presumes to limit what men can *attempt;* one only enquires what the silent forces are which determine what can *last.*

What, in our own society, is the possible future of measures dealing with divorce, with war, with political corruption, with prostitution, with superstition? Enthusiastic idealism is too precious an energy to be wasted if we can spare it false efforts by recognizing that pugnacity, greed, sex, fear, and the like, are permanent ingredients of our being, and set fixed limits to what can be done with us. Is human nature so yielding and characterless as it seems to itself in moments of sated and quiescent appetite, when it appears docile to *any* mould? Do we not know that the aboriginal passions have definite bents of their own, with recurring and relentless cravings, long thoughts, and smouldering revenges, such as no ruler within the self or outside of it does well to ignore? Machiavelli was not inclined to make little of what an unhampered ruler could do with his subjects; yet he saw in such passions as these a fixed boundary to the power of the Prince. "It makes him hated above all things to be rapacious, and to be a violator of the property and women of his subjects, from both of which he must abstain."[1] And if Machiavelli's despotism meets its master in the undercurrents of human instinct, governments of less determined stripe, whether of states or of persons, would hardly do well to treat these ultimate data with less respect.

It is peculiarly the legislator who needs wisdom about the possibility of durable changes in human

[1] *The Prince,* ch. xix.

character, and who in ages of effort to improve mankind by law should have gained some empirical wisdom of his own, since he must deal with masses and averages. And, in fact, we find a kind of official legislative pessimism or resignation, voiced frequently by the wise and great from Solomon to this day. At present it derives large nourishment from statistics. The secular steadiness of the percentages, let us say of the major crimes, shows in the clearest light where the constant level of no-effort lies. When Huxley likened the work of civilization to the work of the gardener with his perpetual warfare against wildness and weeds, he pictured a philosophy for the legislator. The world-wise lawgiver will respect the attainable and maintainable level of culture, a level not too far removed from the stage of no-effort.

Indeed, there are many who believe, at present, that our social pilots would do well to relax their strain in the field of conscious character-building and turn their attention back again to the stock. Perhaps nature was sagacious after all in making her improvements primarily at the point of reproduction. If anything extensive is to be accomplished, may not eugenics offer a better prospect than eternal discipline? The future of the race may conceivably be found in a new and scientifically developed aristocracy of blood.[2] With the old material nothing important can be achieved.

[2] I say 'aristocracy,' because evidently under our present arrangements the lesser breeds would necessarily continue to exist side by side with the new stock for some little time, and the gap must widen between the two. How to induce these rear-guards to seek Nirvana is one of the awkward problems of the eugenic program.

How different from this legislative pessimism is the above-mentioned pessimism of religion. The great religions have spoken ill of original human nature; but they have never despaired of its possibilities. No sacred scripture so far as I know asserts that men are born 'free and equal'; but no accident of birth is held by the major religions (with the exception of Brahmanism) to exclude any human being from the highest religious attainment. In spite of the revolutionary character of their standards, they are still, for the most part, committed to the faith that these standards are reachable. And they have so far entrusted themselves to this faith that the entire accumulation of scientific knowledge regarding the determination of character, regarding heredity, and especially regarding the instincts, leaves them unmoved. This may be a case of the usual indifference of religion to "progress"; but more probably it is a deliberate rejection of the view that the *born* part of man is decisive. Religion declines to limit the moral possibility of human nature.

Thus in the world of practical endeavor as in the world of theory the two extreme positions in the problem of possibility still confront one another. One might suppose, since the question is a practical one, that experience would long ago have settled the matter. And probably, if experience could have settled the matter, it would have been settled long ago.

For after all, how would you judge from experience what the possibilities of human nature are? All the remaking agencies, religion added, have failed to make a world of saints, or any resemblance thereof. True; but they have made *some* saints. And in a question of what is possible, negative experience counts for nothing if there is but a single positive success.

As for the rest, their failure may indeed be due to the incapacity of average human nature. But there are many other conceivable reasons for it, such as lack of effort, lack of faith, political pessimism itself, and finally, lack of *wish*. Is it altogether certain that the saint of history is the one human success and hence the pattern for all mankind? To the coldly political eye, his leaven seems to lose much of its distinction as it spreads through the lump,—as if the rôle hardly fitted the majority. Indeed, those who pursue to the end the counsels of perfection tear away from the mass; and the best examples stand in splendid isolation. May it not be true that the goal of character which seems possible only to the few is closed to the many only because they cannot be brought wholly to desire it? A revised conception of what is desirable may bring a revised view of what is possible.

We turn, then, to consider the status of our third problem, What do we wish to make of human nature?

CHAPTER IV

WHAT CHANGES ARE DESIRABLE?
LIBERATION VERSUS DISCIPLINE

OF all the doubts that invade our primitive assurance, the last to arise, and the most disconcert-
ing, is the doubt whether we know what we want. We
inhale our ideals as we accept our mother-tongue: and
so great is the momentum of the vocabulary of lauda-
tion that it is long before we discover that not all eulo-
gistic epithets can be embodied in one being,—not even
in a god. Mr. Bosanquet has instanced Falstaff as
disproof of the notion that right and wrong are ultimate qualities of the universe:—for who can approve
Falstaff's principles, and yet who would willingly
consign him to hell? But is not the difficulty this, that
the praiseworthy and delightful qualities of Sir John
would be hard to unite with certain other reputable
qualities, such as responsibility and temperance; and,
generally speaking, that among the ideals which we
all accept *seriatim* there is conflict? If so, the natural
inference is simply that these ideals, taken one by one,
are somewhat false and abstract. Neither singly nor
jointly do they furnish a true picture of what we wish
human nature to be; and, in brief, we do not (concep-
tually) know what we wish it to be.

In this unavowed condition of groping ignorance,

mankind has made (equally unavowed) use of certain guiding principles, among which is this: that if anything is impossible, it is not wholly desirable. Ideals are attainable; ergo, what is not attainable is not an ideal.

Every failure to impress a nominal ideal upon human nature, therefore, works two ways: it strengthens the critics of human nature, the legislative pessimists, and the rest; but it also casts doubt upon the validity of the nominal ideal. Men who, in quest of such ideals, have submitted to much discipline have sometimes come to rebel, not because they have reached their limit, but because the friction of the process has led them to suspect the authority of the goal. Such seems to have been the experience of the Buddha, who after six years of exalted austerity in the Uruvilva forest suddenly turned his back upon his Brahmanic guides. And such, in another vein, may have been the experience of the pleadingly defiant Omar. In such cases, when 'Nature rebels,' she rebels not as a traitor, but in the name of a different conception of rightful rule. The average man, I presume, has always doubted in his reticent way whether those counsels of perfection are altogether what they claim to be; whether the gain in brilliance and purity has not been purchased by some loss in the virtues of reality and concrete serviceableness; whether, on the whole, something more like "Follow Nature" may not be a truer guide to a wholly desirable human quality.

There have been eras in history, eras of liberation,

when the general voice of this average man has set itself against the tyranny of prevailing discipline. They have been eras like the Renaissance in which the hypocritical seams in the traditional strait-jackets have become especially visible, as well as the too-interested character of the profession that men are free to become what they are commanded to become. But every age has its party and its prophet of liberation, its Rousseau, its Schlegel, its Whitman, its Nietzsche,—prophets always more or less philosophical, and sometimes political as well. The principle of the Liberator is, Follow thine own inner nature,—Express thyself. As legislator he is anything but a pessimist, not because he thinks that the older discipline is possible, but because he thinks that whatever ought to be is possible, and that merely a minimum of discipline ought to be.

The general influence of the philosophy of evolution has been liberating in this sense. Not long ago, Spencer deduced from his *Biological View* the obvious doctrine of any naturalistic ethics, that (other things being equal) all 'functions' ought to be exercised. For what else do functions exist but to be exercised? There is a flattering piety in thus following the intentions of Nature, which are, besides, much more certainly decipherable than the other oracles of God. It is true, we are obliged to do a certain amount of guessing: but at least one trend of Nature may unhesitatingly be affirmed,—a tendency to the increase of life, measured in terms of these functional activities. The rule for human culture takes a shape like the rule of the medical art: Regard life as a quantity; conserve and increase it; avoid all forms of repression.

The evil of repression—an inevitable accompaniment of discipline—is primarily simply that it is repression, i.e., subtraction from life. But beside this quantitative evil, we are assured by Freud and his school that repression is the root of numerous psychical disorders. Freud's importance to the cause of liberation lies in his showing the very mechanism of the process by which the ignoring of Nature is punished. The repressed tendency is not destroyed; and though it must persist in sub-consciousness it continues to act in its prison; and because it cannot act normally, acts to the distortion of fancy, of thought, of personality itself. This hypothesis of the persistence of the repressed impulse[1]—ascribing to it a distinct and indestructible reality, like that of a quantum of energy— is in its origin a clinical hypothesis for the explanation of abnormal mental states. But it does not remain a theory for explaining mental disease alone. It writes a new chapter in general psychology, the neglected chapter concerning the persistence of mental energies, their transformations and equivalents. It appears as a basic proposition to the effect that original human nature is *not* characterless, that it *has* a bent and current of its own, that it cannot be overruled without limit by the censorious artifices of convention nor the ideals of morality and religion. Through all such disciplines, what you primevally are wins its way. Thus

[1] Discussed below, pp. 98, 193.

the 'new psychology' becomes a theoretical support for the gospel of self-expression, and a revised ethics.

The rule of life which these researches immediately suggest is formulated by various writers.[2] The ethical problem reduces to this: to find such a mode of satisfying any wish that all other wishes may also be satisfied. This is clearly the principle of a democratic society applied to human desires. The only admissible remaking in a régime of this sort is such mutual adjustment of the methods of satisfaction that our numerous impulses may live together in harmony. The sacrificial choices of the older discipline are not merely unintelligent; they are immoral.

It is clear that the freedom which interests these prophets of liberation is not the freedom discussed in the previous chapter,—freedom to control and modify desire: it is the freedom to *assert desire*. If we affect freedom in the former sense, a freedom which can only be displayed by submitting to self-imposed demands, we do but punish ourselves. Such freedom, they hold, is no more than a Quixotic liberty to imprison our own nature. The rights of self-government are not properly to be vested in any such transcendent 'ruling faculty' as the Stoics tried to enthrone: these rights should lie with those primary impulses which emerge, with life itself, from mother earth.

It might be imagined that the religions of redemp-

2 Notably by E. B. Holt, *The Freudian Wish.* See also H. E. Hunt, *The Hidden Self and its Mental Processes;* H. C. Miller, *The New Psychology and the Teacher.*

tion, with their dubious view of the worth of original human nature, and demands of rebirth, would find themselves at odds with the Liberators. And so, to some extent, it has been. But the Liberator is mediatory, and can offer an interpretation of regeneration itself, such as liberal phases of religion are not wholly disinclined to consider. Let us say that 'to save' means simply 'not to waste,'—not to destroy, not to lose. Regard religion, then, together with ethics, as a general economy of life, having definite applications in the field of public justice.[3] The work of religion is to conserve a maximum of energy, of value, of experience; to prevent friction and mutilation, to turn all things to account. A large part of the older meaning of conversion, it is true, must be emptied out. Into this view, no 'twice-born-ness' of the type depicted by William James can be admitted: the precursory sickness of soul, the horror of being cosmically lost, are outgrown trials. The way of the mystics, wherein overcoming the world meant mortifying the flesh, is no longer to be followed. Hell has burned out: for God, himself remade in the image of the expansive spirit, is no longer thought of as one who can whole-heartedly exclude any individual or denounce any thing. The 'agonized conscience' of our forefathers may be satirized as the passing gesture of a 'genteel tradition' now empty of vitality.[4]

The liberal religion of to-day largely accepts this view, and makes no battle for the ancient discipline;

[3] As in the recent writings of Professor T. N. Carver, *The Religion Worth Having; Essays in Social Justice.*

[4] George Santayana, *The Genteel Tradition in American Philosophy.*

contemporary Christians incline to the Confucian doctrine of the native goodness of man, and saving only a
plea for some kind of moral order, accept the general
trend toward the restoration of the original Adam to
respectability. The temper of our age is expansive: it
is for giving freedom to everything that can show a
claim of right; it is partial to every under-dog,—and
are not the primitive passions the under-dogs in our
psychical charade?

It is perhaps well that partisan cries for the return of
discipline are few; for any such cry can be effective
only if it is the voice of our own experience. If our liberalism is at loose ends, there will be signs that we are
conscious of it. If its psychology is defective, our psychology will become aware of the fact and write a still
newer chapter. If the freedom to control oneself and
make oneself over is as genuine a part of freedom as
the freedom to be ruled by original desires, a suspicion
that the Liberators in their plans for satisfying human
nature have somewhere thwarted it will show itself in
various quarters, in letters, in politics, in education.
And even in the course of the continued thinking of
the greater Liberators, a discovery might be anticipated that some sort of censorship is a part of original
human nature itself. Such we shall see to have been the
case.

Meanwhile, we may observe for ourselves that the
simple program of the Liberator's ethics, "So satisfy
each wish that every other wish may also be satisfied,"
is not without its embarrassments. Some of our wishes

are *appetites,* and make for enjoyment, more or less quiescent; others are *impulses,* and make for action. The impulsive man and the appetitive man seek different types of expression, and lead to modes of life not easily reconcilable.

Thus, the natural man of the Nietzschean ideal is a type that would find little in common with the natural man of Rousseau: he is far more strenuous, less disposed to avoid pain and hardness, rather disposed to make himself at home with them. Nevertheless, like his predecessor, he regards himself as a freed man, finds his law within, and defines his good as the venting of his energies upon the world. He is a hater of Christianity chiefly because Christianity seems to him to check those salutary surgical processes among men, eliminating the unfit, which a liberated pugnacity would naturally carry out. We make ourselves soft, we suffer more, we try to ecape suffering by still more softness and sympathy,—in this way we set up a vicious and endless process of decline in manhood; rather give free expression to a normal hardness, in personal relations, in competitions, in war,—in the end all will suffer less, and the over-man will be born.

The Western world has come too newly from initiation into the inwardness of the processes of mutual destruction to lend a ready mind to the Nietzschean type of liberation. We are ready to judge, perhaps, that the word liberation, by itself, is not a final answer to the question, What do we wish to make of ourselves? Human nature wishes freedom,—that is so nearly a truism that it stands at the beginning of our problem, not at the end of it. Freedom is a great word with which to fight oppression, but is it a word to guide the building of any positive conception of human nature? It has been so effective as a fighting-tool that Liberators have commonly fallen into the natural delusion that it can also, without further ado, construct an ethics. So far as they have done this, they have become the typical word-worshippers of our day, and have left the real problems of human living untouched. But the greater minds among them have seen that they cannot stop at this problem-concealing word, liberation.

CHAPTER V

THE LIBERATOR AS DISCIPLINARIAN

LET us first follow the experience of some of the older Liberators, of Rousseau and the Romanticists.

Rousseau is usually regarded as a Liberator, pure and simple. His cult of Nature has the ring of a plea for the undisciplined man, man as his impulses unspoiled by social convention and law would make him. But Rousseau worked his way through that cult, and lived to write against it. The opening words of the *Social Contract*, "Man is born free, but everywhere he is in chains," sound like a renewal of the onslaught on those 'chains,' and a reiterated assertion of the glories of natural freedom. But the situation is quite the opposite; for, as he proceeds to say, it is now his intention to "justify" those chains. The Rousseau of 1762 was not the man to bring fagots for a general bonfire of human fetters. These are some of the words in which he gives his idea of the relative value of original nature and a liberal political discipline:

Passage from the state of nature to the civil state produces a very remarkable change in man, by substituting justice for instinct in his conduct, and giving his actions the morality they formerly lacked. . . .
Let us draw up the whole account in terms easily compared. What man loses by the social contract is his natural liberty,

and an unlimited right to everything he tries to get and succeeds in getting. What he gains is civil liberty, and the proprietorship of all he possesses.

We might add over and above all this to what man acquires in the civil state, moral liberty, which alone makes him truly master of himself. For the mere impulse of appetite is slavery; while obedience to a law which we prescribe to ourselves is liberty.[1]

Rousseau had experienced something like an intellectual conversion; and for our present purposes we should like to know more about the logic of it. But we shall learn less on this point from Rousseau than from other examples of the same process.

Germany, in the short interval between Kant's *Critique of Practical Reason* and Hegel's *Philosophy of Right* passed in ponderous and explicit argument through the entire gamut of these changes. Kant is the unmatched exponent of the cause of discipline, perfect prey, therefore, for an entire school of Romantic liberators. It remained for Hegel, imbibing all that was valid in the Romantic movement, to fan into an impressive flame the embers of Rousseau's genius. Hegel had no crusade to preach against human instinct: Kant's idea of a transcendent autocrat in the shape of formal duty found little response in him. Disjunctive choices, the either-or's of life, are wrong choices; right decision, he thought, reaches a synthesis, a *both-and*. So far, Hegel is of one voice with Romanticism,—also with Freud and Holt.

[1] *The Social Contract*, Book I, ch. viii.

But what Hegel saw (as Romanticism did not) is that this original nature of ours which is to be given its liberty is something very different from a bundle of co-ordinate wishes. It is quite as much a bundle of thoughts or ideas, with demands of their own. Of all the primitive elements in man, the deepest are his reflective and social dispositions; and if *they* are to have any freedom at all, they will impose a certain order upon his goings. Like the talent of an architect which can find complete scope only in productions having a substance and system of their own, so these general human talents can find scope only in the law and custom of a social order. What man is, thinks Hegel, is best described by the word 'spirit,' and if this is true, human freedom, like the freedom of the Absolute Spirit in creating the world, will take concrete shape, and will look very much like submitting to bondage. Human nature can only blossom out under various forms of discipline, such as we find in the economic order, the family, the state: without conformity to some rule, no liberty.

So far, Hegel's point is well taken; yet Hegel has failed to convince the world at large that his variety of liberty is genuine. He has failed to convince, not because he seemed to have in mind the Prussian order rather than the French or the British order, but because he *supplied no clear way of distinguishing between a better order and a worse.* Agreed that only a full set of social regulations can set us adequately free, it still makes an immense difference how those functions are adjusted,—all the difference between a conformity that is far ahead of, and one that is far behind, the freedom of nature. It is the lack of a sharp and usable *criterion* in Hegel's thought which has given the seven devils their opportunity. To advise an uncritical acceptance of the *status quo* was probably no more Hegel's intention than it was the intention of Burke when he celebrated the value of prejudice as a source of English stability and strength. But both thinkers were so mightily impressed by the fact that existence, historical existence, *Wirklichkeit*, is the great and fundamental merit, that both neglected to save themselves from the appearance of endorsing whatever thus exists because it is actually there. We shall therefore dwell no longer on Hegel. In him, German liberation had turned disciplinarian; but his failure to make connection with the needs of an expanding popular and industrial life in Germany, like the failure of Burke to appreciate the demand for reform in England, made it necessary for the nineteenth century to work out the same problem in another key.

It is precisely this, then, that our own naturalism and liberalism have been doing. They have tried to make thorough and literal earnest of the proposal to set human nature free, and have accordingly been drawn into the attempt to set up a thorough and literal inventory of all the ingredients of human nature, all the instincts that are to be satisfied. It is not surprising that they have found, as Hegel found, certain propensities which could hardly be appeased without being allowed to assume control of the other propensities.

They have reported as an empirical discovery what Rousseau and Hegel asserted *a priori*, viz., *There are some elements of human nature whose liberation* is *discipline*.

It cannot be said that there is agreement among our empirical students of human nature what these controlling functions are; but it has become evident that our gregarious tendencies, our sexual and parental tendencies, and our curiosity, are not interests simply co-ordinate with our food-getting and defensive dispositions, to be somehow averaged or synthesized with them. Satisfaction, for them, means *organizing the whole life on their own principle*.

It is an element of strength in Nietzsche's philosophy that he not only sees this conclusion, but seizes it and builds on it. He revolts against the discipline of Christianity, that is true: but he revolts still more against an amiable and indiscriminate expansionism.[2] His type of liberation was one that demanded the utmost severity of self-pruning, because he proposed to give freedom to one of the *masterful* elements of human nature. *Geist,* he said, *ist das Leben das selber ins Leben schneidet;* and almost furiously, in his demand for the sacrifice of the unfit in self as well as in others, he parodies the Christian paradox that life is to be saved by losing it.

Thus Nietzsche expresses the logical outcome of

[2] For this reason, Professor Irving Babbitt's classing of Nietzsche with Rousseau as a Romanticist, in his vigorous and enlightening *Masters of Modern French Criticism*, seems to me a partial truth which is in danger of missing what is most characteristic in Nietzsche's thought.

nineteenth century naturalism. As a goal for the re-making process no superman yet depicted can hold our complete allegiance: but so much can be said,—that our question can no longer be between discipline and liberation; it can only be a question of what discipline a completely free man will have.

Is contemporary expressionism moving along the same path? There are some signs of it. The psycho-analytic movement of the Freudians began with an emphasis on the evil of repression: its present empha-sis is on the necessity of 'sublimation.' Sublimation is a way of giving vent to pent-up impulses; but it is a peculiar way, a way quite different from inviting them to strike out for themselves. It is a way of satisfying them which is *also satisfactory* to something like a con-science or a social standard. But why consider these standards? If they are to be considered at all, it is, from the psycho-analytic point of view, only because a man cannot be at variance with them without being at vari-ance with himself. Not that Freudianism gives up its polemic against the censorship: there is something mis-chievous, it insists, about a nominal ideal which is out of the reach of nature,—such an ideal makes hypocrites or lip-servers of all of us. "Society has permitted itself to be misled into putting its ethical demands as high as possible," instead of putting them where men can readily follow. But to complain of ideals as being "too high" is not to complain of their existence: and if they are allowed to belong to the normal equipment of man, the censor ceases to be an anomaly and a tyrant. Freud has recently gone so far as to permit himself to wonder whether a measure of the sort of hypocrisy involved in having ideals may not be a necessary means of progress; which may be his chosen way of saying that one of the inseparable qualities of an ideal is to be difficult.

The 'new psychology' is thus visibly at work on a new chapter to the effect that not all repression is evil, —that there are two kinds of repression or constraint, one of which is abnormal, the other inseparable from personality.

What is it in the experience of expressionism that is working this gradual change?

Is it perhaps a perception that pure expressionism contains a contradiction? To liberate human desires singly may result not in the liberation of human nature but in its disintegration. Expressionism takes man piecemeal, as a bundle of propensities each one of which has to be heard in independence of the rest,—one desire, one vote. If the art of human life consists in this kind of pluralistic attention to the pack of native impulses and appetites, that amounts to a surrender of the belief that it has any meaning as a whole. But it is only the man who has some total meaning that can have any sense of freedom. Apart from such a unity of purpose, it is the same whether he says he gives freedom to his desires or that he is at their mercy. *He* is free in doing a thing only in so far as he can find himself in what he does, i.e., only when he does it *because* it is an element in, or a means to, what on the whole he purposes to do in the world. Drop out the purpose, and there is no *self* to be found in any of the several satisfactions that may fill the day's program, and therefore no freedom.

Expressionism, whether in psychology or letters or ethics, seems to imply an equal respect for every impulse. In practice, however, it appears to be an exaggerated respect for the sexual and physiological man; this is natural enough not only by way of reaction, or as protest against prudery—no longer needed, but also because it is in dealing with the 'neglected and tabooed' portions of human nature that novelty, or the sensation of novelty, is easiest to obtain. And further, expressionists must despise reticence on principle, not alone because reticence is unscientific, but because reticence is bound up with the belief that human nature has unity. Admit the unity, then no fragment stands alone,—every fragment must enquire, "What is my function?", has to be judged not by itself but by its meaning in the whole. The animal-man in particular can no longer set up an autonomous state: it is, in a special sense, the *property* of the person who uses the phrase "my body." Down with the totality, then, that the fragments may be free. Every destruction of unity has its exhilaration, every repudiation of debt gives radical relief and sends the blood pulsing: maintaining a self is a costly and burdensome program. But destruction of a self is even more costly, and thoroughgoing expressionism in the nature of the case can only co-exist with a mental going-to-pieces.

Hence it is that the pure liberators are gone—or are going! They are in the way of contributing the missing element of the Hegelian theory of freedom through restraint. For the restraint they will find is one which belongs intimately to human nature itself, and has the power to choose among its masters, not merely docilely accept what is put upon it.

CHAPTER VI

AN INDEPENDENT STANDARD

IN a century of thinking, then, we have made headway. We have learned much from our Liberators about what we do not want. We do not want to suppress or get rid of our primitive passions; whatever is to become of them, they are to remain with us, a part of what we permanently are. We do not want to overlay them with a "veneer of civilization,"—that kind of artifice is even less substantial than its name implies. Nor do we want to engage in a persistent struggle against them, as if against gravity, or against the tendency to revert to a wilder type: we do not want any ideal which implies living in a perpetual moral tension. If human nature is to be changed at all, it is to be only in ways that will leave it more completely satisfied.

We have learned, too, that human nature cannot be satisfied in pieces, because among the original passions there are some that make for structure and unity, and give substance to the common turn of speech which says, not "My desires are satisfied," but "I am satisfied."

But with all that we have learned or are likely to learn from experience about the needs of human nature, it does not follow that we can learn from empirical psychology, however accurate, what positively and definitely we want to make of ourselves.

Psychology, studying the facts of the mind as a thing of nature, is at a disadvantage for determining what any of these facts mean. Thus, when psychology studies perception it finds in its hands an image (Berkeley's 'idea,' Hume's 'impression') and therewith a pair of problems, viz., how this image, as a mental fact, can *mean* an object, and how, as a particular fact, it can *mean* a universal. The word 'essence' comes again into use because these problems exist; it calls attention to the truth that what psychology finds, as mental existence, is simply not *knowledge,*—the knowledge-element of perception has leaked out of it. Similarly when psychology studies human wishes, it is likely to find everything except what they *mean.* But it is what they mean that must satisfy them, and not what they are as psychological facts.

There is thus a logical possibility that the goal of human remaking, without being contrary to nature, is yet *beyond nature,* in the sense that nature, taken by itself, fails to define it.[1] And what logic suggests, the quandaries of our thinking on this subject seem to bear out. What is it, after all, that our 'nature' would have us become? Is there reason to think that we can find what will satisfy nature by a study of what nature is more successfully than we could find what will satisfy hunger by a study of what hunger is, apart from all knowledge of the fruits of the earth?

If we make the mental experiment of putting 'instinct' in control of our behavior, we shortly discover

---

[1] After the analogy of those schoolmen who taught that faith without being contrary to reason is beyond reason.

that the dictates not alone of instinct in general but
of every particular instinct are ambiguous: instinct,
as guide, shows a fatal lack of sense of *direction,* and
one suspects that even where it seems to show the way
it is covertly depending on counsel from another source.
The attempt to follow a leader that cannot *lead* may
compel the discovery that our real guidance is to be
sought elsewhere. This need not mean that the pre-
tender should be slaughtered, nor even excluded from
the company; he need only fall in behind the new guide.
Nature may well exercise a veto power, or a second-
ing power, without having the capacity to make definite positive proposals. If there is anything in these
surmises, we should have to look beyond human nature
itself for the thing which human nature should become.

Such an attitude toward nature, considerate, yet
independent, appears in the ethical thought of Plato,
and in his theory of education. For Plato, the goal of
education, as of philosophy and religion, was the attainment of a blessed vision, a state of insight into
things as they are. The conditions for attaining this
goal included the ascent of an intellectual ladder, the
dialectic; but they involved also a purgation of the
desires, a genuine remaking of the natural man. The
original love for particulars and sensible objects must
be transformed into a love of the universal and absolute. It is clear that a goal of this description cannot
be deduced from the rule of any social instinct, nor
of any other instinct observable in the primitive
human animal. And Plato has often been regarded as

thoroughly hostile to the empirical side of human nature. It has commonly been thought that the dualism
of Christian anthropology, with the excessive self-dis-
trust of mediæval piety, traced largely to him. But
while Plato was unquestionably an aristocrat in his
attitude toward the 'senses,' what he required of the
natural impulses was far more like 'sublimation' than
like 'repression.' No one can read The Banquet in
the light of recent psychology without realizing how
completely Plato understood the transformability of
passions and desires; and how completely in his view
of the goal of human endeavor the original fund of
desire—considered as a quantity—was *saved*. For
him there existed a single passion, neither unnatural,
nor yet given by nature, into which all our various
natural impulses are to be emptied and translated.

Plato, I must judge, was not hostile to nature. But
he had certainly not lost the power of exclusion. And
it is not out of the question that liberal religion, too
far acquiescent in the amiable expressionism of the
day, may regain significance for its concepts of evil
and conversion or rebirth through a new contact with
the immortal Greek. For Plato could still liken the
philosophic life to the pursuit of death. The direction of our remaking effort he conceived to be as distinct from the natural slope of our minds as, in the
philosophy of Bergson, intuition is distinct. In Plato's
universe, death and matter and night are still realities; and the destiny of souls has still its infinite perils;
terror and repentance are rational aspects of experience; the way to life leads through a strait gate.

I need not have gone back to Plato to find an illustration of the doctrine of the standard which is independent without being ruthless in its disciplinary demands. Nor yet to Spinoza, who sought to preserve and yet merge all passions in the sense of necessity, the intellectual love of God. Thinkers have always existed who have found the following of 'nature' as vague and inconclusive as the following of fixed law is schematic and unreal. At the present moment, there are those who seek ethical and educational wisdom in a general "theory of value." Such a theory must give an account of what is common to all the different goods in the world, i.e., to all things whatever that appeal to the human being as having worth or interest. And if it looks inward, to the valuer, and backward, to the origins, it will be likely to ascribe them all to 'feeling,' or 'desire,' or 'instinct'; and a theory of liberation will emerge merely from the method of attack on the problem. If, however, it looks outward, to the objects of value, and forward, to their *standards,* it is likely to find itself dealing with an ultimate court which gives laws to nature, rather than receiving laws from nature.[2]

[2] For the most part, present writers seek to refer the phenomenon of the 'normativeness' of our values to some unity within the self, some "Einheit der Gefühlslage," not defined directly in terms of the several elements unified. To some it appears as 'the will' (H. Schwartz, *Psychologie des Willens;* W. Wundt; H. Münsterberg, etc.); to others as 'personality' (Lipps, *Dis ethische Grundprobleme,* ch. i; A. Riehl, *Einführung in die Philosophie;* M. Reischle, *Werturteile und Glaubensurteile,* referring all values to a Gesammt-ich-Gefühl; C. Sigwart); to others as some function of reason or logic (A. Meinong, *Psychologisch-ethische Untersuchungen,* whose reference of moral values to a conceptual

We shall be prepared, then, to find that that which guides our wishes and instigates all the remaking is a spark not lighted in 'nature,' as we commonly understand the term. But if there be any such independent source of standards,—and we shall not here prejudge the question,—a study of the facts of human nature, and of the ways in which various agencies do in fact work upon it, should make that further fact apparent. For what we *are* must at least conspire in our own remaking with any independent principle; and with what we at first take to be the 'leadings of nature,' any such foreign impulse will no doubt be mixed. If it exists, it may be expected to reveal itself in the course of our empirical labor. Without attempting, therefore, a prior critique of pure will, we may now address ourselves to that labor.

impartial spectator revives memories of Adam Smith; J. C. Kriebig, *Psychologische Grundlage eines Systems der Werttheorie;* W. Urban, *Valuation, Its Nature and Its Laws).* Yet again, there is here and there a tendency to abandon the search within the self and to refer the whole matter of ultimate standards to the structure of the world we live in, or to the conditions for improving the race (R. Goldscheid, *Zur Ethik des Gesammtwillens,* also *Entwickelungswerttheorie,* etc., Leipzig, 1908).

PART II

THE NATURAL MAN

Argument

↗ possible point

MEN are born human: that is to say, they inherit from their an- ①
cestors something of vast importance. There are psychologists who
would persuade us to the contrary, making out that heredity is of
little moment, whereas the active environment, social tradition and
education are all but omnipotent in determining what we become.
William James believed that the humanity of the human infant was
wrapped up, so to speak, in a large equipment of 'instincts' which
duly ripened in him as he grew up. Professor Dewey and Mr. John
Watson, behaviorist, deplore the notion of instinct as a bit of psychological mythology.

Now the concept of instinct will stand criticism. It is a vagrant
concept and has in its day covered much superstition. It has also
covered something real; and we cannot obliterate that reality by
denouncing the word. While Mr. Watson rejects 'instinct' he admits
a multitude of 'unlearned responses'! His objection evinces chiefly
a linguistic sensitivity (as is proper for one to whom thinking is an
inaudible exercise of the vocal organs). The substance of the matter
remains: human babies are born with dispositions which fit them ②
to become men rather than pigs or ostriches, and a psychology which
cannot duly estimate that fact is truncated at the start.

The attack on instinct is thoroughly justified in so far as it denies
to the human child the lump-inheritance of mechanically ready
responses. Except for the numerous fragments of behavior involved in crawling, balancing, vocalizing, and so on, the inherited
dispositions of human beings are not so specific as those of animals.
But the more general tendencies,—food-getting, curiosity, fear,
sex-love, pugnacity,—are not absent. In them, he has something in
common with the pig and the ostrich; but they are in him with
radical differences. They are (1) less determinate at the outlet, (2)
better balanced by counter-impulses, and (3) more completely
merged in a central impulse.

(1) The instinct of fear, for example, is present in man; though the shape it may assume is less determinate than in the rest of creation. A man can be afraid of more different things, and try to evade them in more different ways, than any other animal. Yet the fear and his response display his heredity rather than his personal experience and reason, in promptness, in energy, and in mode. (2) Attending every strong instinctive impulse in man there is a shadow of aversion, inhibition: thus to hunger, sex-love, anger, grasping. Thus man is balanced in instinct as in physical build, and equipped for hesitation and a balance of power outside the instinctive drive. (3) All the more general instincts merge in the central current of the will: they are not so much separate drives as separate ways of manifesting a single disposition which becomes, as it learns its own sense, the purpose of the individual person.

This central and original impulse is simply that vital push by which the human being strives forward into the business of living, holding to what good he sees, shaking off evils, and hoping for an unknown but possible satisfaction. The "will to live" is not a bad name for it; yet all names are bad. Since it makes for action and effect, as much as for enjoyment, the "will to power" tells part of the story. Perhaps the "will to reality" is nearer. In any case, human nature from the beginning has its unity, and seeks not alone goods but *the good*.

CHAPTER VII

THE ELEMENTS OF HUMAN NATURE:
THE NOTION OF INSTINCT

IT is no longer possible to share the confidence of
Hobbes or of Rousseau that original human nature,
in distinction from all that education and civil life have
made of it, can forthwith be described. Certainly not
by direct introspection can any man draw the line between what is natural and what is artificial in himself.
Neither can we find examples of the unaffected natural
state: there are solitary wasps, but there are no solitary human infants; and with the first social exchange
the original self is overlaid. Further, this very modification of native character by interplay with an outer
and social world is a condition for the normal appearance of later dispositions; an experimental isolation
of a human being for the sake of observing his natural
behavior would thus be self-defeating.

Our idea of our own original nature, therefore, must
always be a result of abstraction. We have to reach it
as we reach other non-isolable ingredients of things,—
namely, by framing hypothetical definitions of elements
that seem to show a degree of constancy, and allowing
these formulæ to show their power, or lack of power,
to express simply the facts of experience. An 'instinct'
is such an hypothetical unit.

The notion of instinct survives a long history and much rough usage, literary, scientific, and pseudo-scientific. It is a vagabond concept; it has served to indicate in a single word the powers that animals have and man has not; but also to describe the profound traits which man and animals have in common; to impute a mysterious discernment or guidance to certain special types of knowledge or action; but also to explain the blind beginnings of all action; or again to cover up with a term of solemn obscurity our residual ignorance about the sources of any action whatever. It has served the purposes of the naturalists who wish to tie human nature to its physical connections; and those of the theologians who wish to make fast its permanent susceptibility to the supermundane. If such a turncoat concept has gained scientific standing, it is only because it is indispensable.

It is indispensable because it expresses in the simplest way the fact of *heredity,* taken piecemeal. For instincts are simply the elements of our heredity (so far as that consists in dispositions to act in certain ways rather than in others) regarded in its common traits, not in its individual characteristics. The inheritance of each individual includes much that is peculiar to his parents, his family, his racial group: it includes also certain basal traits common to the species. It is this latter part that is meant by his 'instinct.' But as the individual peculiarities may be regarded, for purposes of analysis, as due to unique proportionings of common elements, we shall not go far astray in a search for the common clay of our original endowment, if we enquire in this region covered by the word instinct. We shall use the term without ascribing to it any occult or explanatory powers, without implying that an instinct is a 'force,' an unpushed push, or an ultimate source of energy, or even that instincts *exist* as separable units of character. Our hypothesis shall be that if we are to analyze the original human endowment at all, instinct is the most concrete unit of description we can use.

We shall adopt it, further, because it affords us at the start common ground with the biological understanding of human nature. We wish to accept, for the sake of the argument, the naturalistic view, namely, that man is an outgrowth of the series of living forms on the earth; that he is natively a group of instincts, due to that derivation. We shall allow this working-hypothesis to show its value, and the limits of its value.

If we turn then to the biologist, first of all, with the enquiry what characters are transmitted in 'heredity,' and how they are transmitted, we are invited to think of the original organic capital as a set of 'dispositions' to make typical 'reactions' to typical situations. These dispositions are most simply conceived in the psychological form of the 'reflex arc,' a set of nervous connections whereby an element of the situation acting as 'stimulus,' the disturbance is routed to those specific muscles which affect the 'response,' with an adequate release of energy by the way. And if we distinguish between simple reflexes and more or less intricate

groupings of reflexes, we arrive at the traditional notion of the physiology of instinct, namely, an hereditary arrangement of a group of reflex-arcs whereby
its members follow a more or less regular serial order
to a significant conclusion.

The serial order is apparent in any of the conspicuous animal instincts, as nest-building or wooing and
mating; or in such a sequence as carrying objects to the
mouth, chewing and swallowing, at that point in the
seven ages of man when these actions are still instinctive. The mechanism of the serial arrangement is also
fairly obvious: the conclusion of one stage of the process furnishes the stimulus, or a necessary part of the
stimulus, for the next stage. Thus, in general, the series
can follow but one order; and when once begun tends
to continue to the end.

In many instincts, perhaps in all of them, the stimulus is not single but manifold; an internal stimulus
must co-operate with an external stimulus before the
response can take place, the internal stimulus serving
as a sign that the organism is ready to act in a certain
way, and attuning the senses to especial alertness
toward the external stimulus, as thirst makes one keen
to all signs of water. If the internal stimulus is persistent (appearing in consciousness as a craving) while
the external stimulus is occasional, the course of the
corresponding instinct may appear irregular, may be
latent or interrupted. The hen ready to brood is presumably subject to an inner source of restlessness
which persists, like a hunger, until in presence of the
nest and its contents the long-deferred behavior sets

in with well-known determination or obstinacy.[1] It is not difficult to invent a scheme of nervous connections which could be conceived to operate in some such way as this in human beings. All such schemes are indeed too simple to account in full for even the simpler cases of actual behavior: but the biologist, like other scientists, lives by faith to this extent,—he inclines to regard his problem as solved when he can see how in principle it might be solved. And for the present we may assume that he is justified in his faith, if not by it.[2]

To each instinct there will necessarily belong a set of motor organs which may be assembled, in structure, as a single organ-group, or may be dispersed. To the swimming or flying or spinning instincts are bound the distinctive apparatuses. With the beaver's building propensity goes the beaver's tail. And vice versa, with every such group of motor organs[3] will be found an instinct for its operation. There is thus a very rough correspondence between bodily shape and instinctive equipment: the instincts are inherited with the body, as its behavior-charter, so to speak.

But to the biologist, the notion of instinct contains much more than the picture of a mechanism and the

[1] Professor Wallace Craig has rendered an important service in calling attention to the prevalence of these organic factors of 'appetence' and 'aversion' in instinct. Following him, Professor McDougall goes so far as to say that "it is probable that all instinctive action depends in some degree on Appetite." *Outline of Psychology*, p. 101.

[2] A carefully devised set of graphic schemes has been developed by Professor Max Meyer in *The Fundamental Laws of Human Behavior*.

[3] Any given muscle, it must be understood, may appear in a number of such groups. The distinctness of one instinct from another lies in the motor group, not in the motor units.

mode of its operation. The mechanism is regarded as a unit not simply because its activity has a definite beginning and ending, but because this activity reaches a conclusion which we called significant. More accurately, it brings about a situation which in general favors or once favored the survival of the organism or of its species. Instincts as modes of behavior common to all members of a species or sex of the species, characterize its way of life, outline its 'habits' in the major concerns of food-getting, defence, reproduction, etc. As hereditary paths of least resistance, they serve as a sort of initiation, a foreshortened education, for the vital activities of the species.

To be useful in this way, it is evident that they must be successful with a minimum of training, or with none. Social imitation helps the first efforts at flying, swimming, song; but it is the untaught and unteachable skill that marks instinct. Few, if any, instinctive actions can be said to be perfect at the first attempt (unless such unique actions as breaking through the egg-shell, and even then, a preliminary rehearsal or a second birth might well produce improvement). But the instinctive action is effective from the beginning, as it could not be effective had it to wait for either experience or instruction.

This relation of the instincts to the wider interests of the organism implies a further fact about their physiology. Their nervous circuits include branches that run through the highest nervous center. The instinct is under cerebral control; and, after its first quasi-mechanical operation, is subject to modification through its bearing on other processes reporting at the center. It is the destiny of most instincts to become habits shaped by experience of the owner; hence they must work under the supervision of the owner. They are not, like the winking-reflex, for example, incidental reactions of a part of an animal; they are reactions of the whole animal; they constitute the whole business of the moment of their operation. It is the whole animal that must turn from other business to this business, and retain through all such changes the continuity of its general routine or program. Hence the release of an instinctive operation is never accomplished by the sense-stimulus alone, as if some outer hand could fire a train which must then run its course through the organism, whether it assent or no : there is a releasing or inhibiting function at the center of highest co-ordination.

The language we have been using may all be interpreted physiologically. But for us, the significance of an instinct comes from the fact that its physiological aspect has at each point some bearing on the primitive mental facts of which we are in search. That a nervous loop passes upward through the higher centers means to us that an instinct is an element of consciousness as well as of sub-consciousness; it falls within what we call a mind, a memory; it builds into a continuous experience, and, while adding to it, adds always in such a way as to make part of the *same mind*.

From the conscious side, the 'stimulus' appears as an object of perception. And the circumstance that this object tends to stimulate, to provoke a response, implies that the perception will be accompanied by desire or aversion as well as followed by action. Some vaguer desire, or appetence, commonly precedes the perception and gives it, when it comes, the significance of an opportunity, whereupon desire takes a definite form: *"this* is what I have been wanting." As the nervous channel is the *physical* link between a particular stimulus and a particular response, so a desire is the *conscious* link between a particular perception and a particular action. Without this link of desire, the other two mental facts would not be parts of one mind: for the desire (or appetite or aversion) serves as the conscious excuse for proceeding from the perception to the action. At a certain level of reflectiveness the desire becomes the 'motive,' the 'purpose,' the 'reason' for the act; but at every level, the conscious *ownership* of the act implies that it is 'purposive,' i.e., that there is some change of experience desired and intended throughout the activity as its goal.

With the desire often appears feeling or emotion, especially if the response requires a large change in the energy or direction of the existing mental current.[4]

4 Since an activity perfectly adapted to its task might be perfectly mechanical, and therefore not only devoid of emotion but devoid of consciousness as well, and since instinctive action is held to belong to the more stable and quasi-mechanical adaptations, it has been held by many that it is not characteristically attended by emotion. If flight, for example, is attended by fear, the emotion is a sign not of adaptation but of mal-adaptation, and is therefore extraneous to the instinct itself, which is solely concerned with the efficiency of the behavior. It sometimes happens that in sudden peril an instinctive response is made with a steel-like accuracy and "presence of mind," as if all powers of intellect

But whether the stimulus arouses emotion or not, it always invites interest, developing various degrees of animation and excitement. As the kitten finds fascination in a moving string prior to any experience with mice, so every object that plays on instinctive tendencies seems invested with an unexplained claim upon attention. It has a seemingly intrinsic value, though experience discovers that its value is derived from that something-else whose desire the stimulus arouses, and which it therefore points to, or 'means.'

This 'meaning' of the stimulus is more or less vague and premonitory according to the extent of one's experience with that particular instinct and its result. But I judge that a stimulus has from the beginning some anticipatory meaning, since it must render its account to the mind into which it falls. It seems probable to me that even at first sight, a pond of water must have to a gosling some such meaning: it is an

and of skilled adjustment were heightened in an emotionless blaze of supernormal adroitness; while the emotional tremor and disordering of function may supervene ''after it is all over.''

If one identifies the emotion with the disturbance, and not with the state of heightened faculty itself, it is certain that the emotion is not a state of perfect adaptation; but it may still be a state of *transition from one adjustment to another,* and so a normal attendant of that change of energy-flow and focussing which must occur at the onset of any instinctive action. If the transition is brief, the emotion will be equally brief. But brief and violent transitions may mean incomplete organic preparations, and hence an excessive prostration after the heightened effort is over. The mental aspect of the deferred emotion seems to be most pronounced in the most self-conscious, and to consist in part of the effort to maintain the sense of self-identity in the violently different states of cœnæsthesia. While the instinct has enabled one to act with supreme immediacy and effect, the reckoning with self-consciousness has to come later.

object, I imagine, which not only engages attention, but also invites with dim promises joined with premonitory stirrings of unused swimming mechanisms, while making direct appeal to the waddling abilities already acquired. If this is the case, instinct on its conscious side would involve an idea-content and an active-tendency of an essentially *a priori* character,—not an *a priori* knowledge precisely, but an *a priori* expectation, involving representative images, however indefinite, not derived from the previous experience of the individual organism. I see no sufficient reason for rejecting this view,—a *tabula rasa* at birth the mind certainly is not. But however it may be at the first appearance of a stimulus, in the course of time any such instinct-object comes to mean definitely the whole instinct-process and its end. The 'stimulus,' then, as a fact of consciousness, is the pre-perception of the end as the meaning of the beginning.

Because of this demand upon attention and interest, always more or less unexplained, an instinctive impulse frequently appears as a stranger in the house, curiously external to the 'self' that dwells there. Thus fear or anger may invade a mind as an intruder with which the self deliberately struggles, in the name of reason or of principle. In working out the issue with fear of the dark, a child commonly reaches a stage in which this fear is almost an objective phenomenon within himself, and may be personified as an enemy to be overcome. The instinct with an impetus and course so much its own (as if constituting a separate self in a minor way) is indeed something other than the pre-existing self. Regarded from the standpoint of biological wisdom, the instinct in making for results favorable to the species has been interpreted as the representative of the race at work within the individual.[5] Now it is certain that so long as my mind remains mine, I can be lured into working out the weal of the species, before I understand that weal, only if the end-situation has in it something which my individual self also can value: the purposiveness of instinct must be primarily purposiveness for the individual. But it may well be that the value-for-me which invites the self into an instinctive course is felt by that self as a pretext about which obscure and as-yet-alien values are gathered. There is an unrevealed *more* in its meaning. Hence, perhaps, a certain dread frequently felt at the brink of instinctive behavior, even when it presents itself as a path of satisfaction.

Yet in this externality of the instinct—naturally clearest in the aversions, the negative instincts—there is a paradox. It is in instinctive action that one is most himself. During the moment in which the object of perception, the stimulus, may be purely 'interesting,' the self stands outside the instinct; but the fascination which that object exercises, whether auspicious or baleful, conveys an invitation to identify that self with an attractive process of action. To yield to the invitation is perceived as a route of high satisfaction, even though (as in anger) there is involved an intense effort and possible pain. The instinct is a

[5] Cf. A. Myerson, *The Foundations of Personality*, pp. 108, 109 and note.

channel down which the current of life rushes with exceptional impetus; once committed to it, we reach our highest pitch of personal self-consciousness, our greatest sense of power and command. The self becomes identified with its major passions: the experience of passion is a fateful experience; and the same self emerges as also not the same, because it has discovered missing elements of *itself* by the way.

To resume our view of this term, instinct, so commonly invoked, and which we hypothetically adopt as a unit of human and animal nature: As a physiological mechanism, we have noted the orderly and progressive sequence of reflexes that compose it, the contribution of this series, as a whole, to the vital interests of the organism or species, the central connection which marks its response as total, and its destiny to be modified by experience and to become an individualized habit. As a fact of consciousness, we have described instinct as accentuating the interest of certain objects of perception, endowing them with a meaning to be worked out in a course of conduct whose prompting is the essential part of the instinct, giving zest, momentum, and assurance to that course of conduct,—a zest not unmixed with the thrill of dread as something fateful for the history of the self,—and leading to a situation of repose whose value is the conscious justification for the whole process.

If the entire human being is originally a bundle of such instincts, this 'self' which at any moment seems to be contrasted with a given instinct may be regarded as the representative at that moment of all the *other* instincts. I doubt whether this will prove to be a wholly satisfactory account of the 'self,' but it may serve us for the present as a part of our working hypothesis.

CHAPTER VIII

THE RANGE OF INSTINCT

IN forming our notion of instinct, we find at the same time the criteria by which an instinct is to be recognized. To external observation, the presence of an instinct would be indicated by the trend of the entire species into a distinctive mode of livelihood, by an untaught skill in pursuing these characteristic ways and by the peculiar organs or organic contours that correspond to them. An observer would look also for outward signs of the inner states which accompany instinct, for the expressions of spontaneous interest in certain objects, of desire or aversion, of characteristic emotions, and, finally, of a degree of urgency and insistence in the behavior. For the impeding of instinctive behavior in animals commonly excites first vehemence and then anger. Arts which can be attributed to random action and the discoveries it brings, or to deliberate trial and error, or to ingenuity, are in so far not due to instinct, whose successes are neither accidental nor yet reasoned. Effectiveness beyond what either chance or the existing intelligence would account for is thus an important criterion of instinct. But behavior which is both unreasoned and unreasonable, as being maladapted to existing conditions, is often understood as instinctive, if it appears a recognizable persistence of dispositions serviceable in savagery or more primitive states. To long-continued observation other marks may furnish clues. Thus, since instinctive action is an attractive experience, it is likely to be not alone recurrent, but also the basis of play, and, in subtler expression, of the more enduring interests, bents, and powers, sometimes of exaggeration to the point of mental disorder.

But these criteria are not all equally serviceable or conclusive. For the most part, the identification of an instinct tends to rest upon the simple question whether there is an untaught and unreasoned skill, the other marks being merely corroborative. With these criteria at hand, what range of instinct can we attribute to original human nature?

At first sight, the human equipment seems comparatively slender. We have already referred to the relative absence of fixed traits in the human infant, the predominance of random action rather than of specific responses to specific stimuli. Lengthened infancy implies lengthened parental guidance; and what instinct must do for less favored animals it would better leave undone for a creature whose conduct is to be so variously ordered and so radically experimental. Bergson has recently reaffirmed the once current belief that man, with the vertebrates generally, has largely surrendered instinct in the interest of intellect. This "running to intellect," i.e., an innate propensity to master vital problems by dissecting and reconstructing, such as men take to with more or less of untaught skill, might with some justice be called the essential instinct of man, a substitute for all other instincts. In him, the vital impetus makes for curiosity, and for the invention of hypotheses, and of tools.

It is true that many observers, from Darwin and Spencer onward to Chadbourne and William James, have been impressed by the number and variety of instinct-rudiments in man. But we are looking for fundamental factors in the building of a mind, not for relics and fragments of an admitted animal ancestry. We wish to know whether there are instincts which, as McDougall claims, provide the nucleus of all human values: we are less concerned whether there are vestiges that explain the peculiar ways in which we laugh or cry.

In animals other than man, instinct attracts attention partly because of the conjunction of apparently superhuman cunning with subhuman powers of thought; in part because of the remarkable bodily structures which accompany them. Man lacks these striking organic instruments almost entirely. He has no horns, wings, humps, claws, quills, tusks, shell, or sting. His body offers no visible foothold for notable functions of offence, defence, or craftsmanship. He is a relatively smooth and unmarked animal. Internally, also, his organs are undistinguished. Except that he is obviously neither fish nor fowl, his structure does not mark him for this or that habitat or diet, nor for special mastery over any part of nature. Physically, he is, as nearly as possible, animal-in-general.

From what we can infer of primitive psychology,

something analogous must be said of the inner man. He shows no great native skills nor passions. He is not strikingly social nor solitary, warlike nor submissive, benevolent nor selfish. Hobbes and Grotius were both in error, the one in representing us as dominantly pugnacious, the other as dominantly amicable. Montesquieu showed greater insight. The natural human being, he thought, shows no conspicuous powers, whether of loyalty, mastery, or achievement, interested or disinterested. Sufficient evidence of this may be the wide disagreements of those who have ventured to draw up lists of the principal instincts. Apart from fear, hunger, pugnacity, and love, few names commonly recur in such lists; and none of these can show a wholly undisputed title. Thus, psychically also, we seem to be dealing with a generalized creature, not with one specified in character by many instinctive traits.

But there are reasons why in the case of the human being, the coarser criteria of instinct may not at once reveal what is there. Three such reasons occur to me:

1. *The balance of instincts.* If any organ or function is inconspicuous, it is always possible that it does not exist, and this is no doubt the most obvious supposition. But it is also possible that supplementary organs or functions have grown up beside it, balancing its action, and tending to conceal it. So far as human instincts are concerned, the latter supposition seems the true one. Anatomically, it is the balance of powers rather than the lack of them that distinguishes the human type. The erect posture, for instance, implies

not the lack of a ventral musculature, but rather the growth of an equivalent dorsal musculature. Likewise with the instincts. If no one impulse is dominant in human behavior, it is not because the impulses are lacking, but because in any situation two or more impulses are likely to be concerned. Man is not fated to predation, nor yet to a life of fear and flight. It is not prescribed by nature that he should live in immense herds, nor in mutually repellent families, nor alone. Yet impulses in all these directions are present in him, and he is the field of their conflict and adjustment.

2. *Variety of pattern*. For the sake of simplicity we commonly picture the physiological pattern of an instinct as a triple arrangement of sense-stimulus, central adjustment, and muscular response,—for each instinct a complete individual set of these three parts. And where an instinct conforms to this simple design, following a path of its own and using a specialized group of muscles as in eating, vocalization, locomotion, it will hardly escape detection. But few of our instincts have such clear-cut rights-of-way: for some of them few muscles or none are set apart. Thus, fear-and-flight and anger-and-combat are highly contrasting impulses: but they arise from similar stimuli, and the muscles as well as the visceral changes involved in one largely coincide with those involved in the other. To instincts of this pattern, structure will furnish no definite clue.

And there is, unless I am much mistaken, a still more obscure pattern,—one in which the muscular changes involved are variable, and in some cases comparatively unimportant, because the function of the instinct is to effect adjustments within the nervous system. If there is an instinctive basis for æsthetic values, for example, it is probably of this pattern; surely there is no typical series of muscular events which can be said to be characteristic of our response to beauty! An investigator whose eye is fixed upon the pattern of sensible stimulus and determinate muscular response will be inclined to deny the existence of such instincts; but we cannot so dogmatically close the question.

3. *Coalescence of instincts.* There is a tendency among instincts of all but the simplest patterns, not alone to share in the tracts of physical expression (as above), but also to participate in the satisfactions one of another, vicariously. Are we prepared to say, for instance, that a successful wooing provides satisfaction for the mating instinct, but none for the instinct of acquisition (if there is such) or of self-assertion (if there is such), or, for that matter, of self-abasement? If not, we must acknowledge that no enumeration of instincts in which one is supposed to be wholly different from the other in clean-cut division, is likely to do justice to the actual situation.

When these sources of possible error are borne in mind, it will appear, I believe, that the human equipment of instinct is by no means a meager one. We shall now endeavor to make a rough survey of it.

CHAPTER IX

SURVEY OF THE HUMAN EQUIPMENT

FIRST, there are numerous clear-cut instincts of simple pattern which we may call 'units of behavior,' because they are used in various combinations. In the human economy not alone are there few muscles that are used for only one achievement: there are few of the simpler instincts which appear in only one vital function. The operations of reaching, grasping, pulling, shaking, are such units. They are sometimes referred to jointly as an instinct of prehension. But evidently there are few of the major instincts into whose course they do not enter, as in the beginnings of locomotion, in climbing, food-getting, curiosity, love, pugnacity. It is as if in man the elaborate instincts of his animal forbears had been broken into fragments, or analyzed after the manner of human intelligence itself, in order that duplication might be avoided, and new possibilites of combining realized. Instead of a one-piece instinct of locomotion, we have many partial instincts which further the co-operation of various groups of muscles in the numerous postures of which the body is capable, in crawling, standing, walking, running, climbing. Doubtless many of these innate connections have yet to be isolated: no one knows what instinctive hints and guidance may come to the aid of the first leap or of the first dodge or fall. Food-getting when it reaches the mouth becomes almost a specific instinct, though sucking, biting, chewing have a degree of separability, and so of other employment. The tendency of all careful study of instincts, guided by the formula of sense-stimulus and specific response, is to fragmentize in this manner the older instinct categories. "Curiosity" disappears in a group of instinctive movements of attention and of manipulation such as we mentioned above. The result is an elaborate gamut of units of behavior.[1]

Some writers decline to include these units of behavior among the instincts on the ground that they approximate too closely simple reflexes, that they are not adaptive in any significant sense when taken severally, and that there is no distinctive emotion or affective coloring associated with their exercise.[2] That may be left as a question of nomenclature, with the remark that these simple dispositions cannot be omitted from the account of our inheritance, as they are most evidently not acquired.[3]

To some other writers, these units of behavior are, strictly speaking, the only true instincts. The wider categories, curiosity, hunger, etc., these writers believe should be recognized either as convenient and misleading class-names, representing no real unitary instinct or, if they describe actual dispositions, as acquired habits of reaction built up by incorporating

---

[1] See the lists of James and Thorndike noticed on pages 76-79.

[2] W. McDougall, *Outline of Psychology*, p. 117.

[3] They are accepted as innate by some who otherwise disparage the use of the concept of instinct. Cf. Z. Y. Kuo, *Journal of Philosophy*, Nov. 24, 1921, p. 658.

many of these units into compound patterns shaped by experience and training.[4] It is not evident, however, why a combination of such units to a single serviceable end might not be prearranged by nature quite as truly as the units themselves. It is a question of fact, not of nomenclature, whether such more inclusive instincts exist, i.e., whether such dispositions as pugnacity, sociability, food-getting, are an integral part of our heredity, as well as the simple motor-mechanisms which they employ. Flight, for example, under the impulse of fear, seems a thoroughly instinctive performance, making use with untaught skill of many units of behavior. It is noteworthy also that the order and variety of these units is not fixed: the end-situation to be brought about by flight is describable only in general terms, as well as the means of reaching it. The end is to get *away;* and it is a secondary matter what place I reach, or whether I run away, creep away, or climb away. I should recognize flight as a genuine instinct, identified by its vital meaning or end and by the general character of the process. And since both the end and the process are to be described in general rather than specific terms, this instinct might be called a *general instinct*. Most of the traditional instincts are general in this sense. Fear, which names an emotion rather than an instinct, expresses itself not alone in flight but in contraction, concealment, rigid immobility, or

[4] A similar problem arises in the outlining of species. ''In a handful of small shells the 'splitters' may recognize 20 species, while the 'slumpers' see only 3. Thus Haeckel says of calcareous sponges that, as the naturalist likes to look at the problem, there are 3 species, or 21, or 289, or 591.'' Thomson, *Outlines of Zoölogy*, p. 14.

heightened adroitness. Yet it also has a definable end; and its unity seems further guaranteed by its genetic position at the head of a group of defensive reactions. I should recognize fear as the (rather inaccurate) name of an instinct of high generality.[5]

It is among these general instincts that the tendency of the human equipment toward *balance* is most readily recognized. Some of the units of behavior are paired, as pulling and pushing, taking into the mouth and spitting out, laughing and weeping; many again have no specific counterparts. But the general instincts fall naturally into pairs, as follows: instinct to general physical activity and instinct to repose (including the various modes of rest and sleep as units of behavior);[6] curiosity and aversion to novelty; sociability and anti-sociability. This last named pair is itself highly general, including within itself such instincts, also general, as those of dominance and submission, sex-love and sex-aversion, and parental love,—which seems to have

[5] Lloyd Morgan recognizes (*Scientia*, October, 1920) three levels of instinct: simple motor tendencies, mid-level instincts, and high-level instincts. The latter two levels correspond to our general instincts, the "high-level instincts" (self-preservation and race-maintenance) being tendencies of high generality. I should raise the question of fact, especially in regard to race-maintenance, but I am glad for this confirmation of the existence of the general instinct.

[6] In the first edition of this book, it was with much hesitancy that I included these instincts to general physical arousal and repose-seeking: in the tabular survey, p. 56, I marked them with a query. I was inclined to include them because the ways of making these transitions in activity and alertness, affecting the set of all other instincts, are highly characteristic of animal species. Since then, I have been confirmed in this judgment by observations of Szymanski, Claparède and McDougall (*Outline of Psychology*, p. 165 n.). W. H. R. Rivers' "instinct of collapse" would seem to me to belong also in this place.

no more express counterpart than a repugnance to children, which in most persons is a submerged trait.

It is possible that all of these instincts are derived, as G. H. Schneider thinks, from a pair of primitive reactions, expansive and contractive in nature. I should, in fact, be inclined to group all the assertive and outgoing instincts under one highly general instinct of activity, or expansion, and all the negative instincts under a highly general instinct of retraction or aversion. Pugnacity would be a general instinct, comparatively late in development, uniting in itself the qualities of aversion and expansion. The most primitive reaction to opposition is contraction, withdrawal, 'fear': nature's second thought is that a reserve of energy may be devoted to remove the obstacle—and here pugnacity, with its own characteristic units of behavior, enters the scene.

In speaking of pugnacity, however, we touch upon a highly interesting development in the system of instincts. In a wider sense of the word pugnacity, it may be said that every instinct is pugnacious; that is, it is characteristic of instinctive action of all sorts, even of fear, to meet opposition with irritation and an increased appropriation of energy. Professor William McDougall has made this fact the defining character of anger and the instinct of pugnacity. That quality of spiritedness which makes an obstacle a spur rather than a discouragement is unquestionably a more general form of the fighting instinct. But the point of particular interest in this wider form of pugnacity is that it is an *instinctive control of instinct, an instinct of the second order*. There are other aspects of the instinctive regulation of the course of instincts. *Play* is a lightening of the instinct-pressure, so to speak, under control of sociability; as pugnacity is an enhancement of pressure, under control of anti-sociability.[7] Every instinct may be expressed playfully as well as pugnaciously; and the preponderance of one or the other of these tendencies of the second order marks the difference in temperament between the gay and the serious-minded. It may also be said that every instinct is *curious,* for every instinct, in man at any rate, tends to lend interest to objects in any way bearing upon its own operation; or, conversely, curiosity may be regarded as a function of control or guidance applicable generally to instincts of the first order. Curiosity as an appendage of food-getting, construction, sociability, etc., doubtless precedes in order of development the curiosity which appears as an independent hunger of the mind.

This latter kind of curiosity is typical of that important group of general instincts which in our last chapter we spoke of as *central*. These introduce a question so critical for our theory of instinct that we treat of it in a separate chapter. It will be in place here to throw into rough tabular form the survey so far as completed, while recognizing the impossibility of representing in

[7] Play and pugnacity, in this regulative capacity, furnish another instance of balance, and we frequently find them alternating. But their relation is not simply that of contrast and balance. As instincts of the second order, the domain of each includes the other, i.e., we often play at pugnacity, and are sometimes pugnacious in the pursuit of play.

SURVEY OF THE HUMAN INSTINCTS

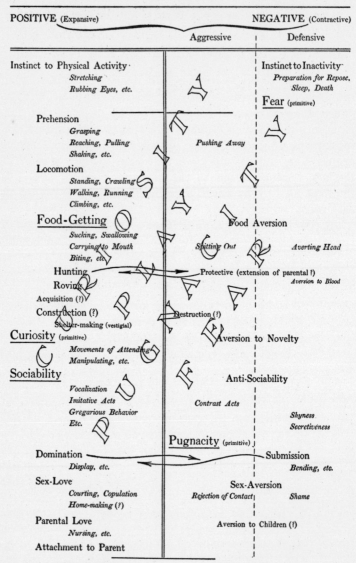

POSITIVE (Expansive)   **NEGATIVE** (Contractive)

Aggressive | Defensive

Instinct to Physical Activity ·   Instinct to Inactivity·
   Stretching   *Preparation for Repose,*
   Rubbing Eyes, etc.   *Sleep, Death*

               Fear (primitive)

Prehension
   Grasping
   Reaching, Pulling   *Pushing Away*
   Shaking, etc.

Locomotion
   Standing, Crawling
   Walking, Running
   Climbing, etc.

Food-Getting   Food Aversion
   Sucking, Swallowing
   Carrying to Mouth   *Spitting Out*   *Averting Head*
   Biting, etc.

   Hunting   Protective (extension of parental ?)
   Roving   *Aversion to Blood*

Acquisition (?)
   Construction (?)   Destruction (?)
   Shelter-making (vestigial)

Curiosity (primitive)   Aversion to Novelty
   Movements of Attending
   Manipulating, etc.

Sociability   Anti-Sociability
   Vocalization
   Imitative Acts   *Contrast Acts*
   Gregarious Behavior   *Shyness*
   Etc.   *Secretiveness*

       Pugnacity (primitive)

Domination   Submission
   Display, etc.   *Bending, etc.*

Sex-Love   Sex-Aversion
   Courting, Copulation   *Rejection of Contact*   *Shame*
   Home-making (?)

Parental Love   Aversion to Children (?)
   Nursing, etc.

Attachment to Parent

NOTE. *Instincts of second order written across page.*   Units *of behavior in* Italics.
Indentation indicates degree of generality, not genetic priority.

two dimensions—or any other number—the relations between psycho-physical entities of this kind.

NOTE. For comparison I append several lists of instincts:

P. A. Chadbourne, writing in 1872, was one of the earliest in this country to give attention to instinct in man. William James was influenced to some extent by his work. His attitude is modern in one respect at least: instead of arguing from the inadequacy of instinct to the necessity of reason in man, he argues from the incompetence of reason to the necessity of instinct. Because reason, in the following respects, is unable to adapt man to his world, a group of instincts is needed at each point:

1. For the life of the individual and the species, a set of instincts common to man and animals, and sufficiently designated as 'appetites.'
2. For progress of the individual and the race:
   The desire for society;
   The desire for knowledge, property, power, esteem;
   The impulse to confide in persons, or faith;
   The disposition to do for posterity.
3. For benevolence (i.e., for maintaining the social and moral life):
   The sense of obligation. "It is plain that we feel under obligation to do certain acts for the doing of which we can give no reason except that we feel the obligation." Shown in four ways:
   1. Impelling to choose the end for which we are made;
   2. Impelling to every act judged as means to that end;
   3. Impelling to certain acts whose relation to that end is not seen;
   4. Impelling the "comprehending power" to do its best to furnish the most favorable conditions for realizing our obligation.

4. For religion (i.e., for adaptation to supernatural environment) :
  The impulse to prayer, etc.

William James, writing in 1890, gives a list based largely on Preyer and G. H. Schneider, remarking of it that "no other mammal, not even the monkey, shows so large an array." Approximately the first twenty correspond with our 'units of behavior.'

Sucking.
Biting.
Chewing and grinding teeth.
Licking.
Grimacing.
Spitting out.
Clasping.
Reaching toward.
Pointing (and sounding).
Carrying to mouth.
Crying.
Smiling.
Protruding lips.
Turning head aside.
Holding head erect.
Sitting up.
Standing.
Locomotion.
Climbing.

Vocalization.
Imitation.
Emulation or rivalry.
Pugnacity, anger, resentment.
Sympathy.
The hunting instinct.
Fear.
Acquisition.
Constructiveness.
Play.
Curiosity.
Sociability and shyness.
Secretiveness.
Cleanliness.
Modesty, shame.
Love.
Jealousy.
Parental love.

In making his list, James was guided by a method of "physiological analysis," and he regarded his results, though confessedly incomplete, as having clear advantages over such a "muddled list" as that of Santlus (Leipzig, 1864), who had classified human instincts under three heads,—instincts of being, of function, and of life.

Professor William McDougall allows the name of instinct

only to what we have called general instincts, holding that while an instinct "may make use at need of a large array of motor mechanisms" it may employ differently such units on different occasions and hence "does not essentially comprise in its organization any motor mechanism" (*Journal of Abnormal Psychology*, 1921-22, p. 311). An instinct must be defined by the nature of its goal, i.e., the change of situation which it tends to bring about: its essence is the purposive striving toward this goal. On these grounds McDougall recognizes (*Outline of Psychology*, 1923) thirteen instincts, as follows:

> Parental or protective instinct.
> Instinct of combat.
> Curiosity.
> Food-seeking.
> Instinct of avoidance, repulsion, or disgust.
> Instinct of escape.
> Gregariousness.
> Self-assertion.
> Submission.
> Mating instinct.
> Acquisitive instinct.
> Constructive instinct.
> Instinct of appeal.

In addition to these, McDougall recognizes certain minor and specific instincts (sneezing, coughing, scratching, excretion, laughing) approximating reflexes, but not serving as units of behavior in other instincts, and also suggestibility, imitation, and sympathy, as innate tendencies of a different pattern.

The most discriminating inventory is that of Professor E. L. Thorndike, in *The Original Nature of Man*, 1913. Thorndike is as much of a "splitter" as McDougall is a "slumper." This is the inevitable consequence of his attempt to apply consistently the scheme of stimulus-response. It would be impracticable to reproduce here the net result of his painstaking studies in the form of a list, and also somewhat unfair, as he regards the list as decidedly provisional.

But a specimen of his reducing process may be given. To recognize groups of instincts resulting in food-getting, habitation, fear, fighting, anger, is a matter of convenience, not of strictly scientific relationship. When named by situation and response, the following innate connections, among others, may be regarded as probable:

SITUATION	RESPONSE
Eating	
Sweet taste.	Sucking movements.
Bitter taste.	Separating posterior portions of tongue and palate.
Very sour, salt, acrid, bitter, oily objects.	Spitting and letting drool out of the mouth.
Food when satiated.	Turning head to one side.
Reaching.	
Not being closely cuddled (in young infants).	Reaching and clutching.
An object attended to and approximately within reaching distance.	Reaching, maintaining extension until object is grasped.
An attractive object seen.	Reaching and pointing, often with 'a peculiar sound expressive of desire.'
Acquisition and possession.	
Any not too large object which attracts attention and does not possess repelling or frightening features.	Approach, or if within reaching distance, reaching, touching, and grasping.
Possession of object grasped.	Putting in mouth, or general manipulation, or both.

A person or animal grabbing or making off with an object which one holds or has near him as a result of recent action of the responses of acquisition.

The neural action paralleling the primitive emotion of anger, a tight clutch on the object, and pushing, striking, and screaming at the intruder.[8]

[8] *The Original Nature of Man*, pp. 50-52.

CHAPTER X

THE CENTRAL INSTINCTS: NECESSARY INTERESTS

WE have had several occasions to refer to the place of curiosity in the group of human instincts. However large the difference among men in the degree of their inquisitiveness, this trait is evidently in some degree a native character of the species, in both sexes. It shows itself in certain units of behavior of the simplest pattern, such as grasping, tasting, pulling to pieces. It bears an evident proportion to other instincts: wherever animals are scantily armed and slightly pugnacious, there is generally a compensating development of fear or curiosity, or of both, as in the timorous and yet inquisitive herbivora. These tendencies, whether in animals or in men, to spy out, examine, test, dissect, appear to be untaught, effective, and frequently absorbing. Sometimes they reach morbid intensity and become a "questioning mania," or "*Grübelsucht.*" Thus there are substantial reasons for including curiosity among the instincts.

If it still seems anomalous to find the activity of intellect, customarily contrasted with instinct, brought within that category, we may remember that while the intellect finds reasons (which are certainly something else than instinct), it does not begin by asking the reason for finding reasons. The motive or value of its own activity is, during that activity, unreasoned and untaught. The *exercise* of thought, as has often been remarked, is a matter of our impulsive nature; and it is the underlying craving for action, rather than the particular type of activity, that primarily betokens the instinct.

Yet if we ask what we should regard as the 'stimulus' in the case of curiosity, we find it impossible to bring it under the usual reflex scheme. "There is no one class of objects," McDougall points out, "to which it is especially directed, or in presence of which it is invariably displayed."[1] Curiosity is commonly excited by what is novel; and what is novel is relative to the previous experience of the individual in question. The idea of a 'stimulus' as a group of sensations that when repeated will invariably excite the given behavior is thus excluded in advance,—the conditions for exciting curiosity negate the very definition of a stimulus. Curiosity is also frequently aroused by signs of concealment or stealth in others; but try to express concealment or stealth in terms of a constant group of sense-impressions, and one forcibly realizes that these are objects, not of vision, but of interpretation in terms of social consciousness.

And if we ask what we should regard as the 'response,' we find a similar difficulty. Curiosity has its manifestations in physical behavior like any other instinct; but the behavior is now of one kind and now of another,—listening, peeking, testing with hands and

[1] *Body and Mind*, p. 266.

mouth, pulling apart, smelling, shaking, tiptoeing and creeping up upon, or later, reading, asking questions, 'stopping to think,'—there is no one-to-one correspondence between the impulse of curiosity and any type of physical action.

This does not mean either that we are dealing with a multitude of fragmentary instincts, or yet, as McDougall infers, that we are dealing with a purely psychical process which has no complete physiological expression. What it does mean, I suggest, is that we must recognize a kind of process in which the 'stimulus' as well as the 'response' are primarily central. It is the existing state of consciousness which determines whether, and in what quarter, curiosity shall be aroused, and what constitutes its satisfaction. In physiological terms, curiosity is a function of the condition of the centers. It has analogies to hunger or appetence; but the basis of this particular craving is not visceral, nor reported to the brain in a stream of sensations by way of the afferent nerves. Though typical external puzzles—such as unusual behavior, situations exploited in mystery and detective stories, challenging problems and 'projects'—may provide the strain characteristic of curiosity, the readiness and restlessness thus aroused are conditions of the brain itself; the hunger to know is especially keen in the maturing brain.

It seems probable that there is a group of tendencies, quite as native as any modes of muscular behavior, which, like curiosity, have their inception and do their work within the higher nervous centers. If certain central conditions are natively unsatisfactory and certain others natively satisfactory (which can hardly be doubted), it is a question of organization whether there will also be native ways of bringing about a change from the former to the latter of these conditions. Whether we extend the word instinct to them, in view of their deviation from the primary pattern, is a matter of choice in definition. In their case, the term instinct becomes strained, and we reach the border of its usefulness in describing original human nature. It is justified in so far as these tendencies are innate rather than acquired, and are universally distributed. It is misleading in so far as their whole process differs profoundly from the reflex type. If the term instinct is to be retained, they should be distinguished as 'central instincts.' Or, since they would depend in the first place not on specific routing of nervous energy, but on the nature of the nervous system itself, the needs in question would presumably be the same in kind though not in degree for every animal having a nervous system; and it would be proper to speak of them as 'necessary interests.'[2]

That this theory may be of some use in explaining our æsthetic tendencies, we have already suggested. Consider the universal tendency to rhythmic expres-

[2] Note that the necessity of these interests is here described not as a logical but as a constitutional necessity. This necessity depends solely on what modes of central nervous operation are satisfactory modes, from the standpoint of the functions of the central nervous system. It is thus a fundamentally different kind of 'necessary interest' from that which Professor R. B. Perry recognizes in the satisfaction of interests generally: this latter is a logically necessary interest, i.e., for a mind sufficiently reflective to make a class of its own interests.

sion, as in dancing, music, design, various forms of
play. There are many signs that the appreciation of
rhythm is as necessary a consequence of the economy
of nervous functions, as rhythmic behavior is of the
economy of muscular function, of respiratory function,
etc. When we want to gain the full flavor of any sense-
impression, we repeat it at intervals, as in tasting,
stroking, feeling textures, etc. So, too, with those perceptions in which thought is mingled with sense. In
realizing the proportions of a façade, a series of but-
tresses or a segmented cornice aid the "grasp." Even
a small surface, as of a coin, seems more completely
known when divided: the spatial perception joined
with the perception of number gives, as it were, a perception of higher order. The principle may be this: that
to appreciate any experience in its totality we must
resort to the device of really or mimetically building
it up from numerable parts; so that whatever we desire
to hold vividly before consciousness we will necessarily
tend to divide and recompose by segments or in rhythmic intervals. Rhythm would then be a general character of art forms, i.e., of the forms we choose for
heightened perception, because of a necessary condition of the neural substratum of cognition. In this sense
we might speak of rhythm as a necessary interest.[3]

Can these necessary interests be enumerated?

It seems evident to me that many names which have
rumbled through theories of instinct without gaining

[3] Mr. Joseph Lee includes rhythm in his list of instincts. *Play in
Education*, 1915, ch. xx.

any definite lodgment have been aimed at this place.
We have heard of an instinct of self-preservation; and
as no definite stimulus or response can be alleged for
such an instinct, it has been dropped from the books,
and some of its ingredients retained, as pugnacity or
self-assertion or fear. The 'will to live' and the 'will to
power' have been allowed a possible place in metaphysics, but with the distinct understanding that they have
no status in psychology. 'Sociability' or 'gregarious-
ness' is commonly regarded as a native trait; yet it will
be found as difficult to define a sense-stimulus and response for the social propensities of men as for their
curiosity.

My judgment is that the most significant of original
human tendencies are tendencies of this central sort.
I should include among these necessary interests our
sociability as well as our curiosity, and hence certain
major ingredients of ambition and the family affections. I have mentioned our formal interest in rhythm,
and there are other formal interests which appear to
be equally native, and to play a part in æsthetics and
logic, such as the interest in simplicity, unity, harmony,
etc., possibly also the prejudice in favor of thoroughness, clean-cut-ness, which runs a long gamut from the
careful toilet-making of animals to the passion for
separateness and purity of many of the saintly-minded.
As for 'self-preservation,' I incline to recognize in the
phrase a fact of human nature more elemental than
pugnacity or self-assertion, which might be understood
as follows:

The will to live, for a being with a mind, must always

mean the will to be mentally alive as well as to be physically metabolizing. The presumption is that the simple fact of *being conscious,* other things equal, is a satisfactory condition; and that a self-conscious being would with a necessity both constitutional and logical (in Professor Perry's sense) tend to preserve the fact and to increase the quantity of his liveliness or awareness. If it is not merely the contents of experience that are valuable, but the process of experiencing, it is clear that so far as a being is self-conscious he will necessarily have a 'will to live,' or an 'instinct of self-preservation.'

In these necessary interests, we have the most significant but also the most obscure of original human tendencies. It is they that have been the chief stumbling block in the theory of instinct; for while that theory becomes comparatively trivial when they are omitted, it has always been muddled when they have been included. The attempt to assimilate them to the type of stimulus and response could hardly have ended otherwise than in confusion. On their physiological side, they are elusive, inaccessible to observation, and refractory to experiment: they are consequences of the fact that the stuff of which we are made works better in one way than another, and not of an arrangement of connections whereby muscles can be set moving by an impact from outside. On the other hand, to cut loose from the reflex-arc pattern has been too often to cut loose from the control of empirical categories altogether in completing the tale of our original endowment. If we are to believe that "the behavior of man in the family, in business, in the state, in religion, and in every other affair of life is rooted in his unlearned original equipment,'[4] that equipment must be a capital stock of large moment; but if at the same time we can reach no agreement as to what it is, and no better description than such terms as 'the will to live,' we can understand a revolt against the use of the conception of instinct in psychology and in the social sciences.

The chief difficulty of reaching a clear and exhaustive enumeration of these tendencies, and hence the chief reason for the all-but-arbitrary variety that has prevailed in the lists of the more general instincts, does not lie, however, in their peculiar mechanism: it lies in the fact that they are *not distinct and separable entities.* They are in reality various aspects of one fundamental instinct or necessary interest. The variety of partly overlapping terms for the more general instinct is due to the variety of approaches to the same object. Could we identify this object, we should at once have the clue to this variety, and be freed from its confusion and from the futile effort to enumerate all forms which the central instinct could take.

If we cannot identify it, we can at least draw attention to its existence, make evident the fact that the general instincts have a region of coalescence, being related as the fingers of a hand rather than as the separate twigs in a bundle, and indicate that this common region is of the first importance for our estimate of original human nature.

[4] Thorndike, *Educational Psychology,* I, p. 4.

CHAPTER XI

THE WILL

IT is notoriously hard to read the motives of other men's acts. And while we have a position of advantage in judging the motives of our own acts, the chances of error are still large. A writer of fiction might fairly be allowed to claim knowledge of the minds of his own creations: yet even here, if I am not mistaken, there is a visible dread of dogmatism, and romance is tending to return to the psychological reticence of the drama, which reveals the mind chiefly through situation and behavior.

This new demand for objectivity need not mean that 'motives' are fictions. It may well mean that our theory of motives is unsatisfactory. The question whether one who joins the colors is actuated by pugnacity, or by love of country, or by ambition, or by mob consciousness, or by need of shining in the eyes of some woman, is a futile question: but it is futile, less because the truth is so hard to ascertain than because of a false assumption in the question. For, since the presence of one of these motives need not exclude another, the either-or assumption of any such question is gratuitous. All actual motives are mixed. Synthesis or fusion of motives, which to Holt is the chief moral obligation, is in fact the universal and natural practice.

But the question I wish to raise is not whether

motives are compounded: it is rather *whether they are originally separate*. It is here, I believe, that we find the root of the difficulty.

Can we say, for example, that curiosity is one thing and the love of power or security a different and separable thing? The interest with which civilization reads its morning paper, the disposition to gossip and to hear gossip, the most flagrant acts of prying or eavesdropping,—is it certain that these are to be put down to intellectual hunger and not to the 'instinct of self-preservation' (since ignorance is undeniably a state of peril), or to the 'instinct of self-assertion' (since knowledge promises control of persons and events)? If the superficial observer finds it hard to decide such questions, is the psychologist in a happier position?[1]

Is not the situation this: that motives can have no such separateness as their names suggest? A mental experiment may throw some light on this matter. Imagine a mind at the beginning of its career, responding to its first instinctive impulse; and then to its second. Assume that this second experience is as different from the first as possible, involving different sense-tracts, different viscera, and different muscles throughout. By what sign would the second experience belong to the *same mind* as the first; i.e., how could we distinguish these two from experiences in two different

---

[1] Speaking of the motives of "those dangerous journeys of discovery, etc., by which the whole earth has been mapped out during the last four hundred years," Graham Wallas suggests that "perhaps, indeed, it is this desire for Fear, rather than the impulse of Curiosity, which has been the most important single cause." *The Great Society*, p. 89.

minds? The answer is both obvious and simple: if
the second experience is an experience of the same
mind, it will appear with the memory of the first experience attending it, and hence as bearing the character expressed in the word "another": it will appear
as *another experience*. No matter how different the
scenery of the adventure, the new craving is still
another craving, the groping activity takes on a tinge
of expectation because another groping had preceded
it, and the end when it comes will be *another* settle-
ment. In brief, what marks these two experiences as
belonging to the same mind is the incipient classing or
generalizing, whereby the two interests appear as two
interests, i.e., as two cases of a common value-mean-
ing. Only when successive experiences, whatever their
differences of content, have this in common, that they
affect for better or for worse an identical concern in
fortune, is there any self at all. And conversely, *wherever there is a self, there all experiences are referred
to a common interest:* they are being perpetually sorted
as satisfactory or unsatisfactory by a test in which no
one can instruct any mind but itself. To ask, then,
whether the various goods of life, or the various values
indicated by our instincts, have a common character
is to ask a self-answering question. No satisfaction is
such except by grace of the fact that beneath all differences it presents to an identical self an identical meaning with every other satisfaction.

A self might be described as a permanent principle
of selection. It has no *a priori* knowledge of what the
world contains, nor yet of the dispositions which we say

it already has. Only experience can reveal to a self what qualities are possible, and what are to be judged as agreeable or otherwise: it learns empirically what *things* are good. But *what good is* it cannot learn empirically; since the use of this knowledge is implied in the first judgment. Nevertheless, experience has everything to do in bringing this knowledge into the foreground of consciousness.

Experience must first show what goods there are in the world: one cannot desire good-in-general while yet it covers no particulars. Experience of hunger-and-eating makes it possible to desire good-in-the-form-of-food; experience of music makes it possible to desire good-in-the-form-of-music. Enjoyment precedes desire, so far as desire becomes definite; pain precedes aversion. Experience must, further, bring about situations requiring choice between concrete goods, and so compel that effort to find the 'preferable' or the 'better,' which in turn compels some sense, however obscure, of common measure and so of common quality. The goods led to by the different instincts appear incomparable enough: what have hunting and courting, feasting, building, caring for children, to do with one another? Are they not so many activities, unrelated save as they might all find a place serially in a lifetime? Even so, the satisfaction of *activity within a workable life-picture* is a common element, and a point of attachment for more that is common. For after all, choices between hunting-activity and courting-activity, etc., are effected; and by something other than blind fiat. If the choice is *one's own choice,* defensible to himself if to no one else, it is because he finds more of himself, under the circumstances, in the one than in the other,—more of *his good*. And so, by dint of much choosing, among all possible pairs of goods, what one's good is begins to appear as a distinct item of self-consciousness. Meanwhile, experience has aided the emergence of the notion in a third way. For while enjoyment precedes definite desire, the desire which follows enjoyment is never desire for exact repetition of the enjoyment. In taking the pleasure up into the mind, it is developed and improved (by imagination, we sometimes say) ; and what we then desire is *a better good*. What experience has given is varied in a direction which we name the 'ideal'; the ideal is a joint product of experience and the *latent idea of good*, whose nature is shown to some extent in that deflection.[2] Thus, by a history of accepting and rejecting, choosing and dream-building, and, further, of sorting out dreams according to their realizable or not-yet-realizable character, one's working idea of the good-common-to-all-separate-goods pulls forward from the background of consciousness into the definable foreground. The dawning of such self-possession means the achievement of a more or less stable *policy* toward incoming suggestions and impulses. And to have a stable policy is to have, in the specific sense of the word, a *will*.

Will in this sense is a matter of degree. At an alarm

[2] It is minimization of the rôle of the ideal that makes it possible for Dewey to describe the will as a mass of habits (*Human Nature and Conduct*, pp. 24, 25). Habit gives the will volume, momentum, and assumed applicability; but there is such a thing as a will to change habit.

of fire, a schoolboy may respond by running to the scene approximately 'without a thought': in a few more years the same stimulus encounters an order of life having a momentum of its own, and if it wins the day, it is by an act of 'will.' Will exists when, and in so far as, any instinctive impulse has first to obtain the consent of a ruling policy before pursuing its course.[3] The policy of a self is its acquired interpretation of its own good, i.e., of its central and necessary interest.

And thus, if men are alike in nature, we should be able to perceive at the center of all "central instincts" or "necessary interests," and indeed within all instincts whatever, a nucleus of common meaning which we would be justified in calling the fundamental instinct of man, the substance of the human will. No one description of this central instinct is likely to be sufficient: we may at once renounce the idea that a final and satisfactory definition can be given. The native hold which man has on his good, his instinct *par excellence,* is likely to evade capture in any neat vessel of concepts. But the *perception* of it is difficult only as all perception of what is both intimate and always present is difficult; and the effort to improve our conceptual

---

[3] In this sense, instinctive action is a precondition of volitional action. But without arbitrary line-drawing, there is no moment at which we may say, Here will begins. For will is only the original and permanent purposiveness of the self made definite to the self by its own experience: it is what that purposiveness has always meant, and it begins therefore with experience, and develops with it so long as the individual continues to learn his own mind.

vessels is not to be abandoned merely because there is always a remainder. Thus "the will to live" was used by Schopenhauer not to indicate an instinct among many, but to indicate the instinct of man: and the phrase is not a false one, except that it allows the impression of an impulse primarily directed to the subjective, perhaps vegetative, fact of existence. The "will to power" escapes this danger, doing better justice to the outward direction of the primitive energies. It has a savage history, but it may be possible to control and amend its meaning so that it will serve us. Let us enquire how much it can convey of what is common in some of the major instincts.

It is not hard to see that many of the simple and general instincts deal with the fluxes of power, in one way or another, and may be referred to a general vital interest in conserving or increasing power. Food-getting instincts reach their apparent goal in the satisfying of hunger; yet it would be a bold psychology that would affirm that eating, to the human species, has no more general meaning than quenching this craving. Hunger, I dare say, is felt as a diminished status, a sign of a dependence on material intake, which eating both confesses and temporarily removes. It is perhaps the element of physical humility which makes the taking of food a fit occasion for sociability: for here is the most natural and permanent democracy, that of equal dependence on material nature for continued life. But the social instinct would hardly make so much of a mutual confession of dependence if there were not also a mutual emancipation. Eating, by itself, is a form of conquest, surrounding what is alien and making it a part of ourselves. The satisfaction of food to a thoroughly hungry man is less a matter of the æsthetics of taste than a consciousness of making something his own, a sense of mastery. But beyond this, he is aware of eating as releasing the springs of his rightful attitude toward the world, his control of his own fortune. In both ways, the satisfaction of hunger is at the same time a satisfaction of an impulse which makes, immediately and unreflectingly, for holding toward the not-self a relation of potency.

Play hardly bears the conventional aspect of the will to power. It seems to consist, as we noticed above, in a social soft-pedalling of the major instincts, rather than in any distinct tendency of its own. Yet the play world may be accurately described, on its psychological side, as the world of *practice in mastery*. In play, growing humanity carries on a career with plastic materials, such as it can control with its small powers, until it is ready to throw away its playthings and try a fall with realities.

Fear is a negative expression of our concern for power. The general element running through all the scores of situations which excite fear is the presence of an environment for which none of our instinctive powers fit us. In water, or fire, or chasms of air, or the world of ghosts, our instincts lose their grip. In such event a residual instinct, felt as fear, tends to remove us from the uncanny world to one in which we may once more say, I can. Thus fear also is a form of the fundamental impulse to be in a relation of power to experience.

The instinctive side of sex-love clearly involves in various ways an effort to attain and exert power. It belongs to the era of mature physical and mental forces; it implies that one is able to see life whole, to administer it, to call it into existence. It means readiness to assume responsibility for the welfare of another human being, though the feat of being responsible for oneself has taxed competence. It means, at the same time, quest for a missing element in one's own self-confidence, for, until one can win that completeness of regard which acceptance conveys, one's status in the world lacks an element of security. Sex-love is potency in search of a sanction.

I do not doubt that other instinctive tendencies will show themselves, upon examination, in a similar light; for the will to power is perhaps the nearest name that has yet been found for the central thread of instinct. The will to live is in some ways a less misleading name. But in man, the will to live must take the form of the will to live *as a man;* and this involves much more than the cherishing of existence,—it involves dealing with a world of objects and resistances, and holding intact one's validity in the midst of that intercourse. More than that, it implies the process of the artist, that of imposing upon the external mass an element of form and order that is first one's own. This active and creative quality is better suggested by the phrase, the will to power.

This phrase need not be regarded with prejudice because it has been used by Nietzsche; nor because it allies itself with the most glaring defects of temper. Nietzsche's error is not that he struck a false note in human nature; but firstly that he supposed his expression to be adequate, and secondly that he thought of power as intrinsically competitive, a good which can be gained by one only at the expense of another. In our use of the phrase we shall at the outset reject both these errors. We do not regard the will to power as an adequate name for the central instinct. And we reject the competitive relation as necessarily implied in the concept of power. Power over nature is the type of all actual commonwealth. And the power of men over one another may be at the same time a power-for,—as the power which a parent has for, and over, a child. And the rightful position of one man toward others cannot be described without this conception: for this position does not consist merely in being amiably disposed toward them, but rather in standing *in loco Dei* toward them, and acting as a Providence to them. To love mankind and to seek this power are not separable; and it is well to be reminded that love without this element of responsible ambition is not fit to survive.

The instinct of man is Protean; but so is also the will to power. To point out the unity of impulse is not to deny its manifoldness. The will to power cannot be satisfied in its generality: it must be satisfied in changing conditions. If power is hindered by ignorance, then it will make for a transition to knowledge; 'curiosity' and its subordinate mechanisms will be called into play.

If power is hindered by an antagonist, then we shall have 'pugnacity' and its mechanisms. The various instinct-names retain their usefulness, since they indicate the variety of situation and the variety of situation-change in which the will to power works.

But the recognition of the unity has another importance than that which always attaches in science to reporting the truth, and not presenting as sundered what are really joined. If the instincts are indeed several, then the life program must provide for them in their severalty, or leave us with a mutilated man. But if these several instincts are differentiations of some fundamental impulse, there will be among them a certain *vicarious possibility of satisfaction*. It is not they in their severalty that need to be satisfied: it is the will to power. If they are repressed, it is not they that persist, but only the will to power. Their energy cannot be destroyed; but the thing that cannot be destroyed is not specifically *they*. The energy of motion may, by impact, be transmuted into heat: so, for these partial impulses, their 'repression' *is*, in general, their 'sublimation.'

We shall accordingly adopt this phrase, the will to power, as a working-name for the instinctive center of the human will.

NOTE. Other views of the will: the Freudian view.

We have argued the question whether the self is a bundle of distinct cravings or a single craving with many forms, as if it were a question of logical necessity. Yet it would seem to be a question for whose answer men might fairly be referred to their own experience. And I agree that what the

self is, and what the will is, are empirical questions whose
answer each self holds within its own experience; only, it
sometimes requires a touch of logic to induce the human mind
to face the facts.

Radical empiricism in psychology once meant seeing nothing of the mind but a swirl of separable 'states'; a still later
empiricism professes to find nothing of the mind but a system
of behavior. But empiricism is not incapable of finding connections and unities,—if they exist. The perception of unity
in psychology, though clearer to Plato than to Aristotle, is no
prerogative of a monistic metaphysics. I doubt whether anyone will accuse Buddha of being a monist, and he certainly
did his best to destroy the theory of a soul; yet Buddha, after
referring all suffering to desire, referred all desire to a single
craving which he described as the craving for individuality
or separateness of being. And modern naturalism is not without tendencies of the same kind. If mind has an evolutionary
history, and particularly if it has grown by "differentiation
and integration" from the simple to the complex, nothing
would be more natural than to derive (as G. H. Schneider
has tried to do, or M. Hachet-Souplet) our many instincts
from a primordial instinct or tropism; and nothing would be
more natural than to suppose that these kinships of origin
would remain as kinships of quality and meaning.

But evolutionary psychology, and in fact all genetic psychology, is necessarily a mixture of empiricism with a degree
of speculation. It is therefore a matter of theoretical interest when a group of psychiatrists, presumably on the basis
of clinical experience alone, find themselves reducing all
human desires to a single root as a working hypothesis.
"From the descriptive standpoint," says C. G. Jung, "psychoanalysis accepts the multiplicity of instincts. From the
genetic standpoint it is otherwise. It regards the multiplicity
of instincts as issuing out of a relative unity, the primitive
libido. It recognizes that definite quantities of the primitive
libido are split off, associated with the recently created func-

tions and finally merged with them. . . . We term libido that
energy which manifests itself by vital processes, which is sub-
jectively perceived as aspiration, longing, and striving. We
see in the diversity of natural phenomena the desire, the
libido, in most diverse applications and forms. In early childhood, we find libido at first wholly in the form of the instinct of nutrition. . . . Claparède in a conversation once
remarked that we could as well use the term 'interest.' "[4]
Others beside Claparède have observed that the Freudian
psychology has important philosophical bearings, which are
disguised by the misleading emphasis of its terms.[5] But if
'libido' is too specific in its connotation, the term 'interest'
is too lacking in descriptive force, while *l'élan vital* is not
intended as a psychological term at all. The 'will to power'
escapes all these defects. Sex-love itself, which to the Freudian mind seems the deepest thing in human nature, is far
better placed as a derivative expression of this more primitive
will; for what more profound assertion of power is our nature
capable of than in that impulse which, assuming responsibility for the life and welfare of another, may also summon
a new life into existence? The greatness of the sex-motive lies
in the junction which it is able to effect between the individual
and the super-individual ranges of power. But to invert the

---

[4] *Theory of Psychoanalysis*, pp. 40, 42.

[5] Dr. James J. Putnam has repeatedly called attention to this point.
"Let its name be altered, and its functions be but slightly more ex-
panded, and we have Bergson's *poussée vitale*, the understudy of self-
activity." *Journal of Abnormal Psychology*, August-September, 1913.
McDougall speaks to the same effect in his *Outline of Psychology*
(1923). "The evolution of the animal world may properly be conceived
as primarily and essentially the differentiation of instinctive tendencies
from some primordial undifferentiated capacity to strive. It is this
undifferentiated capacity to strive, this primordial energy, which
M. Bergson has named *l'élan vital*, which others (notably Doctor C. G.
Jung) speak of as the *libido*, and which perhaps is best named vital energy. We may regard the instincts as so many channels through which
the vital energy pours itself into or through the organism." P. 113.

relation and make all will a form of 'libido' is simply ex-
centric; and can yield at best a Ptolemaic system of psychology. Ptolemy's system for an Egyptian of the second
century was a great achievement, and had at least so much of
truth,—that the world has *some* center of gravity.

But what name and character we give to this center of our
instinctive being is not an unmomentous matter, when we
consider that of all our nominally many native hungers this
one alone must imperatively be satisfied if we are to have
mental soundness or normal fulness of life. Only that one
impulse cannot be substituted for, nor sublimated, nor successfully repressed; for it is the substance of all the proposed
alternatives. If sex is this center, then to sex belong these pre-
rogatives. If it is not the center, it has none of them, without
our permission. But by a false belief about what is necessary
to our mental peace, we may create a necessity where none
in nature exists.

CHAPTER XII

MIND AND BODY: THE LAST ANALYSIS

MANY questions about original human nature are left unanswered by a discussion of instincts and the will. For example, we have given no account of individual personality. The will to power is not personality; it reveals nothing of the nature of personal differences. Upon such questions we shall not here enter: for it is the business of psychology to find first what the common clay is, and only then to enquire how it assumes its individual shapes. But if there is a common clay, a craving which in some way underlies and explains the rest, we are bound to take at least a glance at the question *what this clay itself is made of,* or whether it must be taken as an ultimate fact. We shall accordingly make a brief excursion into the field of speculation regarding ultimate analysis.

The concept of *energy* always stands at the elbow, with promises of solving riddles: it seemed likely at one time to afford the common term for the dualism of matter and motion; it has tempted many since the time of Leibniz into a hope of passing from body to mind and back again. If the will to power could be understood, in Nietzsche's terms, as a need to give utterance to the energy that is in us, we should be on the way to a natural understanding of human nature.

All instinctive tendencies, and so of course the central instinct, are inherited with the body; they all expend the energy developed by the bodily machine. The nutrition of the body and of the nervous centers produces a readiness to act, and indeed an uneasiness if action is delayed. If we assume that our craving accompanies this condition of readiness both of the channels of discharge and of the centers themselves, we shall have a physiological picture much more in accord with our concept of a central instinct than any that could be furnished by the schema of stimulus and response. The presence of energy as a tension or charge serves here in lieu of a stimulus, acting immediately, without afferent apparatus. The discharge itself, the transformation of potential into kinetic energy, may be the primary physical basis of 'satisfaction.'

I should not hestitate to look in this direction for a physical theory of the primitive will to power. I should not hestitate, because I am "not afraid of falling into my own inkpot." No one who thinks twice can be in any danger of identifying the energy which is measurable in terms of mv^2 or fd with the 'energy' of his own will or its fluctuating 'tensions' of desire. Yet the ambiguity of these words is not accidental; no doubt the two phases of energy belong together, the one as substance and the other as shadow. But in this fact there is nothing to indicate *which is the shadow*. In truth, when we seek for physical expressions, we have left behind the direct facts of experience and have begun to spin hypotheses for the sake of connecting these facts with others. We do not by this route penetrate more deeply into the nature of desire. If we wish to know what desire is made of, we should do better to seek it within the completer expressions of the will itself, as we know them.

If we can anywhere catch a glimpse of the ultimate character of the will, it should be in our answer to the work of an artist. For it is his work to bring the deepest things in us into active response to the deep things of the world outside. Recently I saw a drama which ventured to bring to mind the travesty which often goes by the name of Justice; and I returned depressed and resentful and disturbed by what I had seen. There had been forced upon my attention a world of man-made necessity, the Law, in whose meshes man himself could perish both as victim and as administrator. I saw the efforts of men to rise humanly above this their own work. I saw a world of blindness and futile sympathies, pompous certainties that are false, and sentimental certainties that are vain; and men going down in despair because no one but the poet saw fiercely enough the realities which should have outweighed the whole pretentious momentum of habit and routine. I knew that the poet spoke some untruth; and also that he saw and spoke more truth than men are usually privileged to see. And I knew also, what is important for us at this moment, that the feelings and desires of men (so many partial applications of will) are made by such perceptions as these.

Desire, or more generally, feeling, is not something disparate from thought: feeling is a mass of idea at work within us. It is a thorough fallacy to suppose that one can feel or care about anything without knowledge, or that feeling and knowledge are inversely proportional to one another. The theory of feeling has been seriously distorted by confusing feeling with more or less incontinent or futile or unstable types of motor discharge, "emotional temperaments" and the like. Feeling is an experience of "making up one's mind," rising to an occasion, appreciating something to the extent of mobilizing the powers of action. The proper contrast to feeling is not thought but *callousness;* and wherever I am insensitive to an interest or concern which finer members of the race care about, I may know that the root of my deficiency is a lack of intelligence or vision.

If we are right in this, feeling, whether in the form of uneasiness, desire, aspiration, or satisfaction, is *thought,* more or less in control of things,[1] and will, in the last analysis, is *thought assuming control of reality.*

[1] In terms of a colloquial phrase, the common element in value is idea "making good." It is easier to see that making good is a desirable state of affairs, than to see that it is the desirable state of affairs. To make good requires that one has first an idea of something worth making, something that has value independent of the process of realizing it. Then to realize it has the additional value of giving me a sense of validity,—my 'idea' has come true. But what we want to find out is the quality of this presupposed value: what constitutes the desirableness of the object of my idea? Realism in the theory of values holds that the value is there, in the object,—an ultimate quality, and there's an end of it. Relativism holds that value is the relation of the object to my welfare, or my instinct, or my desire,—desire, instinct, etc., being assumed as given facts about which nothing more can be said, except to analyze their physiological basis, as above attempted. I hold that either of these solutions, taken as final, simply gives up the problem. What we desire, we do not desire helplessly, because we are so constituted that a given object sets certain mechanisms tingling. What we desire has an account to give to consciousness itself, and,—as we have maintained,—an account which in general terms is identical in all cases of desire. We

It would follow from this that human instincts,—all of them,—while from the standpoint of physical theory they are such stuff as solar systems are made of, are from a metaphysical standpoint such stuff as dreams, ideas, and reasonings are made of. Pleasure and pain, as termini of the simpler instincts, seem at first sight ultimate data for psychology: we are "so made" that we enjoy and seek this, suffer from and avoid that. Yet even these values, the last to yield to analysis, are clearly not ultimate and irresoluble. Sensation changes its quality under change of mind, as one responds to a slight hurt with increased vehemence and concentration of action, and finds relief in shaking a pinched finger. A child takes pleasure in piling up blocks, and Meyer suggests that the sensation of the pile is more intense

must penetrate the nature of the independent good as it appears to consciousness. For example, suppose I care for music and exert myself to be able to make music. There is satisfaction in the achieving; but there must have been a prior satisfaction in the music. It is this prior satisfaction of which I propose that it also is a case of thought making good. The value of music, I would maintain, is that it sets before us a world of which it would be too little to say that it was auspicious to our ears, or with Kant, to our imagination; the value of music is that it summons up through the vehicle of a mass of tone amenable to our thought the entire reality of our experience, in vaguely generalized situations and moods, with reflective or contemplative mastery. It has to do with intensities, masses, and relations of sensation only as these suggest to a mind groping for a favorable attunement to its world some happier adjustment. And I should say the same of our more organic satisfactions. On this basis we can do justice to both realism and relativism. To realism it seems that desire is defined by the good, the good being defined by itself; to relativism it seems that the good is defined by desire. From our point of view the good is defined not by itself, but in relation to us; yet not to us as beings fated to desire this or that,—rather as beings capable of thinking and knowing this and that, and the whole of things through them. To this extent, good is objective.

than that of the single block. But the *pile* gives a satisfaction which the *row* does not give; and why? The pile,
like the row, is an order, a thought; but it is a thought
which reality has with greater difficulty been induced
to accept and even enlisted to sustain. The control of
fact by thought is more in evidence. Has thought anything to do with sex-interest, or sex-interest with
thought? We shall recur to this question; but to those
who know the trouble of the lover, it would seem absurd
to say that either sense-pleasure or the satisfaction of
formal beauty were sufficient so to absorb his mind or
undo his peace. It includes these in its scope only as
they, too, touch the fringes of universal mystery and
insight.

Pragmatic writers, in the interest of showing that all
thought has an active meaning, have sometimes gone
to great lengths in exhibiting the logical qualities of
instinct and tropism. Charles Peirce does not hesitate
to say that "In point of fact a syllogism virtually takes
place when we irritate the foot of a decapitated frog."[2]
But the force of such interpretations is not to show that
logic is permeated by psychology: it is rather to show
that psychology is permeated by logic. That which from

[2] Instinct has sometimes been called an unconscious reason, not because there are any actual syllogisms in play, but because in reaching
what to consciousness is pleasant, it reaches what to nature is fit,—*as if*
it knew and planned the utility of its behavior. It is hardly supposed
by those who use this phrase that pleasantness is a dim recognition of
the fact of fitness: this would be to reduce the value called pleasantness to a function of a cognition,—a highly speculative procedure, to
say the least. We certainly have no need to assume that what consciousness means by its end is coincident with what 'nature' means;
it may be far simpler, and yet none the less real.

the standpoint of nature seems instrumental becomes, when we take a truly psychological instead of a biological view of the object of value, the substance of the end itself. Instinct, too, in the last analysis can be understood as a wholly ideal activity,—an activity of ideas. If there is any virtue in giving a name to the ultimate stuff of human nature, it would be more like thought than like physical energy; and, if I may venture a final leap of speculation, more, I believe, like conversation than like solitary thought.

The body is the symbol of the mind, not the mind of the body. The mind is the substance of which the body and its energies are the visible behavior-language, the accessible and measurable signs, but still,—the shadows. What ideas they are that enter into this original stuff we do not here enquire in detail. But one question we can no longer postpone. We have made no place for a moral quality in original human nature; yet it is by this quality that man, according to an ancient tradition, is thought to be chiefly distinguished. This question is the subject for our next study.

PART III

CONSCIENCE

Argument

ORIGINAL human nature has in it, besides its equipment of instinct, a principle of judgment and of self-judgment. Our account of the natural man is not complete without considering this natural judge, domesticated in each person, making it possible for him to become a self-changing creature.

A part of this self-judging activity is moral self-judgment: the human being, we say, has a conscience. Whether or not this sharply distinguishes him from other creatures,—according to the traditional view,—he at any rate has moral sense. What is this moral sense? And how does he come by it?

We are told by many genetic psychologists that conscience is nothing innate and peculiar; that it is not present in infants; that it is built up by social experience working on an instinctively sociable and docile mentality. Parents say "You ought" to their children; in time they begin to say "I ought" to themselves.

It is necessary, in our day, to be severely clear with plausible genetics which explain everything except the kernel of the matter. "You ought" may perhaps stimulate an "I ought" in me, if the capacity for that "I ought" is in me; but the "ought" *cannot be imported,* nor transferred from one head to another. Pressure from outside is alien to the nature of conscience: if I adopt a suggestion from outside, and confirm it, as an obligation of mine, it is by an original discovery and a free act.

The same consideration prevents us from considering conscience as a product of evolution, in the sense of a mere hereditary relic of past social punishments and fears. Ancient pains and fears are no more potent than present ones to transform prudence into "I ought." This "ought" is always contemporary, always lighting on new things to command or to forbid.

Conscience is not an instinct. It is total human nature reflecting on the activities of its parts: it is the will to reality commenting on particular deeds and tendencies. It stands on the growing edge of human nature and judges whether the direction is up or down: it is the index of the way in which what I do affects what I am.

Conscience makes the difference between the *mistakes* of maladjustment or organic defect (such as may make the criminal a patient for the social physician) and *wrong* or sin. The Liberator would be more successful in banishing the sense of sin if that sense were an artificial theological horror rather than a deliverance of our own nature. What the Liberator points out is that primitive impulses cannot be sinful,—and that is true. No impulse is sinful in and by itself. But in the human mind, *no impulse is by itself,* and crude impulses are not justified in remaining crude. Sin is failure to make our several impulses contribute their part to our total will.

Conscience indicates that sin affects what I am; and if what I am affects what becomes of me in the wider universe, that would not be unnatural. Religion has always maintained that the moral condition of the soul has consequences which reach beyond present experience: the assertion is anything but absurd. The question may be referred to metaphysics with an open mind.

CHAPTER XIII

THE INTEREST IN JUSTICE

WHEN Aristotle said that man is by nature a political animal, he did not leave this notable saying uninterpreted. It is the faculty of speech, he explains, which marks man for a civic existence; and by speech we are to understand not the simple power to make articulate signs, as do many animal species, but the power to coin signs for general ideas, and particularly for ideas relating to justice and injustice. We may put Aristotle's meaning in this way: the communities which men make are political communities, as distinct from simple defensive or co-operative aggregations, because men are fitted by nature to frame ideas of fair and unfair dealing, of right and wrong, and to use them. The life of an idea consists in being recognized and applied in the concrete; a state is a community in which the idea of justice has a chance for life.

We need not debate here the question of priority,—i.e., whether political society exists for the sake of a morally reasoned life, or whether the moral reason exists for the sake of a political society. Biological interpretations of human life would prefer the second alternative, at least as a preliminary hypothesis. I shall simply point out in passing that a psychological interpretation would have much to say for Aristotle's way of putting it.

For our social impulses, when we examine them, can be seen to depend to a large extent upon a need to put our various thinking powers into operation. We have spoken of sociability as if it were an instinct by itself, and of curiosity as if it were another instinct by itself. But if we should subtract from the natural interest in social life whatever comes through the enquiring sides of argument and conversation, and through persuading others, managing and planning for others, we should deal sociability a severe blow. And if we should subtract from our natural interest in public life—the political development of sociability—whatever comes from the discussion of personalities, laws, principles, quarrels, wars, strands of history, legend, custom, on their ethical side, we should lose much of its normal motive. Political life is, as Aristotle later described it, an arena for distinguished action, a conspicuous jousting-place for contending principles and men having much energy to discharge. And if you will watch where the interest is hottest you will see that it is there where questions of expediency, of bread and butter and prosperity, have merged into questions of rights and obligations; or where questions of a man's ability and record have deepened into questions of his character and honor. It is there where the responses of indignation, chivalry, applause, resentment, loyalty, condemnation, the responses of our ethical nature, have been called out. We are social and political creatures, at least in part, because we need to inject our reasons and our moral perceptions into the world's work. We build states, at least in part, because of *this* will to power. So far we can follow Aristotle.[1]

But here our question arises. If this particular form of mental activity is characteristic of the species, and helps to produce such distinctive products as laws and states (surely as indicative of man as the habits and homes of the beasts), we must find some place for it in original human nature. Shall we say that there is a native moral sense in man, a moral instinct; or if these expressions are inept, what account shall we give of the untaught value which humanity places upon justice? It is usual for writers who view instinct in terms of situation and response not to include moral behavior among the original tendencies, but to regard it as derivative and composite. It could be thought to develop in the form of altruistic sentiment from the maternal instinct (Sutherland); or from pugnacity, as pugnacity becomes a 'disinterested resentment' (Westermarck) turned first outward and then inward. For McDougall

---

[1] And we may also agree in the place that he gives to speech. That impulse to "vocalization" which we included among our units of behavior would not exist in us as it does unless it were destined to take part in a more comprehensive tendency. Thorndike very justly observes that it first appears as an aimless impulse (*The Original Nature of Man*, pp. 135-138); but it is one of the common facts of our more elaborate tendencies that their ingredients assemble themselves in separate and leisurely manner in the course of growth. It is quite compatible with its primitive aimlessness that the talking impulse should be a part of some more general tendency, be it reason, sociability, or 'the political faculty.'

Behaviorism would read the relation the other way around. Thus John R. Watson (*Behavior*, 1914, pp. 321, 319): "The lack of language habits forever differentiates brute from man"; remarking, "We say nothing of reasoning since we do not admit this as a genuine type of human behavior except as a special form of language habit."

moral judgment is a complex attitude in which the 'self-regarding sentiment,' interacting with social likes and dislikes, has the chief rôle. Thorndike does not positively exclude it from our native endowment, but so far fails to verify its presence. He says (*The Original Nature of Man,* p. 202) : "No innate difference of response to 'right' from 'wrong' acts is listed here, in spite of the opinions of a majority of students of ethics, and the authority of Lloyd Morgan, who says emphatically:

Among civilized people conscience is innate. Intuitions of right and wrong are a part of that moral nature which we have inherited from our forefathers. Just as we inherit common sense, an instinctive judgment in intellectual matters, so too do we inherit that instinctive judgment in matters of right and wrong which forms an important element in conscience ('85, p. 307).

So much, however, is clear: that no account of human nature can pretend to have touched the important points unless it shows, in terms of its own theory, how it is that a man can *become* what we call a moral agent, or a political animal. And we have a double concern in this subject, since the human conscience is at once, in some sort of germ, deposited in man's original nature, and at the same time one of the chief instruments in his remaking. What account, then, can we give of the moral aspect of human nature?

CHAPTER XIV

CONSCIENCE AND THE GENERAL WILL

THERE is no need to assume an original moral sense in order to account for the expression, "You ought," or at least for some closely similar expression. If human nature is equipped with instincts such as we have described, and with the preferences that go with them, and if these interests are mightily affected by the neighbor's behavior, a generalizing animal would hardly fail to perceive the value of an habitual disposition on the neighbor's part to consider the feelings of others; and a language-using animal would hardly fail to invent a term to express to his neighbor his sense of the importance of that disposition. What most of us strongly prefer you should do would inevitably be conveyed to you by a phrase such as, "You ought to behave thus and so,"[1] in which the 'ought' would imply that this line of conduct is such as would follow from the fixed habit of 'consideration.' It would remind you simply of a certain permanent condition of peaceable living, that

---

[1] 'Inevitably,' I say: but note that this word 'inevitably' assumes that it would occur to us, instead of simply growling at your encroachments, to appeal to your intelligence and self-control. This is a large assumption, and may be found to be the whole genetic question. Such an appeal is used only when the addressee is supposed free and competent, i.e., something of a psychologist, as we said. And conversely, only then can the members of a group be treated as free, when they can be approached with an 'ought.'

of being a reasonably good practising psychologist in regard to the interest of others.

Every inducement would exist for an attempt on the part of your fellows to give your permanent habits a shape auspicious for them. For this work they would hardly be content with the pressure of the ordinary atmosphere of approval and disapproval,—if a stronger pressure were available. They would gather all possible prestige about this notion of "You ought." They would presumably call upon the instinct of fear, heightened by such religious or other imagination as could be pressed into service, to aid in the shaping of the other instincts. There would be, as there is, a shade of menace in the attitude with which the 'ought' bears down upon you. And there would also be, as there is, a vigorous enlistment of the 'self-regarding sentiment' through the general refusal to permit the man of refractory habits to think well of himself.

Everyone would thus acquire a high interest in accepting the guidance of the social 'ought'; and if not everyone, yet everyone's progeny, would end by taking the interested spectator as well as the disinterested spectator into his own bosom, seeing himself habitually through the eye of the social judgment, and assigning a certain authority to that judgment, together with his own. The moral Rubicon is crossed when once the question is admitted as legitimate, "What *sort* am I?" And the persistent presence of social reaction, with a little generalization, would most reasonably be admitted to raise this question in the mind of each member, and to

keep it there, even if it succeeded in lodging no permanent standards for answering it.

Given, then, a being with a social instinct, and under
the kind of social pressure we have described, some
vocabulary analogous to the 'ought' vocabulary could
be conceived to arise and something like conscience to
emerge, without appealing to any original moral deposit in human nature. But would this socially moulded
'conscience' be identical with conscience as we know it?
The resemblance is, in reality, superficial. It is impossible that the 'ought' as we mean it in its current use
should be a social product, as will appear if we consider how the meaning of this word is ordinarily
conveyed.

No doubt children listen with frequent perplexity to
the abundant You-oughts which are offered them. No
doubt they have to learn this word as they learn other
words for invisible things: making the assumption that
some meaning it must have, since the grown world uses
it; noting the circumstances in which it is employed,
the accompanying frowns, rewards, and other appeals
and sanctions; then devising various hypotheses about
its meaning until some one seems to fit the cases and
survive. The history of the mastering of this word is
not outwardly different from the history of the mastering of other difficult words: it is late in finding a firm
place in the mind. But when it arrives, there is a clear
distinction in meaning between ''I ought to do thus and
so'' and ''It would be prudent for me because others
prefer it.'' This distinction has been called out by something in the attitude of the person who uses ''You

ought" not noted in the foregoing derivation. The "You ought" is neither a command, nor an item of information concerning the general will. The reaction to one who is supposed to have violated the "You ought" is not one of simple anger; it has an ingredient of regret. It addresses itself not alone to his future discretion, but also to his past decision: it deplores the process by which he reached his choice. It assumes, rightly or not, that he was capable of a better process, and that he knows it. In brief, the "You ought" addresses itself to an answering "I ought" within; and unless the "I ought" responds, it has missed its target. This "I ought," since it is presupposed in the meaning of "You ought," cannot be conveyed from without by means of the "You ought." It can only find its way into our sign-language by being taken as understood.[2] While we ply our moral epithets, we wait anxiously and all but helplessly for evidence that our meaning has struck home: for we know that every new person must find this angle of vision for himself. The social use of the word is thus never purely instructive: it is also, and primarily, *awakening*. It appeals to a strand of self-judgment which is original with every individual, and in this sense belongs to original human nature.

[2] In establishing a system of signs, there are always certain signs which cannot be mutually agreed upon, since in order to agree upon any sign, certain other signs must be used as already understood. These must be thrown out as hopeful ventures, and confirmed first by the nod of understanding, then by successful use. The sign for 'ought' is in this position.

CHAPTER XV

CONSCIENCE AND INSTINCT

IF the moral point of view must be achieved by each mind for itself, may the tendency to do this be regarded as an instinct among the other instincts?

It is conceivable that the inner scruple, finally aroused by the moral batteries of our early environment, is itself an inherited relic of ancestral experience (giving Spencer the benefit of the doubt about the methods of heredity). According to Lippert, who certainly improves upon Spencer's psychology, the race has acquired a group of "secondary instincts," acting as counterbalances for the more violent of our primitive impulses, those of pugnacity, sex, and acquisition; and these comparatively new tendencies to respect and refrain are the essential ingredients of conscience. From the Darwinian standpoint, it appears reasonable enough that only men in whom these primary instincts were well mated and checked could form stable societies, and hand their natures down to us. Conscience would then be fairly regarded as the last touch in the process of balancing human instincts.

Without doubting that certain specific inhibitions, such as shame or the indisposition to inflict bodily injury, may be accounted for in this way, conscience itself is certainly not this kind of instinct. Our sense of ought does not limit itself to any ancient categories of behavior. It does not behave like an echo of racial experience, but lights upon new types of action as keenly as upon old types: it impels the return of 'conscience money' quite as clearly as it provokes remorse for murder. It seeks out its own applications, and is capable of a development like the sense of beauty, rising in some persons to the point of genius. Further, it is not attached unchangeably to any specific types of behavior at all, whether new or old. Its demands have a more general character, and descend upon particular actions only through a process of subsuming. The grain of truth in the wild assertion that "the *mores* can make anything right" is sufficient to discredit the view that the moral sense consists of a set of acquired reactions to specific situations.

If there is anything innate in conscience it must be sought in whatever about it is characteristic of the species, i.e. (in other words), unchangeable and universal. And if all branches of the human family have a conscience, there is at least so much that is universal, despite all variations in the particular scruples it adopts.[1] And we should be able to indicate certain very general traits of moral behavior which are con-

[1] If one should answer the thoroughgoing relativist that amid all variations in the moral code there was always a moral code, the answer might justly be called empty and formal. But the criticism is irrelevant: the answer, empty and formal as it is, is sufficient. To refute absurdities, one falls back on formalities. So if it should be said that all moral codes have at least one common content, that of approving mutual benefit above mutual injury,—the statement would properly be called a banality. But the proper function of a banal truth is to meet a banal error, such as this that because things vary there is no constant element in them.

stant throughout these variations. Thus, while customs vary enormously, conscience is generally inclined to set a value upon custom. And while totem gods and other gods give extraordinarily different commands, the tendency of conscience to respect these commands is always there. We should come near to stating a universal trait of conscience if we took what is common to both these cases,—the disposition to find an object of devotion, and to set this object up as authority in details of conduct, finding what one 'ought' to do not directly but indirectly through suggestions from this source,—be it family head, totem, ruler, god, custom, or law.

Thus conscience behaves somewhat like a general instinct, craving an object of loyalty. It finds these objects through its social context, and so is a close ally of the social instinct. Indeed, every associate is probably to some degree a moral authority, though the disposition to centralize the sources of suggestion is marked. But conscience is not identical with sociability. It is not seeking neighbors, but authorities: and while it seems to light on the objects of its devotion often with an unreasoned tact, and adhere to them with a blindness that savors of the tropism, it does not authoritatively accept its authorities. It chooses them with the same originality as hunger shows in the selection of foods; it chooses what satisfies itself, not what satisfies the tribe. It is convenient and usual that one can worship where his tribesmen worship, and eat where and what his tribesmen eat; but the hunger in each case is one's own. What the authority does is to

eke out the resources of the spark of moral originality
in each individual, so that it can perform the task of
regulating a whole life-full of actions. In custom, law,
and religious precept, we find not so much other men's
consciences as the remainder of our own. The same
motive that leads to the adoption of authority may
lead to its rejection, and the setting up of conscience
versus custom, etc. Thus, the authority-seeking trait
is symptomatic of conscience, and is well-nigh universal; but it is not conscience itself.

The essential and universal thing about conscience,
in fact, seems to set it apart from all other innate tendencies. For conscience is the principal inner agency
for the remaking of human nature; hence it must stand
as a critic over against everything that is to be remade,
and so over against all instincts. It plays the part of
censor, for the most part permissive, and hence silent:
but *de jure* it is cognizant of every act of will, and of
the total policy of the self. All that belongs to the will,
including every form of the will to power, must be
bringable under its scrutiny: it might appear, then,
that conscience is not itself any part of the will,—certainly not an instinct,—but something outside of all
these, like self-consciousness pure and simple. On this
showing, original human nature would contain, besides
all its instincts, something different from instinct, a
self-consciousness applying certain standards of value
to the control of behavior.

But if so, what is the nature of these standards, and
what is their source? Are they something uniquely

different from the will to power, and possibly opposed
to it now and then? Or is the standard simply the whole
will to power itself in its most adequate and far-sighted
interpretation?

My own view is that conscience stands outside the
instinctive life of man, not as something separate, but
as an *awareness of the success or failure of that life
in maintaining its status and its growth*. It is a safe-
guard of the power at any time achieved. It interposes
a check when an act is proposed which threatens
'integrity.' What conscience recognizes is that certain
behavior increases our hold on reality while certain
other behavior diminishes that hold, constitutes what
the old Southern Buddhist called an *asava,* a leak. The
remark of conscience is: "That course, or that act,
promises to build, or threatens to tear down, what you
metaphysically are."[2] Conscience is native to human
nature in the sense that it is within the capacity of
human nature to be thus self-conscious in perceiving
and controlling its own cosmic direction. It is not an
instinct. It is the latest and finest instrument for the
self-integration of instinct. And it is an instrument
characteristically human.

[2] Conscience can come into existence only when such an increase or
decrease of being could itself become an object of perception. One can
be stronger or weaker, fresher or wearier, without noticing the fact;
if it occurs to one to remark on his own condition, that is a turn of experience analogous to conscience. In structure, it must take a form such
that some higher differential of the whole nervous process at the center
becomes available in regulating that process. See an article by the
author in *The Psychological Bulletin,* May 15, 1908, "Theory of Value
and Conscience in their Biological Context."

If we are right in thus placing conscience upon the growing edge of human nature, we can understand the importance which men have assigned to its working. While the occasional ciphering of many another innate tendency passes without comment, the world has made a particular tradition of the failures of conscience, and has bewailed them as the essential failure of man. Intellectual blunders it adjusts itself to with comparative resignation. Against moral errors it renews its warfare from day to day.

Our description of conscience so far has been rather to locate it than to interpret it. Our conception is still vague. Perhaps we shall always understand our moral faculty better on its negative than on its positive side. For it is in dealing with 'sin' that the moral nature comes to its most vigorous and definite expression.

CHAPTER XVI

CURRENT FALLACIES REGARDING SIN

IF a man is caught in a lie, the discoverer commonly
feels justified in calling him a liar. There is obviously a large logical distance between the discovered
fact and the appellation. It is something more than an
inductive leap from the single lie to a lying habit: it is
a reference of the habit to a flaw in the moral substance
of the individual. To call a man a liar is to make a
metaphysical assertion.

If this logical leap can be justified, it is by aid of the
premiss that unless the flaw existed, the single lie would
be impossible. Character is a disposition which makes
a person 'incapable of' this and that: it sets up universal negatives. If a person lapses at any time, it is obvious that he was 'capable' of that lapse. Hence he who
has ever stolen is a thief; and one indiscretion is enough
to establish a woman's permanent status.

These fragments of moral logic are common enough
in the form of unexamined attitudes, sentiments, prejudices. We do not as commonly recognize them for
what they are,—forms of the ancient Oriental inference to the effect that he who has sinned is fallen, is a
sinner. When we inspect this argument in its magnificent sweep, we incline to shrink from it. Many repudiate
it *in toto;* though the repudiation is for the most part

rather a hygienic and educational maxim—a pragmatic reaction from the morbid agonies of Calvinistic tradition—than a theoretical criticism of the inference itself.

Yet the healthier mind of our time would be disposed, I think, to reject also the theory of the argument, "A sin shows a sinner." A sin may show an individual unduly strained or unduly depressed. The distribution of blame is at least as difficult a problem as the distribution of wealth. The head of a woman's prison tells me that her murderesses are, as a class, her best citizens. As men grow wise, the judgment of moral censure tends to be replaced by the judgment of misfit: if someone has gone wrong, it is very likely that he is in the wrong place; give him the right work and the right neighborhood, and going right follows of its own accord. Or, what we call sin may be an incident in the normal process of groping our way into our place. Nobody can do anything righter, we think, than live out his powers, his instincts, conduct strongly the great adventure, a soul-building process which must lead through an occasional swamp as well as over mountain highways. "Through angers, losses, ambition, ignorance, ennui, what you are picks its way." When we think of "what you are," as Walt Whitman does, under the figure of a substance, the notion of sin reduces to that of aberration in an orbit, a quantitative matter, for the most part merely the extravagance of your virtues. Instead of thinking that a sin shows a sinner, shall we not say that a sin, taken by itself, shows nothing at all?

In truth, there are signs of bewilderment in our current moral judgments on this point. We see clearly that there is something disproportionately dark in the thoughts of Augustine and his followers; we do not see clearly what to put in their place. General amnesty is hardly more successful than general condemnation of the race. Let me try to get rid of the idea of guilt, substituting for it the idea of illness or misfortune. Let me take into my employ a man with a 'record,' believing that society is part-responsible for every crime, —I find that I feel far more confidence for the future if my unfortunate brother condemns *himself* than if he chimes in too heartily with my own point of view. There is a margin of indulgence in the moral bookkeeping of society, perhaps also of the universe, and all of us profit by it; yet if anyone demands this indulgence as a right, he disqualifies himself. If we think we can omit the moral sermon and substitute the hygienic measure or the change of place, we find the rebuke is still implied in the need for these measures: the 'ought' is none the less active for not being verbally invoked. The sense of sin seems to have at least so much pragmatic force,—it *does not quite work to omit it*, as a prevalent modern attitude tries to do.

I presume that both the Calvinistic and this modern attitude are wrong, and for similar reasons: one assumes that wrong cancels merit, the other that merit cancels wrong, like the positive and negative numbers of algebra. This, I venture to think, is a fundamental fallacy. It is much as if we should balance off the black of one part of a picture against the white of another

part and declare the whole a muddy gray. Nothing
is more natural than to feel one is making up for
a wrong by good offices of some sort, or that a misstep
is destroying a good record; but the result of such a
balancing process is that our moral self-consciousness
tends to become nondescript. We tend to revert to the
simpler state of mind in which we have no more moral
qualities, but simply are. There is relief in this rever-
sion, but as an abandonment of a theoretical difficulty
it is not a place to remain in. The difficulty has a
solution.

The solution lies, I believe, in a simple distinction
between the logic of physical things and the logic of
consciousness. It is characteristic of physical nature
that algebraic opposites neutralize one another: acid
and base combine in a neutral salt. It is equally characteristic of consciousness to retain both components
without neutralization: it is this which gives consciousness its 'depth.' Thus, in the physical world, all that is
real is present: the past exists only in the form of
present traces, records, ruins, hereditary dispositions,
brain paths, momenta,—so many present facts. The
geological past is typical, existing in the order and
shape of contemporary rocks and scratches. But in
consciousness the past retains its character as past: the
glacial moraine calls up to it something which no longer
exists in nature; and the depth of memory, the journey
of thought as it reads its own strata,—the journey from
the present to the beginning and back again,—is one of
the dimensions of a mind. For physical purposes, two
equal and opposite forces produce a resultant zero. For

consciousness, two equal and opposite efforts remain two and opposite: in the state of deadlock or equipoise, the elements do not lose their identity. In consciousness there is many an *a* minus *a*, but never a zero nor a neutral.

This principle holds good for the moral sense. When we fall into the dull optimism which ventures to hope that after all deductions there will still be a moral balance in our favor, we are transferring a physical calculus which our fresher judgments know nothing of. When a fresh wrong has to be dealt with, it is no one's first impulse to check it off against all previous right-going: it stands by itself whole and intact,—the right-going falls into irrelevance, for after all why should one not go right? And when there is a deed that calls for honor or thanks, where is the shabby calculator who brings to mind the offsetting failures or mistakes? On such a day, the critic fearing to be disloyal to his criticism is likely to join half-heartedly in the praise; unless he is set free by perceiving the fallacy of the process of balance. The deed of the hero is not dimmed by his crimes; nor are his crimes wiped out by his heroism. Consciousness is not a cancelling ground: it is the region in which opposites are preserved. Character, that mysterious entity which we surmise through single deeds, is much more versatile than the psychology of either Calvin or Augustine or Pelagius allows, 'capable of' harboring many an unsolved antithesis. But a corollary of this truth is, that with all our good will to stand up for ourselves as men in presence of the Adamic title of 'sinner,' that epithet and its logic remain as something to be reckoned with.

But our disinclination to hear much of sin has other roots than the fallacy of cancellation. It is due in part to the fallacy of custom; by which I mean that the usualness of a given type of wrong-doing diminishes the psychological sense of its wrongfulness, and with our increasing knowledge of evil, all types of wrong-doing appear usual. Our knowledge of evil to-day is no longer the knowledge of personal experience and hearsay; it is the knowledge of social and statistical science. It is a knowledge spread broadcast by journalism, by a literature of disillusionment, and even by the necessities of a popular government which makes every man responsible for knowing how the other half lives. And in dealing with sin through all our institutions we accept a sort of complicity in all that we know. The work of the jury is not simply to discern the external fact regarding the behavior of the accused: the jury are chosen as his peers, that is, as those who can perceive the fact, because they understand his will, being of like circumstances and like mind with him. In truth, the villains of the world are a shade more comprehensible to us than its saints. The latter, if we are cynical, we reduce to villains in disguise in order to understand them. If we accept them as genuine, we account them somewhat more than human and endow them with a halo of supernature. The real villain is remarkable chiefly for the absence of that nimbus of mystery which still enwraps the common man. He is one who has yielded to the obvious reason, the universal drag toward overt advantage, the material day of unmodified instinct. Evil is the thing we understand, through an unhindered participation in its motive.

But on the other hand, by a principle of human psychology, the very extent of our knowledge of moral evil tends to rob of tragedy the statement that "all men are sinners." The sense of sin, which is at home in the solitude of individual conscience, can hardly survive in the universalizing atmosphere. There is no better balm for the conscience of the *nouveau mauvais* than the assurance that "everybody does it." Or if this cannot be said, then the more general, "We all make our mistakes," or "To err is human," may be used. It is a general principle of values that whatever introduces a wider horizon into an experience, such as conceiving it as the common lot, sweetens it and enhances its worth. It is for this reason, in part, that the *mores* have been able to do so much toward making the uncouth (an ancient) good. But beside this, every man, as we were saying, is something of a moral authority to every other; and whatever one can do in company, or in a mob, is partly removed from the sphere of private judgment. The principle, Judge not others that ye be not yourself judged, is inverted in its application: in order not to judge others, we refrain from judging ourselves.

This checkage of moral judgment in dealing with common errors has many expressions. The touch of nature which is said to make the whole world kin frequently takes the form of confessing a common weakness. Does it not add somewhat to ordinary social negotiability to live genially with the minor vices?— I am speaking of psychological tendencies. Men incline to meet and enjoy each other 'at the sign' of their mutually admitted indulgences. The gaiety, the humor, the color, to some extent the art of the world—not to speak of the world's fighting and the world's work— seem to thrive best in an atmosphere made free by mutual agreement that the censor shall be, to some extent, suspended.

This is by no means pure moral blindness. There is soundness in the common judgment before which the pharisee has always come off less well than the publican. The righteousness which has to be achieved by insulating one's sympathies is justly suspected of abstraction and so far of unrighteousness. In the effort after virtue there is a genuine paradox: to be duly strenuous in the pursuit, and to retain perfect charity for the unstrenuous, are attitudes difficult to combine. By general consent mankind seems to prefer the kindly soul—if mankind must choose—to the more consistent moral aristocrat. In Bohemia, the humane breadth of common weakness, its liberating and inspiriting fraternity, appear to deprive sin of its sinful quality.

It is worth pointing out, therefore, that there is a fallacy here also, a fallacy which can be read plainly enough in the facts of our own experience. For Bohemia finds itself, after all, no universal brotherhood, but a region distinctly localized in our minds: we know by instinct the place for this abstract gaiety of forgetfulness and irresponsibility. It is in the world of art,

of letters, of fairly distant history,—in brief, it is in
the world of *imagination* (for remote history takes on
imaginative quality) that Falstaff, Aspasia, The Jolly
Friars, Lucretia Borgia, Tam O'Shanter, Don Juan,
and all the other heroes and heroines of the morally
unstrenuous life have their rightful sphere. They are
the glorified fringes of our too sharp-cut and self-right-
eous ideals. Their human value lies in the respiration
they afford to repressed possibilities within us, their
conspiracy with our own genius and invention, not in
the actual frailty or vice which they embody. If we enjoy them with a bad conscience, it is because we cannot
accept them in this rôle; we fear that this function of
imaginative release will be mistaken (by others?); we
fear the subconscious inference from the proposition,
To err is human (which is true), to the proposition,
Error is not error (which is false). This is the essence
of the fallacy.

But there is a third fallacy which lends support to
the others, and is, perhaps, their more philosophical
expression. It may be stated thus: Whatever is natural
is right; Whatever is impulsive is natural; hence,
Whatever is impulsive is right. The common misdeeds
of humanity, springing as they do from impulse, are to
be dealt with not as moral wrongs, but as effects of
natural causes: if the effects are unwelcome, they are
to be changed by changing the causes. As nobody can
do anything that cannot with equal reason be referred
to nature, this reasoning would at a stroke abolish the

category of sin. If this category is to hold its own, we must be able to state what sin means, in terms of human instincts.

CHAPTER XVII

INSTINCT AND SIN

THE early manifestations of instinct are crude enough; but crudity and sin are not identical. Many of the early assertions of natural impulse in children are inconvenient to ourselves; but they are not on this account anti-social. Some innate dispositions we may justly call dangerous; but this does not make them wrong. There is nothing in original human nature which taken by itself can be called evil.

This principle may be understood to mean that any instinct is justified by virtue of its existence. Stanley Hall and others, on this ground, are willing to recognize such tendencies as lying, stealing, cruelty, greed, and malice as right in their place. In the main they hold it advisable that these impulses should come to their natural expression, wearing themselves through on a principle resembling the Aristotelian *katharsis,* and paving the way for the more congenial impulses that normally follow them. One is reminded of the Sabbasava Sutta, in which it is held that some of the *asavas,* or native weaknesses of character, should be overcome by due indulgence. In view of these same tendencies, however, Professor E. L. Thorndike feels bound to hold that "original nature is very often and very much imperfect and wrong.'"[1] And had we the same view of human nature as that adopted by these observers, we should be driven to Thorndike's conclusion rather than to that of Stanley Hall. But we cannot agree that these particular impulses are natural, however characteristic they may be of childhood. It begs the entire question to ascribe to human nature impulses to cheat, to steal, to bully, to torture, etc.: the names chosen carry with them the ethical reproach. An impulse, taken by itself, is a promise of satisfaction, and so far, of good. We have a natural impulse to climb; and if we climb trees we may find other natural impulses to take what is growing there. But this taking is not in itself 'stealing': it becomes stealing only in relation to a social environment not involved in the first intention of the act. There is no natural impulse to steal.

The same is true of supposed tendencies to deceive. Children have dramatic impulses which may acquire the character of deception by the entrance from without of a demand for facts. The moral quality lies not in the impulse but in its relation to this demand. So hunger may acquire the character of selfishness and greed, by the arrival of other claimants. It is not so obvious in the case of primitive fighting and sex impulses, in which other human beings are normally concerned, that the moral qualification can be denied; and doubtless it is these impulses that have had to bear the brunt of the traditional condemnation of human

[1] *The Original Nature of Man*, p. 280. He thinks the view that original nature is essentially wrong and untrustworthy to be "probably as fair" as the view that original nature is always right.

nature. Yet here, too, we have to take the ground of the primitive impulses themselves. And primitive anger and love, if they make any excursion into the minds of their objects, picture these objects to themselves as pure enemy or pure lover, and in this light there is nothing in them to condemn.[2]

Crude impulses must be described by non-invidious names. Further, we may notice that the apparent moral defect lies not in the impulse itself, but in the manner in which it reaches satisfaction. With an impulse are organized (to compose the instinct) certain methods of procedure, not inseparably nor exclusively, but as the directest ways to the goal—the "natural ways," we may call them. Thus, it is more natural, at least for Anglo-Saxon boys, to fight with fists and according to the principle "all's fair," than to fight with swords or arguments and according to rule and order. The ways which represent much social modification and technique are called "better": the natural way is less adapted to the latest marches of society. If we have an instinct to hunt and kill, it certainly knows nothing of hook or gun: something much more like Tolstoy's

[2] A wise critic puts to me this question: "Are not these forms of the will to power? Will not the self in its early stage, after finding that he can subject the inanimate world to himself, attempt also to assert his will on the living, as, e.g., in deception, stealth, pugnacity, cruelty? Is there not a natural antagonism, and does not morality rightly arise through incipient immorality?" My answer would be that self-assertion is indeed a form of the will to power, and when tried upon fellow beings is frequently incipient immorality. But if it becomes, let us say, actual 'cruelty,' it is because it goes beyond pure self-assertion and begins to be aware of a conscious and suffering environment.

picture of the boar hunt, or Fielding's picture of the Malayan sacrifice comes to mind. In so far as the natural ways are unfitted to contemporary social needs or sensitivities, or to their own conscious environment, they are objectively evil. But it is only as such unfitness enters the mental horizon of the agent that a moral evil can be alleged.[3]

Admitting, then, that no crude impulse is sinful taken by itself, it does not in the least follow that crude impulses as we find them in human nature are therefore good. It does not so much as follow (as is often stated) that they are devoid of moral quality. For as we find them in human nature, *no impulse is by itself*. The moral quality of any impulse is due somehow to its mental environment, not to its own intrinsic quality; but every impulse (after the hypothetical first) has an environment.[4] It is particularly true of the instincts of

[3] I do not say that the perception of such unfitness is sufficient to constitute a moral quality; I say only that it is necessary. To give an act a moral character, it is further necessary that the person having the impulse should recognize an *obligation* to achieve what is fit rather than what is unfit, should perceive *himself as qualified* by his own act,— subject, that is, to approval or reproach,—and should know, too, that he is *able to refrain* from following his impulse in view of his obligation. These elements may all be present, of course, without any power of analysis on the part of the moral subject.

[4] This fact seems to be overlooked in Dewey's penetrating discussion of the concept of motive. ''A child grabs food . . . greediness simply means the quality of his act as socially observed and disapproved. By attributing it to him as his motive . . . we induce him to refrain'' (*Human Nature and Conduct*, p. 120). The child's eating, we agree, is not 'greedy' as a satisfaction of hunger, but as over-muscular and under-circumspect: the standards of poise and consideration lie outside the instinct. But *not outside the individual*. We should have no right to tell

pugnacity and sex-love, about whose natural rightness much is said and with weighty conclusions, that the environment into which their full strength emerges is elaborate and compact. It is, therefore, thoroughly fallacious to argue that because these impulses taken by themselves are justified by their existence, these same impulses taken together with the rest of a human mind are equally justified in their original crudity. Nothing can be condemned because it is crude; but a moral question may arise at once *if an impulse has an opportunity to be something else than crude*. Sin lies, we judge, in the relation of an impulse to its mental environment. What in particular is this relation?

In our analysis of human nature, we recognized two strata, that of the central instincts, and that of the more specific instincts and units of behavior. These central instincts, we thought, no matter how various their names, were in reality forms of a single tendency, which we roughly described as the will to power. As for the other, more specific instincts, it appeared to us that while each one had its own particular goal and its way thereto, none could be wholly independent of this central current of the will. Because every impulse of a given mind belongs to that mind, it must at least

---

him he was greedy unless in fact he were so by his own judgment. The motive is not something imputed by us: we merely supply a name for a struggling element of his own self-consciousness. We use a normal authority in supplying the name and suggesting an attitude in advance of moral clarity on the part of the culprit. We abuse authority when we try to impose our motive-names and attitudes on an innocent consciousness. There is a place for command and obedience, prior to the age of possible appreciation; but moral qualification is another matter. Motives cannot be superimposed.

appear consistent with its central purpose; more than this, it must more or less fully satisfy that central purpose within its special field. It is here that the moral issue arises. For any given impulse may reject the responsibility to carry any further meaning than that of its own direct goal. I may say, Hunger is hunger, it means bread, and nothing more fanciful; or Fear is fear and its whole significance is that I make good my immediate escape, without responsibility to any other instincts, social or what not; or Desire is desire, and if any vague sense of my total destiny attempts to impose a further interpretation, so much the worse for the vague sense and its pretended claims. The moral issue arises from *this* conflict: not the conflict between one person and another, nor the conflict between one impulse and another in a given mind; but the conflict between a given impulse and the central will, or between the separate and restricted meaning of an impulse, and the wider meaning which because of its human belonging it "ought" to carry. Sin, I believe, is *the refusal to interpret crude impulse in terms of the individual's most intelligent will to power.*

The responsibility of the particular impulse to the central will is, in fact, twofold. It has not simply to be subordinate to the central will and express it; it has also to aid in creating, or giving substance to, that central will. For, as we saw, the self acquires vigor and definiteness of policy only by degrees; all instinctive experience must be laid under contribution to give solidity and consistency to the central trend. The mind is at first a very feeble and general unity, aim-

ing to become more concrete. Its numerous impulses
and hungers, as nature wakes them, establish for it a
lax routine, but no coherent purpose. Ask a young
child what its plans are for the day, the week, the
future; sufficient unto the hour, for the child, is the
pain or pleasure thereof. Indeed, a unified policy is
never completely achieved; there is always a certain
desultoriness or unrelatedness in our many doings—
life is "first one thing and then another": each of us
knows only more or less what in the concrete he most
deeply wants. But just because of this *more or less,*
and because in administering our impulses we can control the *more or less,* human existence takes on moral
character. Sin, we may say, *is the deliberate failure to
interpret an impulse so that it will confirm or increase
the integration of selfhood.*

Consider, for example, an impulse of anger. There
is another will which opposes my own; and the "natural way" of my impulse is to break down this opposition by main force, destroying the opposing will if
necessary. The will to power might seem to be in full
possession; and to some extent it is in possession—but
not, for the human intellect, in full possession. For
power is lost, generally speaking, when an opposing
mind is treated according to the "natural way" as a
physical obstacle, or "thing." If that opposing mind
survives as a mind, it exists (as a physical obstacle
does not) as a force against the hostile self, and so far
as a subtraction from its power. If it does not survive
as a mind, there is so much less for the will to power
to rule over: this will, in human form, has robbed itself

of its normal domain. If, then, I allow my impulse to assume its primitive and separate meaning of destruction, I give it an interpretation inconsistent, in general, with as much of my will to power as I am capable of grasping. I sin. And I am aware of the fact, however vaguely:—this is my conscience.

CHAPTER XVIII

SIN AS BLINDNESS AND UNTRUTH

IN a sinful act, we were saying, one is aware of his own deficiency of interpretation. If he were not thus aware, his act, though objectively wrong, would not be sinful. Yet this awareness is kept obscure by the strategy of the sinful consciousness itself: for purposes of protective coloration, it endeavors to suppress the unwelcome knowledge.

In any full-fledged passion, as of wrath, we can readily detect this trait of wilful blindness It is characteristic of passion to exclude a part of the mental horizon. There is immense satisfaction in radical thought and radical action: by eliminating scruples or further considerations, our mental state gains at once that simplicity and unity in which we have a "necessary interest," for they insure that added intensity in the process of living which is the object of the life *élan* itself. The impeding call for the additional meaning is at a disadvantage, because it appears as hostile to more abundant life; yet as it is the achieved will to power that is attempting to assert itself, it cannot be banished: it can only be thrown into the margin.[1] Sin, in fact, deals

---

[1] One recommendation of this account of moral consciousness over that of McDougall, for example, may be that the problem how the naturally weaker motive acquires such strength as often to overcome the naturally stronger motive loses much of its point. There is no need to

in margins. It involves, as has often been pointed out, an obscuration of knowledge; but what it rejects is only the difference between one thought system and another slightly more complete. Passion is always highly intellectual and alert. The most primitive exhibition of pugnacity is full of such concepts as—''On this issue (simple or complex)—you (with your view of it)—shall submit—shall regret—your obstinacy—shall go down —before this, my attack—longer parley intolerable, stultifying—all evasion shall be swept away.'' It is simply that the marriage between the given course of behavior and its appropriate thought-system is so close that a readjustment in favor of a more complete, and probably less definite, thought-system is rendered difficult.

We see that sin cannot be defined, except very relatively, as a preference of pleasure to reason: there are pleasure and reason on each side. There is on each side a satisfaction of the will to live—we have seen that passion presents itself as a more abundant life than its opposite; and on each side a satisfaction of the will to power, which all human actions must in some degree express. There is, in fact, *no descriptive difference* between the act which is sinful and the act which is not sinful: sin has all the psychological ingredients of virtue, and virtue all the ingredients of sin— even to the mental concentration, the limiting of marginal thought. It is only the wholly individual situa-

appeal to the growing strength of a self-regarding sentiment. For the central will has as much of the strength of all the instincts as at any time the self has succeeded in lending it by its efforts of interpretation.

tion, the reference of a given impulse to an available charge of interpretative thought, that furnishes the criterion.

An assertion of the individual character of sin usually excites the question how it is then that social organization, with its common laws and statutes, describing murder, theft, adultery, disorderly conduct by definite and chiefly external means, is possible,—a question which we have later to consider,—but the principle of the answer seems to be this: There are certain kinds of objective behavior which are so far below the level of average human interpretative power that we can assume with all but complete certainty that the objective wrong implies a subjective wrong. And for social purposes we must assume this, allowing under liberal régimes that strong evidence might still convince us of the contrary. It is, in fact, far safer to assume that an externally anti-social behavior is internally sinful than that an externally correct behavior is internally virtuous. But neither assumption is entirely safe; and in our own discussion we are speaking of principles, not of proportions. In all strictness, no behavior can be defined as sinful by its descriptive characters alone.

But we can perhaps find a still more complete expression of the nature of sin by considering a further development of the "meaning" which an act may carry.

Every day a great volume of money changes hands without a word, the meaning of the transaction being established by some understanding in the background.

The understanding may be an agreement for work and wages; then if, at the week's end, A pays money to B, the acts of A in giving and of B in receiving bear a definite meaning which could be expressed in the form of an assertion. B's act of receiving means, "I have done the work agreed upon, and am entitled to this return"; A's act means, "I believe that you have done your work, and this is your earning." If B has not done his work, his act still conveys the same meaning; but this time, it is a false meaning. His act is equivalent to an untruth. The wrong does not lie primarily in the untruth; but the untruth points out the wrong.

Suppose now that we have arrived at an understanding about the conditions which justify a decision in general, namely, that I shall only then decide and act when I have fairly interpreted my impulses. In this case, any decision or act of mine would have this further meaning: that I have done my interpreting, and am justified in releasing the act, in saying "Now" to my impulse. And as my actions aim at some satisfaction, whether in the acting or in the end reached, it follows that my *pleasures themselves acquire a meaning,* because of the general understanding. Pleasure, to the moral self, ceases to be mere pleasure: it means a justified mastery; it means that so far as I know my own will, it is now being realized; it means that the material of experience is becoming subject to my ideas and purposes. If I have accepted this understanding, and take a pleasure without complying with the conditions, without doing my thinking and interpreting, then that taking of pleasure means a falsehood. I sit down to meat, and my eating does no more than satisfy my appetite, when by the grace of God I profess that it concerns my widest plans and purposes also: in this case my eating becomes a lie in action. Always assuming the understanding, we can agree so far with Wollaston—a keen but little-noticed thinker—that all sin has the character of untruth, because of the unspoken assertions or meanings of our acts. Wollaston had in mind the meanings which acts carry by virtue of social understandings and conventions. Thus if I beat my wife, or betray my friend, I treat them as if they were not wife, or friend: my acts convey untruth. For us, however, the untruth lies farther back than the social usage in treating wives or friends: it is found in the general recognition by human consciousness that human acts, at any rate, must express a well-considered will to power. From such a will, certain ways of treating wives and friends will follow by logical necessity.

Sin, with this understanding, appears as *a reckless Now-saying*, to the pleasure of action or enjoyment;[2]

2 The thesis that pleasure has a meaning is likely to meet a cold reception from those whose scientific conscience requires them to assert in all cases that a primrose is a primrose—and nothing more. Let me say that I do not deny that pleasure is pleasure. What I deny is that pleasure to a human being is ever quite "nothing but pleasure."

What else, then, is it, as a matter of plain psychology? Psychologically, pleasure will be admitted an absorbing experience: it tends to concentrate the attention within its own focus. But what, pray, does it absorb? If it is my pleasure, it absorbs *me;* if yours, it absorbs *you:* it absorbs the self that experiences it. But what is the self when absorbed in the pleasure except that pleasure simply? The self is the pleasure, if you like; but here the plain psychologist is in danger of losing all the significant truth about pleasure: it would be better to state the identity conversely—the pleasure is the self. For the pleasure

and hence as a *false assertion that in that pleasure I
am a complete man.* I accept my wages; I have not
paid the price in labor, or in thought.

is not a fixed entity to whose measure the self shrinks; it is the self
which is a relatively fixed entity to whose measure the pleasure tends
to expand. Child and man may find pleasure in the same object; but
the pleasures are as the child is to the man.

What does the self bring to the pleasure? Its meaning. The simplest
meaning of pleasure is that it is what life is for. It satisfies the self;
it becomes a guide. So much meaning biology is inclined to assert.
But has it any further meaning?

Experience develops further meanings. Pleasure is at first something
discovered; it is not demanded, it is hit upon. It is an enlightening
discovery; it seems to unlock the secret of life, and hence becomes, as
we said, a guide. But what is at first a privilege becomes looked upon,
just because it seems to belong to life, as a right. Pleasure begins to
mean something due, and claimed, and perhaps rightfully fought for.
The will to power takes the form that Hobbes so perfectly describes;
it tries to "ensure forever the way of my future desire." Any particular
pleasure takes on the meaning of an element in a total life-requirement.

For human beings, experience passes through this stage, but does not
stop there, as Hobbes thought. It is found that pleasure, as a private
right, fails to satisfy. With prey in mouth the cat at once becomes a
solitary beast; and with every pleasurable absorption men also tend
to loosen their ties with other men. Since pleasure satisfies my will, it
tends to make me complete in myself; every joy has a centrifugal component,
it tends to be a "joy apart from thee." Yet just this component
nent makes the meaning of pleasure so far attained incomplete. To a
human being pleasure seeks to take on the meaning, not of a private
victory, but of a victory in which my social world shares, either actually
or by consent. Eating ceases to mean scurrying into the thicket with
the snatched morsel; it begins to mean an opportunity for celebrating a
common life.

There is perhaps no limit to the meaning that a simple pleasure may
bear; but even to plain psychology it cannot be called "mere pleasure."

Thus, if one reflects upon the phylogenesis of our capacities for
pleasure, he may light upon the view that every enjoyment in the human
being represents a long history of self-denials on the part of our subhuman ancestors. Pleasure would acquire a further meaning for such
a view; it would mean an inheritance of prehistoric labor and sacrifice.

We cannot forthwith define sin, however, as a *premature* Now-saying to action or enjoyment; it is simply an unjustified Now-saying, and it may also, though more rarely, be *too late*. In a difficult decision delay may itself become a momentary satisfaction: under the pretence of further thought, a lesser volume of thinking may be accepted—too little to win the right of decision. Thus sin may more completely assume the appearance of virtue, and obliterate the descriptive differences. Yet in this guise also, it corresponds to our analysis: it is the refusal to interpret; it is likewise the false assertion, whether by action or by delay, that my action expresses my attainable interpretation.

And because of this meaning, illicit pleasure would mean, as for Mr. G. K. Chesterton, the *exploitation of a deposit,* the violation of a trust, disloyalty to an implied compact with all the elemental virtue that has gone into our human make.

Or, if the horizon in which our will has to work out its destiny is enlarged by thought, until it tries to conceive the world as whole; and if that whole-view perceives a quality in the world which might be called divine; then pleasure will appear as a symbol of this divine quality, possibly as a participation therein. If pleasure is used in such wise as to blur or banish the holiness, or dignity, or beauty, or infinitude of the conscious horizon, it is false to *that* meaning. From this side, *sin is secularization.*

CHAPTER XIX

WHY MEN SIN

IT is possible to analyze sin, and in a measure to describe it. It is not possible to explain it. For to explain it would be to show it as the necessary or invariable consequence of certain conditions; and whatever is necessary or automatic is not sin. Sin implies that kind of freedom in which the fate and character of each conscious act comes for a moment under the control of 'self'; and neither nature nor environment nor God decides what meaning the act shall bear.

It is true that right-doing lies in the direction of effort; and that wrong-doing, as the easier course, has the advantage of the natural slope. Sin is likely to pose as the "law of the members" and to claim the indulgence due to the natively stronger motive. The burden of explanation would thus be thrown upon doing right: we should rather ask how it is possible *not* to sin. But we have deprived ourselves of this recourse, since the will, as the central thread of our meaning, is on the side of the fully interpreted, or right, action.[1] Doing right, however, requires "trying"; and if we were thoroughly necessitated beings, we might explain

---

[1] In a self there is no "stronger motive" except that which the self *makes* stronger. After we have acted it requires no great wisdom to tell which consideration was the prevailing one. But the wisdom which can tell this *beforehand* is still to be found.

the variable vigor of our trying by the varying amount
of the energy at our disposal, and the fluctuations of
that hunger and thirst after righteousness with which
we are endowed. But unfortunately for this type of
explanation, no experience is more familiar than that
of trying more or less hard, within the limits of the
energy and interest we have. The moral issue lies
wholly within the range of what trying we are able
to do.

But in these respects, moral mistakes seem to bear
a close analogy to the mistakes which are inevitable
in acquiring any new art, and may have the same explanation. The beginner at target practice will miss
the mark: that is a safe prediction. He is entirely free
to hit it: and there is no assignable reason why he
must miss it. "Good shooting," said a marksman to me,
"is simply a matter of caring enough about each shot."
Yet the beginner will miss. As time goes on, he will
miss less frequently,—a curve of his progress in learning can be drawn. Some men progress more rapidly
than others, and go farther toward a perfect score; but
there is a similarity in all curves of learning. Is not
sin a missing of the target, and hence a phenomenon
of the curve of learning?

For any particular technique at which we try, the
curve of learning holds; and so with the virtues, so far
as they have a technique. Franklin's scheme of monthly
practice was a prudent one. But right is not a matter
of matching an objectively definable standard. In all
such efforts the full will of the individual is on the
side of striking the mark, and the adjustment is de-

feated by the physical obstacles of imperfect organization and control. In the moral effort there is no difficulty of this sort: the nature of right is to be always within reach, otherwise there is no obligation. The point is that my full will is *not* on the side of striking that mark. Hence the analogy breaks down; and there is no law of learning for morality. The sinful situation is not a failure to reach what was by some organic law beyond reach; it is a defection from what was within my power. I have, as a fact of history, preferred an easier course.

Thus sin is in all cases a matter of history, or better, of biography. Our judgment that all men sin is statistical in part, taking into account the immense number of decisions that men make; and in part it is due to a knowledge of the conditions that favor imperfect choices. It is on this ground alone that we can approach an account of why men sin. In most general terms, sin is possible because of the existence of real moral dilemmas (and later of feigned dilemmas); and every sin has a 'case,' either of innocuousness or of positive virtue. When once we have begun to take part in the world of action, the world sees to it that we are driven from one venture to another: the exigencies of growth compel us to face, from time to time, a new step with all its possibilities of error, while the alternative of playing safe in the old way is itself an error. It might be possible to show the entire history of sin as a history of moral growth. I shall content myself with mentioning a few typical situations.

1. There is one dilemma that attends every moral act; though it is seldom that it becomes acute. It concerns the process of coming to a decision. There is an obvious danger of false judgment in acting before deliberation is complete; but there is likewise a danger of error in holding decision until deliberation can be complete.

For deliberation never reaches anything but a rough completion. Through experience every man finds for himself a degree of certainty which he regards as sufficient for practical purposes: he calls himself 'certain' when this standard is reached, and for the most part his deliberative process rises quickly to this level and passes into action without hesitation. For he has found that if he acts at all, he must act when his action will fit the case; he must reach the best possible view of the case in the time permitted. He is but occasionally aware of what is universally true: that no case has ever been seen by him in its full meaning. And since all of our fiats are issued in partial obscurity, the chance is offered, as they fall through the dark of the mind, for deflection toward the lurking magnets of the cruder wishes. Thus there is wrong in delaying beyond the moment of an action's possible meaning; and yet the imperfect reflection involved is the natural cover of sin.

2. No man can live a moral life in aloofness from society and its various alliances; yet all alliance is alliance with the imperfect. It might be hard to say which is in the greater danger of political error, the party

man or the non-party man. Each has his own peril;
and a cynic would have it, we suspect, both. It is evident, however, that growth lies in the direction of *belonging*. It is at the cost of losing all effect that one
refrains from attachment to whatever is historical and
organized in the world. Institutions exist to lend to
each individual member their over-individual dimensions and scope. It is not alone a practical but a moral
peril if I reject their aid.

It is equally evident that there are no perfect institutions. Whatever is historical inherits the strength and
the weakness of all the past from which it comes; and
whatever is organized must make use of concrete men
whose virtues are mixed with their vices. Is it possible
to be an historical entity without partaking of the evil
with which one must make alliance? It is not politics
alone that involves this threat of contamination and
compromise: nothing historical is free from it, the
church, the professional group, social traditions, societies everywhere,—even friendship, if Emerson's
dictum is right, "Friends descend to meet." It is
possible to be in the world and not of it; but is it
possible to *work with it* and not be of it?

I do not say that it is impossible: I say that there
is a moral difficulty in either alternative. I must ally
myself; but I must vigilantly interpret that alliance,
as Burke interpreted the social contract, as an alliance
with all the honest strivings of my comrades, to the
rejection of the ease and profit of all guilty conformity.
In all positive living, the morally necessary ends are
perpetually pleading the justification of the means,

and who can avoid being carried from time to time
across the evanescent line? Sin has no need to enter
life as a separate deed:—it may be the simple prolonging of a good deed.

3. The moral life must become social, we have said:
growth lies that way. Among the necessary incidents
of this socially moral existence is the use of moral
authorities, which we have already referred to as a
natural habit of conscience. Perfect rectitude implies
an art of preserving solitude of decision amid the mass
of suggestion borne in upon us from our environment:
the distinction between the good and the evil of the
alliances we were speaking of requires and assumes
this power. But we cannot escape the need of moral
authority any more than we can escape the time-
element in decision. And the dilemma lies not so much
in the likelihood that we will choose radically wrong
authorities (for humanity has shown a singular unanimity in its major selections, its heroes and saints)
as that we will take our authorities whole.

It is doubtful whether any leader is not liable at
some point to become a misleader. At such a point
clear judgment for the follower becomes peculiarly
difficult, since it involves a plunge out of congenial
company into solitude. Moral disillusionment is the
severest of experiences. The habit of deference takes
on the psychological quality of a secondary virtue:
when the rift appears in the halo, it becomes necessary
to choose either the distress of opposing an honored
guidance, or that tacit complicity which is the parent

of cynicism, and whose creed is, "All men, even the best, are at heart false."

Such an experience is severe only because there was an initial error in the degree of reliance placed upon the authority in question. The will had been seduced into ease by the presence of an object of too great trust: sin was already there. For this reason, it is natural to plead for the alternative of rejecting authority altogether in moral matters, an alternative in which I do not hesitate to say there is an equal danger of moral faltering, ineptitude, and obliquity, even to the limited extent to which the discarding of moral guidance is possible.

4. If moral disagreement is one of the incidents of moral growth; and if it is the business of men to incorporate their convictions in action,—as it is; there is no escape from the occasional dilemma between fighting for your conviction and letting your conviction fail by avoiding hostilities.

What I conceive as right I am bound to work for, and if need be fight for. The distinction between working and fighting is gradual: in either case I am opposing myself to what opposes my purpose. The difference lies in the amount of faith I have in my opponent, and in the time and effort I can subtract from my work to accomplish his conversion. There comes a time at which I must decide that he that is not for me is against me: to defer this decision is as evil as to hasten it. Yet wherever opposition enters, there is so great a likelihood of the entrance of moral wrong, that we are often counselled rather to forgo the good it aims at.

For when one fights for human rights, is he not also fighting for his own? And when one fights for his own rights, is he not also fighting for his comforts? Since public wrong, as a rule, first shows itself in economic injury, he who fights for liberty and justice has to reflect that his fight intends also to be profitable. His opponent will seldom fail to remind him of this fact, and to interpret his psychology accordingly. And when motives are mixed, the warrior can hardly be too confident about the color of his own purpose. The justest warfare, in its beginnings, is open to suspicion.

And further, however perfectly the belligerent spirit is at first in accord with the necessities of honor, its momentum tends to carry it beyond the point of the moral issue. The activity of fighting has its own instinctive delight; and while the belligerent exaltation is probably intended by nature to make easier the transition from comparative sloth to full activity under a vital demand, it is at least as difficult for this passion as for others to hold itself within the bounds of this function, as means to an ulterior end. And morally, it is more necessary that it should accept this meaning.

Perhaps it is superfluous to point out the moral peril of warfare; yet it may serve a purpose in measuring the moral peril of the alternative. The dangers of hostility are obvious; but those of peace are incomparably deceitful.

It was Thomas Hobbes who adopted the maxim "Seek peace and pursue it" as the first law not of love but of enlightened selfishness. As the wrongs which I have not combatted and might have combatted are indefinitely more numerous than the selfish interests for which I have fought, it appears to me that incomparably the greater bulk of moral error is that which enters the will under the garb of peace. Fighting is hard and distracting work: peace, I say, has easier victories. But what if this more ideal warfare does not take place? Here is my community, for example, in which I do not have to look far for examples of injustice, waste, maladministration, which are bound to affect the health, happiness, or safety of myself, my children, and many others: yet I do not take issue with them. There are philosophers in Europe who have been preaching for some time the gospel of the right of might, or of the strong culture which judges itself the best. I have known of this too, and have not lifted a voice against it. Had those who knew of it risen in time, and had they faced the ills of which this doctrine was but a symptom, the world might well have been spared its last and greatest war. The test of an evil peace is that its fruit is discord and not unity; and conversely, any peace that eventuates in war is thereby shown to have been an evil peace.

The moral seductiveness of peace lies in its method of dealing with wrong: it is apt to deal with it as an unclean person deals with dirt,—by preferring not to recognize its existence, hence leaving it unmet and uncured. The clean soul is militantly eager to find the dirt: the true lover of peace with a similar obsession seeks for the spot that is unharmonized, and makes

an issue of that spot until it is wiped out. He smells
afar off the issues that threaten war, ferrets them out
in advance, and tries to settle them. But the greater
part of our vociferous cult of peace has become foul,
stagnant, attempting to conceal in dark closets the
underlying differences of interest and the unresolved
dislikes of the world. Its policy is the policy of Hush.
It is the cover of our deepest and largest guilt.

5. To generalize from situations such as the above,
the only right ways of behavior are ways which with
a slight change of inner adjustment become wrong
ways. Conversely, to venture a wrong way is a condition of finding the right way. This much the search
after righteousness has in common with the acquisition
of skill. We begin, indeed, with something better than
random movements; but we do not begin with a self-
consciousness quick to discern the point at which the
imperfect maxim usurps the nest of the perfect one.
There is nothing to be achieved in the moral life except
at a risk which is a moral risk. He who will not risk
falling into egotism or undue self-assertion can hardly
win an honorable effectiveness; for the crude plunge
of action, if it has the merit of vigor and decision, will
rarely escape at first the touch of insensitiveness. And
he who will not risk a fall into cowardice or ease will
hardly find the point of an honorably pacific will. I do
not say that we must fall: I say that we must risk the
fall. We must find our moral equipoise through trial
and the risk of error.

But behind the vagaries of such moral self-education, there lies *the good-will to win this equipoise,* which is the redeeming feature behind many an actual sin. It is the total will, not the partial will, which gives the ultimate character to an act; and so a career of moral adventure, if it is a genuine search for truth and not a covert lust for the joys of the taster, may be by conscience itself required of the soul. Or let me rather say, it is by conscience required of every soul; though it also is attended by the subtlest moral peril. For morality that is not original is no morality.

It is with this proviso of a genuine and ultimate will to win moral truth that we look if not with leniency yet with hope upon those statistically certain lapses which make of every individual a participant in the sins of his race. For given this good-will, the forces making for righteousness are twofold: the intrinsic attraction of the good, and the repulsion of the evil. Sin, when it occurs, enhances the force of evil, by channelling deeper the path already easier by nature; but it also enhances the force of good, by awakening the reaction we call remorse. It is a part of our moral destiny, as a race, that we must work out our moral life by the aid of both forces, the quest of blessedness and the sorrowful ruing of our own guilt. In so far as sin is capable of explanation in terms of a balance of forces, the explanation is this: that since we must win moral life through moral adventure, we need to add the push of rue to the pull of the ultimate good, in order to find our adequate and complete moral motive.

CHAPTER XX

SIN AS STATUS

THERE was an ancient theological conception which attained a large social importance, and even a political importance in the days when a widespread fear of future punishment was a factor in allegiance to institutions. This conception can be couched in terms of a rude syllogism, somewhat as follows:

> The wages of sin is death;
> All men are born in sin; ergo,
> All men are, by birth, mortal.

I doubt whether this argument has been refuted: in many minds it has suffered a severer fate,—that of being outgrown by the gradual wearing out of the belief in its premises. Upon the view of sin which we have so far developed there can be no such thing as "original sin": every man is his own Adam. As for death, whether physical death or the cessation of personal existence, we have ceased to see any causal connection between this and moral delinquency. Sin of course has its consequences, both social and psychological; the attention of ethical theory has been largely occupied with these, as is natural in a pragmatic era of thought. But the fact that these ascertainable consequences exist hardly disposes of the question whether

there are also metaphysical consequences. The idea of
a moral causality which runs deeper than the surface
of phenomenal connections is both ancient and modern,
a property of all great religions and of various phil-
osophies. As a metaphysical notion it lies just beyond
the range of our present enquiry. But it is human
nature, and particularly moral human nature, to make
conscious connections with ultimate facts; for this
reason, we cannot fairly finish our own task without
stepping over this border.

We may remind ourselves at this point that we have
been speaking of sin in but one of its two traditional
meanings. Sin has commonly referred to individual
deeds,—and so we have understood it; but it has also
referred to a *status*. As a status, or condition, it has
implied impurity, pollution, liability to banishment,
etc., metaphysical outlawry. The word sinner refers
to this status rather than to the particular deeds. Regarding it in this way we should have to say that so
far from rejecting the notion that there is a sinful
status, we should have to affirm one, so far, at least,
as psychology can carry us.

My moral status, as a fact of psychology, would be
the condition of my preferences—my character. And
my preferences I cannot modify in any so immediate
way as I can modify a deed. Suppose that, whether
by birth or by acquired habit, I simply do not as a fact
prefer righteousness,—at the price of moral effort.
I might not call this condition depravity. I should certainly not call it holiness.

And this, on the whole, seems to be the condition I

am in. The necessary interest I have in blessedness is relatively faint; it appears to me rather as something known about, or heard about, than of poignant, present, and compelling value. And while some shimmer of the beatific vision may lend a distant glow to the pursuit of duty, the actual work of righteousness has to deal rather with the raw materials of which happiness is made than with happiness itself. It is like a price paid in advance, sometimes far in advance: there is a strain upon faith, upon imagination. One "walks out upon his idea"—not upon his immediate appreciation. Such is the balance of my nature; it is this balance which makes it historically necessary that ruing should add itself to the lifting force of the good. And for aught I can see, this balance came with me into the world, as a part of my inherited being. From the first I willed the good with an effort; and so, perhaps, as Augustine argues, what I willed was never quite good. I do not say I should be condemned or punished for this; I am now speaking of statuses, i.e., of simple metaphysical facts.

We need not, however, attribute this judgment to Augustine alone. If Aristotle is right, we are all of us more or less in the position of patients who cling to their illnesses, of those, familiar to psychiatry, who resist being robbed of their delusions, even of their persecutions. It takes the good wholly to prefer the good. The holy will, no doubt, is something to be acquired; it is not innate. If this is what is meant by being born in sin, I do not know how I should deny it.

I doubt whether this apparently somber judgment of

original human nature is primarily a product of theological speculation. It has at least a strong support
in common experience. For quite apart from all theories, self-condemnation, when it comes, has an ex-
traordinary way of applying retroactively: blame
frequently reaches back over a past which seemed innocent of the moral question involved. A new insight
tends to condemn all prior ignorance, not alone re-
gretting, but accusing, the long persistence in the lower
level of life. The lover enters his new vista of consciousness with an embarrassment which is partly
moral,—the symptom of a critical self-judgment which
surveys the whole domain of past choices. He accuses
that past self at least of a moral inertness; it was dull,
as atheists are dull "who cannot guess God's presence
out of sight."

The argument of this retroactive judgment may be
this. That my life has been, if not an active rejection
of the good, yet a long acquiescence in something less
than good. I have failed to shake myself awake to the
conditions of my own welfare. I have accepted without
protest enjoyments I have not earned: I have not en-
quired into the right of my own ease. Back of all my
passivity was an awareness that life has, after all, its
conditions; and I failed to force myself up to the exertion or hardship of learning them. There was a possible subconscious integrity in me which I was disloyal to, all the while there was no one to hold me to
it. I have not known in detail what I ought to do, and
I cannot be judged for what I have not known, but I
judge myself for living in an ignorance which my will

knew could be overcome. I was not without *that* clue, nor *that* desire.[1]

Apart from particular deeds of sin, then, our common moral consciousness recognizes something like a sinful status. As for those deeds themselves, it is a matter of daily experience that they bring a new status with them. Debasement is not an act; it is a condition of choice resulting from a series of acts. Each abandonment of the effort for complete interpretation, makes the next abandonment easier; and what conscience is concerned about is not alone the issue of this act but also, and primarily, the psychological status which it creates. But what is the significance of this status, whether original or acquired? Allowing that we are justified in viewing it with regret, if not wholly with indignation, is there any excuse for the

[1] In greater detail: There have been occasions in which I could not be reconciled with my brother, through lack of available sympathy at that moment. But I know that that sympathy would have been available, had I apart from times of stress been perceptive of facts which it was my business to know, if I had been duly out-living, objective, alive. Or, I cannot think of the right thing to say at a given moment; and who can blame me for not thinking of the right thing? Yet I may well blame myself. For this, too, while a result of present perception, is of a perception built on past alertness. Now I must prepare what I would say, if I am to appear well. But if I were what I would present myself as being, consistently and always, I need "take no thought for what I shall speak"; myself would speak. What I am not accuses me. Even what I am not in intellect traces back to lapses from what I have been admonished to become. Admonished by what? By nothing except by the perception that "life lies this way, rather than that, and for the most part, in living in the object." Admonished, if you like, by the original *synderesis*, adequate to its own work.

terror and guilt of soul, the "anxiety neurosis" of the older theology?

We shall see more clearly if we eliminate the psychological element of blame, and ask again simply for fact. What does this status entail? I do not know. But I am not prepared to say that it entails nothing. If I were told that it entails a form of mortality, I should lend the assertion a respectful hearing. It would seem reasonable to me that a lesser status, in things relating to insight, idea, appreciation, should be a measure of lesser validity in point of reality. If ideas are the most real things in the universe, this would most certainly be the case. If life is to be measured in terms of intercourse with minds with whom I am fit to converse, I can see that this status of inferiority is one that must carry with it a lesser degree of life.

Putting away all emphasis on moral ideals, let me look at things "naturally." It seems in this sense natural to me that men should be sinful. It seems also natural to me that they should be mortal. It is not mortality that looks strange to me; it is immortality. I could not rebel if I were told, without prejudice, that my range of existence would be as the range of my own effective wishes. This, I should say, is obvious justice. Let those who care for immortality take the pains; let the others have their own finite reward. Let each have the degree of life which his own status—by its natural hold on reality—commands.

This would leave us all in calm, were this the last word. For who could regard that a "punishment" which is simply failure to attain an end that one does not want? You thunder at me that unless I repent of my sin, I shall perish. I reply, I am content to perish—indeed, I had never aimed at anything else: I have not insisted on being immortal.

But we are not thus left, by nature, at our natural ease. Having become self-conscious, we have no choice but to see life for the good it is, and to be restless at the thought of exclusion from that good. To lose life, to lose the quality of life, to lose the possibility of responding to what we believe to be the best, and hence the possibility of being with the best, to be unable, as Dostoievski's Father Zossima has it,—to be unable to love, and *to know this inability and this loss:* this is a torment to man as it is not to the other creatures. If man must recognize in himself a status of natural finitude, we must also ascribe to him, in his original equipment, an impulse which repudiates that status and demands a being at the level of his appreciation. If man is by nature evil, that evil is not all of him: he is also by nature ill-at-ease with his imperfect self, fretted by an ambition to become what he is not, an ambition which makes of his conscience an ally and a tool. This is not something different from the will to power; but it is the deepest expression of that will. It is *the will to overcome death.*

Religion has had this service to render: it has co-operated with this human unwillingness to accept mortality. It has constantly reminded man how easily he may remain mortal, and how hardly he may earn immortality. It has made him pray with a touch of fear,

"Take not thy holy spirit from me." There are those who refer to this state of mind as an 'anxiety neurosis': it may become such. But in substance, it is simply the original man in his wholeness facing the fact of his natural status. Others have called it the 'divine spark' which somehow disturbs our clod. Names matter little; but the disturbed state is one of increased, not lessened, awareness of truth. The capacity of feeling the natural bent of desire as invested with the omen of finitude is what constitutes man not only a self but a *soul*. For the soul is the self as aware of, and seeking to control, its metaphysical status. It is original man in his full stature.

This completes our survey of original human nature. We shall now turn to the process of its remaking.

PART IV

EXPERIENCE

Argument

It is an axiom that experience modifies human nature, as for example by building habits. But this is all metaphor. What is experience, and how does it act?

The metaphor suggests that experience is an active something which plays upon a passive material, human nature, and shapes it. That aspect of the picture needs to be corrected at the outset. Experience works nothing in us without our coöperation; it does nothing to a passive mind. Further, while experience is truly a great teacher, it has no language but that of the dumb; what it means to say we must guess for ourselves.

Inasmuch as the human being is most unfinished at birth, his instincts all imperfectly defined, there is more shaping and reshaping to be done in his case than in that of any other animal. Perhaps for the same reason, he shows more initiative in going out to get experience, rather than waiting for it to happen to him. He *experiments;* experimenting is active angling for experience. And before he consciously experiments he *plays.* The habits he picks up at first are less stable and compulsory than for other animals; he lightly disregards them and tries something else. Into his play there enter strands of curiosity and pugnacity, a strange enjoyment of risk and of a spice of pain, to cancel the interest in safety of conservative habit. Hence the human being commonly refuses to let well enough alone, or to regard as settled what experience pretends to have taught, so long as a lively interest turns that way.

Hence for him also, *pleasure and pain,* the instruments by which experience chiefly teaches the animals, are never final evidences. Suppose you are hurt in an experiment; does that stop the experiment. A whip may check a horse, but not a zebra: a pain may make a child pause, but only to devise some other way of doing the same thing.

More significant than sense pains and pleasures is the general depression or elation which follows action. Still more significant is the mental after-image, a reflection of my total self on the course of behavior: a positive after-image may discount a hundred pains; a negative after-image may cancel a hundred pleasures.

The negative comments of experience do not tell me what to do: they only admonish me to *change my hypothesis* about what I want and how to get it. This progressive alteration of hypotheses may be called the dialectic of the will.

Now let us be clear that these negative after-images are *my own,* and the new hypotheses are chosen in an effort to satisfy *them.* Society, custom, tradition are all active in proposing ways to behave; and these ways have a powerful influence over young heads, devoid of strong counter-suggestions. For this reason, some thinkers, like Professor Dewey, consider experience as chiefly a process of running custom into individual vessels where it takes the form of habit, and begets new custom. This assumes that the aboriginal will of the individual has no direction of its own; that the *élan vital* is blind. This is far from being the case. No individual ever reproduces custom without giving it his own cast. Custom is admitted on sufferance, and produces no permanent habit but by individual consent.

CHAPTER XXI

THE AGENCIES OF REMAKING

IN studying original human nature, we have already begun the study of the remaking of human nature. For remaking is in large part a work of man upon himself, i.e., the gradual transformation of the fragmentary and particular impulses by the central instinct, the will. The self-conscious being is inevitably a self-changing being; and what we have called the moral aspect of original nature is simply the self-conscious will taking a broad cosmic responsibility for the work of self-building, making itself a present partner with man's remoter destiny.

The moral consciousness is not separable from any other aspect of self-consciousness. It is not necessarily a moral sense which may lead one to such reflections as "I am awkward, or slow, or peculiar, or inefficient"; yet in judgments of this sort, if there is a *morale* behind them, remaking processes begin. Wherever the human being can catch a glimpse of himself as a whole, self-judgment will emerge, and the central instinct will begin to impose its findings upon each impulse severally.

And strictly speaking, nothing can transform a will but itself. It is easily possible to force a man to behave this way or that, by various sorts of coercion; but this is not to effect a change in his instincts, and unless the

instincts are reached there is no change in the man. To
change human nature is to change *what it wants,* or
wills, and nothing can naturalize within the will such
a change but the will itself.[1]

But the inner factors do no work except in conjunction with outer occasions which furnish the materials
and the incentives for self-judgment. And this co-operation of inner with outer factors of change is what we
mean by the word 'experience.'

It is customary to make a contrast between what one
learns on the basis of his own experience and what he
learns from his social environment. On this ground
we might be inclined to divide the agencies of remaking

---

[1] It is the recognition of this truth which distinguishes modern
education, the education of freedom as opposed to that of constraint:
the principle has been generally understood from the times, at latest, of
Pestalozzi and Froebel.

No doubt, external pressure long enough continued, a long imprison-
ment, for example, will be followed by some change of character. You
may be able to recognize a convict as easily as you recognize a member
of the more liberal professions. But if so, it is because a degree of
consent has domesticated in him as in them, the presumably freer people,
certain of the repeated details and attitudes of his daily program. The
point is, that however little the program itself may be one of his choice,
the habits are *his habits,*—his ways of adapting his will to a persistent
situation. And such habits may, of course, mean little change in the
deeper strata of character.

As a rule, it is true, constraint does finally invade a will incapable
of permanent rebellion. It reaches it through this middle stage of habit;
for habits of any kind, though imposed by necessity, will reveal variations
more or less alluring, and the more alluring may become accepted by the
pliable character as its own choice. Thus force may develop into
seduction, for better or for worse: and no educational theory can safely
neglect the fact that many a horse, driven unwillingly to water, finds that
it *wants to drink.* We have no right to conclude, because all remaking
must be founded on consent, that therefore, in all education, obtaining
consent is preliminary.

into two groups which we might broadly label, experience and training. This distinction must have some justification. Otherwise there would be no meaning in the question whether social pressure, or some particular brand of social pressure, is helpful or hurtful to human nature. Such a question implies that there is a normal course of development which human nature, left to itself, its own data and reflection, would tend to realize. When, for example, Mr. Bertrand Russell says that "those who have had most of 'education' are very often atrophied in their mental and spiritual life"— and no doubt he is right—he implies that this mental and spiritual life of the individual mind has a natural growth and destiny of its own, capable in some way of being ascertained and used as a standard for judging the results of social action. We might then be expected to show what experience would do with human nature if there were no such thing as social pressure and education.

It is obvious, however, that social experience is an integral part of individual experience; since individual experience has neither its complete data nor its working tools apart from social interaction. The various standards of self-judgment gain certainty and vigor only in the give and take of the group; there are no more impressive arguments for changing one's ways than the wholly spontaneous reactions of one's fellows; and the private self hardly knows its own desires apart from the experiences that come through play, submission, dominance, affection, and the like. Isolation, actual or theoretical, would give us as distorted a view of the work of experience as of original human nature. There is thus no point in attempting a distinction between the effects of solitary experience and the effects of companionship: the only distinction worth drawing would be between one's own reflection upon his entire experience, social and solitary, and his neighbor's reflection, especially when the neighborly views are enforced by artificial rewards and punishments.

This is the distinction which we shall undertake to draw, meaning by 'experience' simply that inner digestion of data of all sorts whereby the outcome of every essay in behavior becomes a basis for modifying the next similar essay, and excluding the influence of all deliberate suggestion and training. We shall first glance at the task which experience in this sense has to accomplish.

CHAPTER XXII

THE TASK OF EXPERIENCE

THERE is more reshaping to be done in the human being than in any other creature. This is partly because in him the instincts appear in more numerous fragments, less fixed in their connections and hence less promptly serviceable, as the human infant is less nearly ready at birth for locomotion than the new-born colt. But it is also partly because the great middle group of instincts which we have called the general instincts are *more general*, so that there is more work to be done to fit them to specific circumstances.

No creature can engage in food-getting-in-general: it must get particular items of food in particular ways. Even the most definite units of behavior, as grasping, biting, are generalities needing adjustment to every individual task. All instincts, then, and especially human instincts, have to be brought to earth by building a bridge from the universal to the particular. The human being, so far as his original impulses are guiding him, is in the position of an agent under such widely general orders that he is allowed, and obliged, to use a liberal 'discretion.' It is in this gap between the broad thrust of instinct and the particular emergency that 'intelligence' finds its first employment.

When I say that intelligence—i.e., the idea of a total

end regulating the ways and means to its fulfilment—
spans this gap, I do not mean that it acts unaided.
Nature does not fail to make specific suggestions in
specific situations: in every circumstance there must,
of course, be some nervous route of least resistance.
Nature may produce a veritable magazine of handy
responses, which may be run through more or less
mechanically until some one suits the emergency, as
in the case of an animal seeking to escape from a trap.
But the significant thing is that Nature herself draws
the distinction between these suggestions and the
major instinct: *they* are alterable, loosely attached,
while the general instinct remains controlling the
alterations. The law seems to hold for human nature
that the more specific the suggestion, the more alterable it is.

Take, for example, the instinct to fly from danger—
a general instinct. No highly developed creature is
endowed with such an instinct without numerous
auxiliary responses. When a special sign indicates a
special danger—a loud noise, a "large object coming
rapidly toward one"—nature has one or more proposals to make, also comparatively specific—to shrink,
to retire, to get closer to companions, to call out, to
hide. But it is just these specials signs (stimuli) and
special suggestions (responses) which are modifiable.[1]

[1] McDougall holds that it is the emotional core of the instinct which
persists, while the two termini, the afferent and efferent channels, are
subject to modification. But what persists is more than an emotion;
it is the entire general tendency. As the instincts which McDougall
enumerates are themselves highly general, I should not hesitate to pro-

Thus, birds which by impulse take to flight at any loud noise may learn to sit through the passage of a railway train; while the mere sight of a man on foot will scatter them. The former special stimulus has ceased to have the general meaning 'danger'; the latter special stimulus has acquired that general meaning. A rabbit at large when alarmed will make for its burrow; in captivity, it will make for its box or kennel. The general meaning, 'escape,' can no longer take the former special route—the natural way; the latter response has acquired that meaning. In such modifications of stimulus or response, or both, consists the education or self-education of the animal: they are the work of 'intelligence,' so far as they are guided by the persisting idea of the general end, that is to say, by a mind or self; we call them, also, the results of 'experience'—understanding, however, that apart from the 'intelligence' the experience would mean nothing, and therefore accomplish nothing.

What is accomplished is usually something more, however, than a fitting of a particular response to a particular situation, as the examples given will show. For the new stimuli and responses that are brought under the general instinct are themselves general. The bird has an attitude toward 'walking men' which, though far more specific than its attitude toward 'danger,' is still a general attitude. These acquired generalities we call *habits*. A habit might indeed be

pose that it is *they*, in their entirety, which persist, while the modification affects mainly such particularized channels as form the main object of Professor Thorndike's studies.

fairly described as an acquired (and usually comparatively specific) instinct.[2] It is what experience deposits when the mind has played long enough with a situation that is bound to recur; has played long enough, that is, with its repertoire of responses and its own inventions, to adopt a general method as best, and to turn its experience-interest to other situations.

Thus 'experience' moves through the growth of our natural impulses like a reaper's swath,—concerned at every point with the particular instance, while having before it and leaving behind it only the masses and bundles of grain, generalities of higher and lower level. The result of this reaping of experience is that nothing is left standing in its original relation to Mother Earth. Everything is now brought into relation to the purposes of the reaper. No natural impulse can become a matter of experience and remain unchanged. What we call memory implies that every new stimulus will be invested with all the meaning of what followed at the

  [2] As a connection between stimulus and response, habit has, as Watson justly remarks, the same structure as instinct. It is not impossible that instincts may have originated to some extent through such deposits. But it is an error to hold that there is no essential difference between them (Watson, *Behavior*, p. 185). Habit differs from instinct in its relation to the higher centers. Since habit is not flung off, so to speak, as a full-blown bubble, until the self is satisfied, or,—let me say,—since habit is never even relatively finished, until attention is relatively turned to other sequences, a habit is controlled by a central awareness of the meaning of its sequence as an instinct is not controlled. An instinct, we may say, turns into habit just in proportion as it yields up to consciousness the secret of its destination. So far as action is instinctive, consciousness is increasingly aware of the articulation of parts into a total sequence; so far as it is habitual, the awareness of elements is on the decline, and the centers are dealing with the complex whole as a simple entity, whose meaning is sufficiently grasped.

previous ventures. Every new effort is normally more my *own* than any previous effort. And if a mind is equipped like the human mind with vigorous impulses of curiosity and play, the most favorable result of any item of behavior will not preserve the next following cases of the kind from experimental variation, though it were always for the worse.

But we must now look more particularly at the methods by which experience works in transforming instinct.

CHAPTER XXIII

THE METHODS OF EXPERIENCE

WHEN we picture to ourselves experience as an active agency, working upon a passive and malleable mind, we think of it as wielding the tools of pleasure and pain. These tools are universal and imperative: no man can ignore them, especially, no child. Of the two, pain, the chief change-working tool, is the more impressive and inescapable: it is said to be "prepotent," that is, to assume when it appears a certain precedence over other claims to attention. And there is a degree of justice in speaking of the mind as passive. For while all living and experimenting must be active, and I may launch what ventures I will, I cannot decide in advance whether the outcome shall be agreeable or the reverse. Here I am at the mercy of the world, and of my own constitution.[1]

The general method of experience is not a secret. Whatever experiment of mine results in pleasure will be confirmed, and its occasion will be sought again. Whatever experiment results in pain will tend to be checked or much modified at its next suggestion. Pleas-

[1] To experience is to experiment and to read the returns of experimentation. Experimenting is an active element; also mounting the results. But if experimenting were sufficient to determine the results themselves, as certain forms of idealism suggest, experiment would lose its meaning.

ure heightens the rate and energy of experimenting, and so tends to increase the total volume of experience. It leads the will out, supplies it with information of what there is to live for, and increases the likelihood that new types of pleasure will be found. Pleasure is thus a type of experience which favors its own growth, and so becomes the substance with which 'life' does, or normally should, fill up. Of pain, in general, the reverse is true. Probably some retrospective alteration of the nervous channel is being effected during the experience of pain itself, tending to occlude the channel, as the physiological side of that experience.

But what this change is and how far back it reaches cannot be put down in any simple general proposition. It depends in the first place upon *the mind* that experiences the pain. The burnt animal, generally speaking, dreads the fire, and avoids it. But it is not true that the burnt moth ceases to approach the flame, nor either that the traditional burnt child refrains from further experiments. The phototropism of the moth persists; the interest of the child persists likewise. The child has connected the image of the flame with the experience of being burnt; the moth has not. But beyond this quasi-mechanical linkage, with its inhibiting force, the child recognizes in its own approach to the flame differences of degree, of rapidity, of route; and this recognition is a controlling factor in what its experience *means* to it. In an animal intermediate between moth and man the effect of the burning might be a blank and absolute negative toward all flames. For the human being there are no such negatives:—there are acquired cautions and discriminations. Such experience, in brief, drives a human being to 'think.'

Such thinking is still, like the first exercise of intelligence, a subsuming of means under ends; but here it takes the direction of analyzing, and making hypotheses,—i.e., of induction. In the result it will, if it can, so modify its plan of action as both to gain the good and avoid the evil. There is at once a beginning of science, and of the economic virtues.

But the nature of the change produced by experience depends, in the second place, upon the *kind of pain* (or pleasure)—for different kinds of disagreeable experience give different kinds of thrust to the mind. While it is true that every outcome of an experiment must be either favorable or unfavorable, and that we may call all favorable results pleasurable and all unfavorable results painful, the names pleasure and pain are so restricted in what they directly bring before our thought that they give no adequate idea of the working of experience. 'Experience' works in different ways according as the agreeable or disagreeable results are of one variety or another: it will be in the interest of clearness, therefore, to make a few simple distinctions in the kind of result we have to deal with.

1. *Definite sense experiences,*—pleasures and pains in the primary sense, together with other "original satisfiers and annoyers" of which Professor Thorndike speaks, such as bitter tastes, hindrances of motion, contact with objects of aversion or disgust.[2]

[2] *The Original Nature of Man,* pp. 123 ff.

The relation of any such sensible annoyer to the course of action is a purely empirical fact. Nature might have made flame, so far as the child's insight goes, as innocuous as incense. It might have made those unpalatable lady-bugs pecked at by Lloyd Morgan's deservedly noted chicks as sweet as corn. The attribute has to be learned as a fact, by the method of contiguity. It is imperative that objects of the attractive but dangerous class should thereafter be divided into the nocuous and the innocuous, and distinguished by signs: the fate of our individual may depend on success in finding such a sign. But the imperative is categorical in the sense that it offers no reasons for its existence.

2. *General depression or elation.* Every vital sequence has its bodily reverberation as well as its sensible contents. A general sense of physical well-being or the reverse may accompany the end of a course of behavior, or may come as an after-effect more or less belated. This cœnæsthetic condition may be of the same quality as the sensible result of the behavior, but it may also be of opposite quality, as in the disagreeable afterclap of an agreeable indulgence.

To bring these vaguer physical experiences into connection with the original impulse and its direct pleasures and pains requires some mental span, especially when they are of contrary quality. Thus, after any strenuous exertion there normally follows the depression of fatigue; yet if the direct sensible results of the effort have been pleasant, fatigue seems to have no tendency to alter the sequence. In primitive self-consciousness, the flux of bodily conditions is taken for granted. The same is true in even greater measure of the remoter after-effects. Our orgiastic ancestors presumably suffered from their excesses more or less as we do; yet there are few signs that they habitually put two and two together. But when the causal connection is observed, and the enjoyment (for example) is recognized as a deceitful enjoyment, there will be some modification of the next response to that invitation, whether or not the response is inhibited. And further, there will be a degree of insight into the meaning of this connection of effect with cause; for the beginning of seeing *why* a given cause should have a given effect, is the condition of seeing that there is any causal connection at all. Hence the modification that takes place will not be a wholly random one, but will take the direction of escaping that particular logical sequence.

3. *Mental after-image.* Distinct from all peripheral consequences of a sequence is a central comment which may be subconscious or distinct, but is probably always present in the human being. It is most noticeable, naturally enough, when it is contrary in quality to either the sensible result or the general bodily condition; as when one succeeds in a competition and finds himself somehow dissatisfied with his success, or as when one fails and finds himself at peace in his failure. Such a mental after-image may appear at first as irrationally connected with my experience as the burning with the candle-flame. But it differs from the preceding types of experience in the circumstance that the comment is recognized as being not nature's comment, but my own. There is the same demand as

before for analysis and induction; but this time I am required to understand. This kind of experience has such a crucial bearing upon the process of revising my behavior that we must illustrate it in greater detail.

I have a disobedient child; and upon an accumulation of petty refusals to obey, I act upon the advice of a contemporary sage, "Never punish a child except in anger." I secure attention and compliance, and leave a fairly permanent impression; I go away satisfied. I suffer from no physical depression. But in time, perhaps, my sense of triumph abates, or becomes obscured by a counter uneasiness. And when I analyze the experience, I find that it refers to a defect in my achievement: I gained what I defined for myself,— namely, compliance; but obedience I have not gained. When I gave rein to the pugnacious behavior, my will had defined its object as the destruction of a state of mind too little impressed with the importance of my own. But I have not conveyed to my child any positive conviction on that point, and so I have gained no genuine authority. My strategy has been in some measure self-defeating. The mental after-image of my result is a *negative after-image*.

Such an after-image may have sufficient potency to reverse the judgment of the other types of experience. No one can engage in a brisk fight without incurring much physical pain, and experiencing subsequent depression; yet these circumstances are not in the least competent to deter an enthusiastic fighter. It would be false psychology to explain this as a matter of the balance of pleasure over pain; it is a question of the positive after-image. The pursuit of pleasure among young people is still more or less orgiastic and physically expensive; yet so long as the mental after-images are favorable, the efforts and depressions are judged worth the cost. If they become unfavorable, the degree of pleasure does not save them. We incline to estimate the human worth of a woman by the degree of the deterrent effect which the pain of childbirth may have upon her. By all the laws of effect, if pleasure and pain were the controlling factors, the first child should commonly be the last. It is the mental after-image which normally determines the destiny of that instinctive sequence. In fact, there are few of the vital experiences of humanity that do not entail a weight of pain and labor such as does in fact deter those in whom prudence is the highest virtue. And I do not ignore the fact that the mental after-image varies markedly with one's general theory of the universe. But I am here pointing out simply a law of human nature as a fact to be reckoned with: *it is the mental after-image which determines whether a given sequence shall be confirmed or weakened, and how it shall be modified.* If the after-image is positive, any discomfort is prevented from eating into the allurement of the stimulus; if it is negative, any delight is prevented from enhancing it.

The nature of this after-image should be evident from our previous discussion. It is the reaction of the *whole will* upon the partial impulse, when the full meaning of that impulse is perceived in the light of its results. It is not necessarily a moral reaction; remorse, shame, æsthetic revolt, etc., are its clarified varieties. Its significance may simply be, "This is, or is not, what *on the whole* I want"; "I was a fool"; "I hit it right." In the unfinished condition of our instincts (and the slightness of our experience) every course of action is launched more or less hypothetically. It is my theory, as I make my decision, that this is what I want to do; yet I am aware that there is some doubt about it, and that I shall not be sure until the returns are all in. The mental after-image is the answer to the question involved in this tentative state of mind.

If the after-image is negative, the natural result will be a *new hypothesis* for dealing with a similar situation. And *the transformation of instinct, under experience, consists essentially in the series of hypotheses* which a given mind adopts,—hypotheses about the ways in which impulses are to be followed in order to satisfy the complete will. This being the case, it is evident that the series of these successive transformations must approach, as a goal, an interpretation of the impulse in question in terms of the individual's own variety of the will-to-power. And inasmuch as each successive hypothesis is built on the error of the preceding one, the process might well be called, in analogy with Plato's method of finding true ideas, a dialectical process. The work of experience is the dialectic of the will.

CHAPTER XXIV

THE DIALECTIC OF THE WILL:
THE INDIVIDUAL AND CUSTOM

WE have frequently referred to the effect of experience upon the instinct of pugnacity. Let me, then, illustrate my view of the dialectic of the will by a series of transformations of pugnacity which may represent, somewhat symbolically, the experience of individuals, accumulating as the experience of the race up to a certain point.

I

In its original and crudest form, pugnacity makes for the simple and radical destruction of its object. This is what it 'means.' If this impulse appears in a mind which is incapable of any social interest in its object, the slaying of the opponent may be an entirely satisfactory result. The mental after-image may be positive.

But in most of the higher animals this is not the case. Destruction brings, as we have noted, a degree of defeat of one's total wish; there is at least enough interest in the survival of the opposed mind so that its chagrin, its acknowledgment of the victor, has a value. The hypothesis, "I want destruction," changes into the hypothesis, "I want *revenge*." Shand has collected a number of instances in which animals have with apparent deliberation refrained from destroying in order to take satisfaction in the suffering or discomfiture of the enemy. I wish to point out that this revision takes place quite in independence of any social constraint upon the fighting impulse.

Though the successive interpretations of pugnacity are likely to retain their hold in certain relations while showing their defects in others, yet revenge, like destruction, tends to invade every relation of life. Within members of any given group when murder is recognized as undesirable, wrath is likely to take everywhere the form of revenge, whether in the 'tit for tat' of children, or in the petulant relations of parents and offspring, or in the more deliberate and vindictive eye-for-eye quarrels among adults. Revenge has, however, an inherent inconsistency of motive which is bound to produce, in the regions of denser sociability, a further revision of hypothesis.

For while revenge aims to leave such injury as to exclude the restoration of amicable feelings, and, indeed, to gloat in the persistence of hatred and contempt, one has need of the presence of the despised and defeated adversary as a source of this satisfaction; revenge squints toward the maintenance of friendliness. The solving of this puzzle turns revenge into *punishment*, which is the next stage of the developing perception of what pugnacity means.

Punishment aims at inflicting pain, but without permanent injury. The anatomy of the infant vertebrate commonly lends itself to this interpretation; and some of the animals, elephants at least, have acquired the same technique of punishment as prevails with human parents. Punishment makes a discrimination between the evil of a will and its essential nature, just as revenge made a distinction between the will and the life. Punishment is an interpretation of pugnacity as meaning the elimination of an evil element in the will of another while retaining the integrity of, and the regard for, that will as a whole. Punishment intends to reinstate the original amity of the disturbed relationship.

When this discrimination has once been made, it is not a long step to a direct aim at the restoration of the integrity of that will, and a subordination of the effort to do justice to the defect. It may be an empirical discovery at first, that a soft answer may in some cases satisfy the whole aim of punishment, and have the further advantage of avoiding the bitterness of humiliating memory. It matters not how the hypothesis was arrived at; so long as punishment left in some relations a negative after-image, this revision was bound to be hit upon sooner or later. This complete suppression of the destructive behavior in the interest of a resolute kindliness may not be the last word in the development of the pugnacious impulse: we shall have some further enquiry to make on this point.[1] But it is one of the views to which experience leads.

And my point is that experience, given the human mind to work upon, would be likely to lead to this stage, quite apart from the disciplinary action of society, and quite apart from the teachings of religion, simply

[1] Chapters XLI, XXXI, XXXII, XXVIII.

because the prior interpretations of the anger-impulse are not what the human being, on the whole, wants.

I am intentionally omitting all reference to the contributions which various types of social pressure, economic, political, and others, make to this result. It is far from my purpose to ignore or minimize the extent of these contributions. I have excluded them here, because I intend to speak of them by themselves; and because our present concern has been to find a method of testing whether social transformations tend to distort human nature, and to carry it in directions which of its own momentum it would not follow. So far as pugnacity is concerned, my judgment is,—from the considerations here put down,—that social repressions of the fighting impulse and 'civilization' of its expression are not, on the whole, violently counter to the direction of individual growth. The dominant trend of the human will here seems to be, at least roughly, parallel with the demands made upon it by society.

In a complete treatise each of the major general instincts should be examined for its natural dialectic. I must be content at present to indicate a method of work; and in a later section to sketch some of the tendencies in other instincts.

II

Wherever we find a rough agreement, as in the case of pugnacity, between social demands and the counsels of individual experience, one suspects a causal connection. The individual result may be the cause of the social standard; but it is also possible that the social rule may be the cause of the individual attitude. In view of the strong reasons for regarding the individual, his experience and his habits, as products primarily of society, let me dwell briefly on our main thesis, that the individual will has an independent course of growth, a *direction of its own*.

Everything an individual becomes, every habit he acquires, will bear the mark of *all* the forces that have been steadily at work upon him. We say that his will has its bent, and that whatever his mind becomes will show the trace of it: this does not exclude the fact that society also leaves its mark on every developed trait. Hence one who sees that the social effect is *everywhere* may easily leap to the conclusion that it is *everything*: and that the individual is a mere term in a social process.

Social custom, he will observe, shapes individual habit: individual habit perpetuates social custom: the cycle is self-continuing. Hence social groups breed true: the French type reproduces itself, never by mistake developing a Scotch character; and this is not because the organic germ-plasm is distinctive, but because the group-customs are distinctive, and individual ways of life have no other such potent source as these social ways.

According to Professor Dewey, custom preserves itself not alone in the fact of habit, but in the very conscience of the individual. For "habit is energy organized in certain channels. When interfered with, it swells as resentment and as an avenging force . . . breach of custom or habit is the source of sympathetic resentment,''[2] and thus of the sense of wrong itself.

Now certain it is that human habits do not form themselves *in vacuo* by dint of solitary trial and error, nor yet at the dictation of an all-sufficient hereditary impulse. The marvelous plasticity of the human infant means not only a capacity to receive suggestion, but a high degree of helplessness without tutelage. It needs its social inheritance not less than its organic heredity; it has a hunger for authoritative guidance quite as aboriginal as its hunger for food. Powerful as its instinctive dispositions may *become,* their strength is largely due to social encouragement; and an instinct that is not helped into action, so far from smouldering as a 'repressed' energy, is hardly able to make itself felt as a directed craving. Professor C. C. Josey goes so far as to say that "instinct must be *expressed* before it can be *repressed*";[3] so that whatever repression society exercises is a limitation of what society itself has called into being, and not a curtailment of innate powers clamoring for their rightful outlet. In brief, the human individual cannot be itself except at the cost of becoming one of its kind: whatever its original selfhood or subjectivity may be, it is no sufficient source of conduct. The Bergsonian *élan vital,* when taken as separate from matter, as pure inwardness, is but "a blind onward push or impetus . . . as likely to turn out

[2] *Human Nature and Conduct,* p. 76.
[3] *Instinct in Social Philosophy,* p. 264.

destructive as creative.''⁴ This is the force of the pragmatic and of the kindred Hegelian contention.

But does all this mean that the individual will is not *also* a factor in what it becomes? Does it mean that society can so much as impose upon it a single habit without its own consent and conspiracy? Certainly not.

For the original instinct of the individual is not a directionless *élan vital:* it has a native trend which shows itself in its reactions upon custom. It relies on custom, or some sort of social suggestion, to set its habits in motion; but it receives all custom *tentatively* as an hypothesis in its own dialectic, the mental after-image of every such performance of adoption or imitation is *its own,* and the consequent modification is its own. For note that custom is never adopted without change: hence the social process is not precisely circular. Custom which is taken up into the individual will and reissued as habit bears the marks of the issuer: it is now ''his'' habit, no longer ''society's'' custom. Hence customs are perpetually being readjusted to the will, and not alone the will to custom. ''Impulses are the pivots upon which the re-organization of activities turns; they are the agencies of deviation, for giving new directions to old habits and changing their quality'';⁵ and that which thus gives direction cannot conceivably be a directionless force.

Nor is it custom that produces conscience: for a breach of custom is wholly incompetent to produce a *moral* resentment, however much it may produce trepi-

---

⁴ Dewey, *Human Nature and Conduct,* p. 74.
⁵ Dewey, *Human Nature and Conduct,* p. 93.

dation, unless the custom were already accorded the quality of 'rightness' at the bar of individual feeling. If custom were the source of conscience, all custom must be right, save where it conflicts with other custom: the ultimate court is custom, and "The *mores* can make anything right." But the illusion of the moral ultimacy of custom, and of the consequent moral equivalence of customs in different societies and ages (an illusion to which hospitable minds are subject when immersed in folklore), cannot survive the perception that conscience shows itself most notably in individual deviations from custom, and in an initiative which slowly brings changes of custom after it.[6] So far as the report of conscience is embodied in the mental after-image, it is evident that the dialectic of individual experience carries it naturally in the direction of moral standards. In this sense, man, if not by nature good, has a natural bent to goodness. It requires no grace of custom to make a courteous or a kindly nature, such as occurs sporadically in the wildest surroundings; and whether or not integrity, honor, courage, magnanimity, shine by their own light, they shine, in any society, in contrast to the prescriptive level of the *mores,* and as traits of individual wills.

We maintain, therefore, that the will has a way of its own, through and athwart custom. Only thus can we so much as enquire how society affects that original bent. We proceed to that enquiry.

[6] Cf. above, pp. 117 et seq.

PART V

SOCIETY

Argument

IF there were nothing in human nature itself to give bent to the direction of its growth, there could be no meaning in a complaint that society warps human nature, or that its standards and conventions and laws are oppressive. This theory of the indefinite plasticity of human nature, as proposed by Watson and Dewey, when carried to its consequences, would justify every tyranny; since in the end human nature would adapt itself to whatever social custom required.

What we have to do is to consider what society tries to make of us, and what *resists* this all-pervasive moulding.

In the main, social action is not distorting to human nature; it rather aids and foreshortens the results of individual experience; but since society tends to speak to its members in *its own* interest rather than in theirs, its demands may become oppressive.

Most ideals are colored by the selfish wishes of those who announce them to others; but the self-interest of society is not sufficient to lend final authority to any such ideal. Ideals are subject to a test of right, distinct from either social or individual liking, and therefore capable of commanding the identical approval of both society and individual.

As with ideals, so with laws and institutions; they are not justified in their demands merely because they, as expressions of the great society, exist. They must be brought to the test of the requirements of human nature, in its own course of normal growth. Such tests are proposed in our discussion, in the shape of postulates, that is to say, demands which human nature in its turn has to make upon laws and institutions.

The process of *education* concentrates in itself all this possible clash of interest between the social will and human nature. In education the older generation transmits its entire type of mind to the newer: it reproduces there its mental and moral self. Those who love liberty fear the self-imposition of the old upon the new. Some of them, as Mr. Bertrand Russell, plead that no instruction be given in morals, in religion, in politics, lest we merely propagate our prejudices. The advice is mischievous. Education must expose each generation to the *best* which the older generation has seen, not because it has been *their* vision, but because it is their *best*. Children cannot be bred on a vacuum. But with this best must be given also the means of escaping its possible error and relativity, namely a training in original reflection and criticism, and the arts of self-knowledge. Education must culminate in the self-elimination of society with all the prestige and bluster of the over-mind.

Nothing can withdraw from the individual the right to rebel; nor from society the right to punish. Each, in the absence of a higher tribunal, must be judge in his own case. These are the conditions under which the recurring tragedies of history are engendered. But while there is no higher human court, there are agencies of common discipline, which tend to remould both individual and society, and so to bring their judgments nearer to identity. Art and religion may be taken as typical of these agencies.

CHAPTER XXV

SOCIAL MODELLING

IF human instincts, left to the teachings of experience, would grow very much as society tries to model them, why not leave them more completely to their own growth? Our result so far supplies a good argument for greater freedom from social constraint, if not for anarchy. Social interference with natural growth is based, we know, upon a degree of distrust of human nature: and when we perceive that human nature has its own inward righting-tendency, its 'dialectic,' the distrust seems unjustified: social modelling appears as an elaborate social meddling.

Attempts to steady an ark that will steady itself are worse than unnecessary: they prevent the finding of *real reasons* for preferring one mode of behavior to another. The social reason is always at one remove from the real reason, vitiated as it is by all the motives that play for or against conformity.[1] And further, so far as society loses the invaluable guidance of that still, small voice, the mental after-image, which governs growth, how can we be assured that its transformations shall, in the main, be other than deformations? Working, as society does, through 'sanctions,' that is, through artificial pressures of reward and punishment,

[1] Cf. Holt, *The Freudian Wish;* Herbert Spencer, *Education,* etc., for expressions of this ideal.

the amount of such pressure may be an index of the amount of warping which nature is likely to suffer under its control.

The tabus under which we now live are indeed but phantoms of the ferocities which helped to create the first 'cakes of custom.' Consequently we cannot point to any such mutilations or immolations of nature, such head-hunting or widow-burnings, such foot-bindings or soul-bindings, as cumber to satiety the annals of the folkways. Personal liberty has won many battles; but is its work complete? If such natural expressions as laughter and tears, coughing and sneezing, are still subject to social regulation, what shall be said of the course of our deeper impulses, our antipathies, our affections, our fears? Society is not precisely hostile to our passions any more than it is hostile to our sneezing; but it asserts jurisdiction over the ways and methods of each. And it makes these ways and means so much the essence of the agreement that unless the impulse can be satisfied in the prescribed way, society inclines to demand that it shall not be satisfied at all. There are approved ways of earning a living, as there are approved ways of winning a bride, but who can recognize under the activities of shop and factory and office an expression of natural impulses to hunt, to fish, to gather where one has not strewn? In its ways of food-getting, civilization has listened to advisers more imperious than instinct; yet it insists that unless one follow these ways, he shall not have a man's living at all.

As for the weapons which produce conformity, if

the social lash has lost its barbarity, it has not lost
its sting. Fears of death and beyond-death are seldom
invoked; yet the fears which spring from ambition and
from multiform social attachments and dependencies
are hardly less powerful. Man's need of his fellows is
so great, and increasingly great, that he will not willingly forfeit a large measure of their favor. Besides
this, the knowledge and dread of our own ignorance in
the management of life can be counted upon to herd the
mass of mankind into the beaten path, while ease, certainty, and the feeling of at-homeness serve to keep
them there. For the more adventurous spirits, the finer
but not less terrifying punishments of ridicule and
exclusion are held in reserve. Hence 'convention' is a
word which still conveys a sense of enforced deviation
from the natural. What society imagines it wants imposes itself upon what *I* want, and buries it.

Our attitude toward convention is for the most part
not only docile, but unreasoning. The modelling process, working by suggestion and imitation as well as
by overt control, has done its work before the critical
powers are fully awake. To many minds, it is something
of a recommendation of usage that we hold to it, as to
a religious mystery, with the blind adherence of faith.
Yet we are destined to reach self-conscious judgment
in these matters as in all others. We cannot hold a
custom *against* reason, when once reason has become
competent to deal with it. On the other hand, it would
be a questionable procedure to argue from the general
unreasoning acceptance of any social habit or belief
that there are no reasons for it. While we are bound

to challenge whatever we can see to be unnatural or outworn, yet so deep are the roots of convention that most customs and prejudices deserve a second glance —he takes great risks who denies to any of them a meaning.

To take one example from among many, I find this risk too lightly run in a recent chapter by that always informing and vigorous thinker, Professor E. A. Ross. He is dealing with a number of conventional beliefs which modify behavior.[2] He cites, among others, the belief "that manual labor is degrading," a belief less surprising among the upper castes who profit by it than among manual laborers themselves. Yet these latter also give it an unreasoned acceptance, thinks Professor Ross, as seen in their ambitions for themselves and their children to escape from the ranks of toil into the ranks of the long-nailed mandarins. But why translate this conventional direction of ambition, so far as it is an article of faith rather than a desire for greater income, as a belief that manual labor is degrading? Why not recognize in it a highly reasonable belief that a man should by all means have a mental survey of his own work, and that the particular kind of manual labor which is robbed of all mental interest *is* degrading. There is a false note in the desire to get away from toil; but beside it is a deep and true note in the desire to live, as man was made to live, by a union of toil with wit. As a second meaningless convention, our author mentions the belief that "pecuniary success is the only

2 E. A. Ross, *Social Psychology*, ch. vii.

success.'' No doubt society, less by what it says than by the turn of its eyes, instils an admiration for the man who has made his fortune. This value-attitude, if not exclusive among us, is certainly overdeveloped; but can we say that it is essentially unreasonable? If command of the fruits of the earth is the normal and destined position for man, why should one who has achieved such a position, and in so doing has shown large powers of one kind or another, not receive the recognition that he, in so far, has succeeded? It is a man's work to make a fortune, and under normal circumstances a measure of ability. It is not the only kind of work that can be called a man's work, but it is typical. It has the appeal that the qualities it calls out can be understood by everybody. We must define this convention rather by the values it justly appreciates, if there are any such, than by its myopic aberrations, its exclusion of other values. And unless we are prepared to deny that the normal result of economic effort, the mastery of nature, is a good, we must expect to deal, for all time, with a disposition to admire the man who has become ruler over many things. Another meaningless convention, according to Ross, is ''that the consumption of stimulants or narcotics by women is unwomanly.'' But I desist. There are few prejudices or ceremonial observances for which the users are entirely ready with their reasons. If they were, these elements of mental usage would forfeit the thought-saving merits of custom. But if we forthwith pronounce an observance unreasonable because it is unreasoned, we forgo all possibility of penetrating into its often subtle and subconscious grounds.

Rebellion we have always with us, and we need it. It trims the dead wood, and summons latent reasons into the open. Of the rebellion of to-day, it is perhaps significant that it complains less of the common customs of the tribe, so far as they affect the majority, than of the incidental hardship which any custom, by its uniformity, may work in special cases. Society tyrannizes less by mistaking the conditions for the welfare of the mass of men, than by classifying individuals, who never quite fit the categories.[3] We may approach our enquiry, then, without antecedent bias either hostile to convention or in favor of it, simply as a question of fact. How does society tend to modify individual behavior?

[3] See, for example, Elsie Clews Parsons, *Social Freedom.*

CHAPTER XXVI

MAIN DIRECTIONS OF SOCIAL MODELLING

FOR the sake of proportion, our first duty is always to the obvious. We must remind ourselves at the outset of the most general way in which social rules bear upon the development of instinct. Generally speaking, then, custom *continues the direction of development struck out by individual experience, and facilitates it.*

More in detail: it abbreviates the tedious process of learning from experience; it saves from experiments too costly for the individual,—such, for example, as might cost him his life, or his health; it speeds the whole process of interpretation, through its own acquired skill in imparting its maxims; and on account of all this economy, it carries the process farther than personal experimentation could hope to reach. It also preserves a common direction of growth, and at least a minimum level of achievement in a great number of individuals. Society is to each of its members a storehouse of technique: and as little as the learner could spare the mechanical technique of the socially transmitted arts and sciences, could he dispense with the accumulated capital of wisdom in the ways of behavior, the folkways of his own tribe and time. That is, he could not spare them if what we call 'progress' is to continue.

To say that social action continues the direction of the work of individual experience understates the case: it continues the whole work of organic evolution. Let me mention two ways in which this continuation is marked.

1. The 'vestibule of satisfaction' is prolonged. By the 'vestibule' of a satisfaction I mean the series of preliminary processes which lead up to it. Throughout the animal series, we can trace a growing elaboration of instinctive processes, and hence a prolonged period of suspense between the first stimulus and the final satisfaction. Consider the food-getting processes, and the satisfaction of eating. An amœba 'eats' immediately upon contact with a food-particle,—if this activity of surrounding and absorbing may be called eating. The sea-anemone has to observe a preliminary or two: it must use its tentacles to waft the food-bearing water into its body cavity. When organs of smell and vision exist, they imply that food (as well as danger) is to be discerned at a distance, and usually that the animal thus equipped is to go and get it. Organs of chase and combat indicate still more elaborate preliminaries; with hunting, stalking, and killing, the vestibule is prolonged many fold. An instinct to lay up stores for winter shows that a farther step has been taken in the same direction; and all this is accomplished without appealing either to experience or to social instruction. Individual experience not only retraces the phylogenetic journey: it carries farther the interpolation of

means and conditions in the form of labor and foresight between hunger and consumption. If society, then, intercalates further conditions and complexities, it is but exceeding Nature at her own game. The prolonging of the vestibule goes with a greater reserve of tissue, and a finer balancing of the stimulus; so that the period of suspense is not more than the organism is fitted to sustain. The general principle holds good, that the farther the stimulus is from the satisfaction, the less its intensity, the more it is negligible, and therefore the inconvenience of delay or even of ignoring it is negligible, in the vital economy.

What is true of food-getting is obviously true likewise of mating. If society has interposed apparently artificial conditions, such as the consent of the partner, the approval of a social representative, a ceremonial wedding, it is but embroidering upon the theme which Nature had, in the practices of quest and courtship, already inserted as preliminaries to the mating.

This conspiracy of all the phases of evolution in prolonging the vestibule of satisfaction, can hardly be looked upon as an end in itself, from the biological standpoint, though it implies the complication and development of the animal body. It means simply that the organism is fit to live in a more complex and extended environment, in which the time-factor and the ability to wait are highly important factors in survival. But from the psychological standpoint, the scope of the process, and the fact that satisfaction is hemmed in by an increasing number of conditions, imply an immense development of the meaning of each part of the long sequence, together with enhanced powers of self-control at its beginnings.

2. Limitation of the range of objects with which one deals. The protozoön must deal with the whole world so far as that world impinges upon it; it reacts to everything with like thoroughness of attention. The same organs that imply a lengthening of the vestibule bring also a power of selection. The higher animal reacts to a very small proportion of the total objects that come within its range of perception. The law is analogous to that of the increase of power in an optical instrument; the field is restricted as the reach increases. This discrimination, society carries farther. It prescribes to some extent what I may not eat, whom I may not fight, and whom I may not marry. And this element of artificiality is in continuance of the direction of phylogenesis and of experience, as before.

These circumstances do not sanction the social process in detail. But they make it altogether probable that the gross normal effect of society upon individual behavior is not only of biological value, but favorable as well to that gathering of meaning which is the business of individual growth. For a more accurate knowledge of what I want, a better understanding of what any instinct means, could only be gained by better excluding what it does not mean; and such exclusion would naturally be made effective, in society, by setting up preliminary conditions with which I must comply, and by defining certain objects to which I shall not react. If all custom were good custom, it would in this way add to the meaning, or value, of all behavior. And we are justified in inferring that, of its own nature, *society is not primarily repressive*.

But whether all custom, or any custom, is normal custom these facts can give no hint. In actuality society has been and is repressive; and especially in three ways. (1) The standards and ideals it sets up for me to follow are shaped to its own interest rather than to mine,—for society, like nature, must look first to the group and only secondarily to the individual; (2) the material equipment and scope which it offers me is curtailed by the competing needs of others,—and there are too many of us for the supply; (3) the permitted modes of behavior fall into fixed institutional forms, and hamper the movements of any life that grows beyond them. Social modelling can be good, from the standpoint of the individual, *only if all these tendencies are corrected*.

The old theory, then, that "the interests of the individual are identical with the interests of society" we shall not unconditionally accept. Our argument so far may be taken as a confirmation from a new angle of approach of the notion that in the main these interests tend to agree, but not of the notions of Hobbes, Burke, Hegel, and others which seem to sanction any pressure society might choose to impose upon its members. We have set up the individual life, with its natural dialectic, as the standard to which social pressures must conform; and by the aid of this standard we propose now to outline what none of these thinkers has given us, namely, a set of tests whereby we can distinguish a good social order from a bad social order, considering in turn each of the three ways in which societies are likely to go wrong.

CHAPTER XXVII

IDEALS AND THEIR RECOMMENDERS

A MAN in the midst of a society which is trying to shape him is not to be thought of as surrounded by pure altruists. Whatever behavior is recommended to him will bear some trace of the convenience of the source of recommendation. The virtue of labor in the eyes of its employers is a 'faithfulness and industry' which smacks of acquiescence *in statu quo*. The ideal citizen, for the standpatter, is the 'loyal' vessel of party authority and routine. The ideal child for the overburdened school mistress is by almost physical necessity the 'good' boy, not too beloved of his fellows, more docile than enterprising. It has been said that the excellence of wives as defined by husbands shows similar traits. In proportion to its self-satisfaction,— and the tendency of all aggregates is to be self-satisfied,—any group is prone to condemn its most vigorous as well as its least vigorous members: if it must move forward, it keeps a mean which it calls golden; it learns but slowly the truth of Aristotle's saying, that the best rule is rule over the best. It inclines to shape its members to its own ease, not to their advantage; it supplies them with a set of ideals visibly colored by its own idler interest.

But all conversation assumes an ultimate equality,

even that between master and slave, or between society
and the individual. What is required of me must come
professing to be for my good. Slaveholders, Aristotle
himself, tried to think slavery beneficial for slaves.
Interest may warp the particular judgment; but the
form of the apology reveals the principle at stake. The
interest of society by this involuntary confession, is
seen to have no authority over me unless it is also my
own interest. This is the primary and original 'right'
in the relations of whole and member: a man's right
is to his own development; the right of society exists
only where its own interest and that interest coincide.
And structurally (not historically) these interests do
coincide, not more because the member needs the society than because no society can prefer the less developed to the more developed member, other things
equal. Not even society, then, has a right to make
use of a person as a mere means to its majestic ends.[1]

The test of a good social order, then, will be this:
that I am not obliged to adopt any rule of conduct because of what others prefer I should do or be, unless
I also have or can have that same preference. Let us
state this test in the form of a postulate or demand

[1] There can, of course, be no legal right against political society, by
the definition of a legal right as something created by society (how
mighty are definitions!). By the same sign it would be inaccurate to
speak of political society itself as *having* legal rights, since legal rights
are something which it confers on its members. But those who thus
argue from definitions sometimes forget that the legal right is a specified
form of a more generic relationship; and that under this generic sense
of right, questions of right may arise between two such unlike persons
as state and individual, or society and individual.

which every good society must, and can, comply with:

What others wish me to be must be identical
with what I myself wish to be,—

a principle which we may call the *postulate of identical ideals*. It may be that no society, no actual society, complies with the requirement: but I venture to think that no actual society despairs of complying with it or fails in practical ways to aim at it. The conditions of social life everywhere assume that however wide the original disparity between what I think I would like to be, and what my environment thinks it would have me be, such an agreement *can be found* by some effort of thought, or by the slow working of social arrangements, or both. In point of fact there are arrangements apparently as natural and as old as society itself which help to secure precisely the agreement required by the postulate. I shall mention the most important of these.

1. The direct impact of social requirements comes to the individual through the most altruistic part of the social shell. This is especially true of his most plastic years: he is born among his well-wishers. And while the egoism of parents has also to be reckoned with, the danger of social tyranny lies rather in their lack of originality than in their lack of pride in the personal growth of their child. It is always possible that, as filtered through the medium of the family, the demand of society will strike with too little force rather than too much. For the identity required in the postulate calls for an effort on the part of the individual as well as upon the part of society, especially as the in-

dividual cannot be said to know without much drastic trial what in particular he wishes to be.

2. *Recommendership.* If society were sufficiently self-conscious to perceive that this immensely important ideal-making function is everywhere muddled and adulterated by short-sighted egoism, its own included, it might be imagined as referring this function to a carefully chosen and disinterested third party.

Such an imaginary arbitrator it would be difficult to realize in the flesh. He must be no member of society, either in its capacity as impressing ideals or in its capacity as receiving and using them. He would nevertheless have to know human nature to the bottom, and the necessities of social order. He would have to understand all parties, all social conflicts, and all occupations, and yet participate in none of them.

Political theory has now and again attempted to define such a functionary, inasmuch as the logical problem of a liberal government in preventing the warping of laws by political tyranny is very much the same as ours. This problem is: so to organize a public body that to every possible pair of parties there is always a third party to pass judgment between them, even when the two parties are the public as a whole and any part or member thereof. John Locke tried, in effect, to provide a perfectly general solution for this problem, and all but succeeded. His 'legislative' is a good third to every pair of parties that can be defined among the people, including executive and people, and also including itself as part of the people. He only failed to provide for a third party between the legislative in office and the people, which is precisely the point at which we, in our own problem, need relief. Here Locke had no recourse but the 'appeal to Heaven.' And we look in vain in any subsequent writer or political device for the general solution of our problem.

But Rousseau, approaching the problem from the other end, that of protecting people from their own idleness and ignorance, saw far more clearly than Locke the conditions for finding just social standards. "In order to discover the social rules best suited to peoples, a superior intelligence would be required, which should behold all the passions of men without experiencing any of them. This intelligence would have to be wholly independent of our nature while knowing it through and through. Its own welfare would have to be secure apart from us; and yet it must be ready to concern itself with our welfare. And lastly, it would have to look forward in the march of time to a distant consummation, and working in one century be willing to put its enjoyment in the next. It would take gods to give laws to man.'"[2] Surprisingly like what we thought necessary to protect men from society is Rousseau's view of what is necessary to protect men from themselves; and on the lips of the supposed believer in absolute democracy, the sentiment is striking. But if we ask what provision Rousseau would make to secure this ideal giver of laws we find no answer; for such a legislator is an anomaly in Rousseau's state, and if we may judge from his words, in any state. It is but a fiction, called upon to do the work of a reality. "This sublime

<hr />

[2] *The Social Contract*, Book II, ch. vii.

reason,'' he says, almost cynically, ''far above the range of the common herd, is that whose decisions the actual legislator puts into the mouth of the immortals, in order to constrain by (the pretence of) divine authority those whom human prudence could not move.'' Thus Rousseau also is driven to an appeal to Heaven, but to a merely dramatic appeal. To impute in this way an unreal divine quality to what is after all but a humanly conceived standard of behavior might well provide the needed force; but unless we could also ensure the divine wisdom and justice, this appeal would only deepen the tyranny, as the course of history may show.

Nevertheless, the arrangement which is so difficult from the standpoint of practical statecraft exists, and has existed from time immemorial, in ordinary social structure. It makes use of a common property of the self-conscious mind,—the capacity of being, while immersed in the stream of events, at the same time reflectively aloof from them. The man who recommends to others what were good to be done without having to follow his own teaching, or being in a position to do so, is not an unknown person, nor on the whole an unwelcome person. And it has been found possible to devise circumstances which give his announcement of rules and ideals so much detachment from the usual cares and fears of the casual disinterested observer, that the ''appeal to Heaven'' would be a phrase not wholly unwarranted in his case.

Society, in short, has never been without its professional 'Recommenders'; and it has never failed to

accord them a position of such immunity that their
words are as nearly as possible the words of the freed
spirit. In ancient times, they were the elders, the
shamans, the medicine men, the prophets, the priests.
In latter days, these also, and with them all whose work
is the liberal reflection upon human life,—the scholars,
the men of letters and of art. Such men live voluntarily
both within the society and mentally without it; in the
theological phrase their mental position is both imma-
nent and transcendent. At times they have lived in
security and freedom both political and economic; but
always they have survived only so far as men have
found in them an actual performance in some measure
of the momentous function of delineating the man who
is at once fully himself and fully the servant of the
social order. They have done their work more or less
badly, turbidly, venally; but in spite of the men, mankind has valued the function. In so far as it tolerates
them, organized society bears witness to its own self-
abnegation; through them it secures the unhampered
force of its own severest self-judgment. The original
moral nature we found attaching itself, as if by instinct,
to its chosen "Third Parties"; these it finds naturally
among the Recommenders, and the powers they represent. From both sides, then, that of society and that of
the individual, the Recommender is an agent of progress in the direction of realizing our postulate; and so
far as it can make use of this (free and unofficial)
triadic structure, society succeeds, as it were, in lifting itself by its own bootstraps. The ideals under which

men perforce live thus *tend to approximate* the ideals they would choose for themselves.

3. The particular advantage gained by the detachment of Recommendership is the correction of the *interested* ideal: but like every advantage, this one also is bought with a price; and society needs always to be saved from the besetting vice of its Recommenders, that of *abstraction*. Since Aristotle drew his sharp-cut pictures of the philosopher and the statesman we have progressed far in the art of combining the contrasting careers of reflection and action; but we are still far from knowing how to be wholly immersed in affairs and at the same time adequately to reflect upon them. Hence we need protection from the *abstract* ideal, as well as from the interested ideal.

Contemporary consciousness is keenly aware of this need. We see that by the circumstances of their origin our inherited magazine of standards is likely to fit the men of fiction better than the men of reality; and there are many signs of the inclination to attribute the difficulty to 'philosophy' or to 'idealism,' when it is simply the difficulty of reflective self-consciousness everywhere. Biography encounters it in the form of an apparent dilemma: that between being, on the one hand, realistic and disappointing, and on the other, abstractly heroic and unreal. All history, all art, all reflective description of mankind encounters it.

One of the class faults of the Recommender, an expression of the penchant for keen and sensitive listening that makes him useful, is an over-valuation of the æsthetic elements in our necessary interests,—the unmixed, the clear, the simple, the orderly, the systematic, the 'pure.'[3] Our aversions to dirt or to disorder are not profoundly natural, and in this case nature may be partly right: certainly a highly successful patternism and purism produce distrust by their very clarity. Mature worldly wisdom is quick to detect the shopproduct of Recommendership; and not uncommonly it adopts an indulgent superiority to the whole business of 'ideals,' as a necessary but always transitory incident in the process of growing-up.

But there is a natural corrective for the tyranny of abstractions, less easy than this superior realism, but more honest. It is found in the circumstance that abstractions breed their own critics in opposing abstractions; so that individual judgment is summoned to select between them or to combine them. The overburdened school mistress we were speaking of has, no doubt, an abstract ideal. But the contrasting ideals of the boys' gang, administered through that fear of being thought afraid which makes the life of a small boy with his fellows a chronic, if subconscious, hazing party,— these ideals also, with all their flourish of substantiality, are abstract. So, too, are all the maturer realisms abstract. Whatever common sense any boy or man achieves as a guide of his life must be won by composing for himself the half-truths of his opposing abstract authorities. And in this process of composing, he will

---

[3] Sir Henry Maine's attitude toward the ideals of an equity based on 'natural law' well illustrates the revulsion from this defect. *Ancient Law*, chs. iii and iv.

be guided by that same mental after-image which directs his individual experience.[4]

4. By the play of one authority against another, authority thus sinks to its rightful place as an element, a necessary element, in the circuits of individual growth. But after all, what assurance have we that this playing with authority is not simply a compromise? For the sake of living in society, I bargain away, as by an implied contract, a certain amount of liberty, that is to say, of myself. Recommenders help to make the bargain less costly for me; and their own differences and competitions still further lower the price of the social commodity. But is not the transaction at its best after all a sale, a relinquishment of my free nature?

In fact, we have not shown that our postulate can be complied with; that any real identity of what I want and what others want of me can be reached. The missing link in the logic, however, may be supplied; and perhaps conveniently by considering the *anatomy of admiration,* from which sentiment any ideal must come.

In the boy's desire to be a man, amounting at times to a ruling passion, society finds the need upon which many a hard bargain can be driven. If the Spartan boy thinks that to be a man involves enduring much pain without flinching, no theory of his interest will prevent him from submitting to torture. He is gov-

---

[4] It is in such situations that the dialectic of experience, at first of the simple Platonic form, tends to fall into the Hegelian pattern, the opposing Recommenders standing as thesis and antithesis, while the self undertakes to reinterpret their ideas in a synthesis of its own. Many of Hegel's triads are fair formal accounts of social experience; fewer than he thought express common or universal experience.

erned not by ideals alone, but by his concrete admirations. His principle might be stated: *What I admire in others I wish for myself* (naturally with the understanding that what man has done man can do again). It is logically impossible for him to detach his thought of himself from his thought of others; because in every instance, including his own, consciousness shows him at once the individual and the *type*. In every human event, he is perceiving *man*. But this general principle, that what one admires one admires universally, applies also to the admirations of others: they cannot emancipate their admirations from their experience. Hence admiration is held within the scope of the possible; and it tends to be true of all fundamental values, that *What others admire, I admire*. The connection with our postulate is therewith complete. What others would admire in me tends to agree with what I actually admire in them: and what I admire in them I must admire (and wish for) in myself: hence, what they would admire in me, I must wish for in myself.

It is true that admiration is capable of drinking up much sediment with its cup, imitation being the most indiscriminate of all human proclivities. It is also true that I cease in time to hope to realize in myself all that I admire. I find that I can be neither Lincoln, nor Napoleon, nor Plato. Yet in any such relinquishment, I forgo only the detail and the degree; I persist in demanding of myself that I transplant into my own work and upon my own scale, the *most general quality* of my admiration. For at bottom, admiration is a form of appetite. Men can only admire where they can have interest and possibility. No amount of recommendation can make the ideals of mediæval art an object (*in toto*) of my desire for myself: no hunger of mine leans that way. The individual need is cared for by the spontaneous emphasis of his admirations. I can admire what others admire only so far as I do in reality belong to their species and to their clan. But this organic basis of desire for quality is perhaps the best security that the authorities within one's own age and society will be roughly the authorities meeting one's major needs.

In many simple passes of daily experience we acknowledge clearly enough that the social eye intrudes upon our own more private life not to alienate, but to recall us to ourselves. Imagine, for example, that in that wild place, that arena in which primitive motives are free to appear and be wrestled with,—imagine, I say, that in the family circle some explosion of primitive wrath takes place. And suppose that by inadvertence an honored guest becomes witness of the scene. This accidental intrusion of the disinterested eye is likely to come not as a disagreeable reminder of a false convention; but as lending new vigor—through the chagrin—to certain languishing maxims of self-control which personal experience in the dialectic of pugnacity had already suggested. What my friend wishes me to be, and what I would appear to him to be, is without doubt what I also demand for myself. In this instance, at least, I am recalled to my own freedom. And this is the natural destiny of all the arrangements by which society foists ideals upon individual lives.

CHAPTER XXVIII

LAWS AND THE STATE

IN the making of ideals there is no necessary compromise of individual welfare. But in managing the materials of existence, some compromise is inevitable. If men live together at all, especially if they live close together like trees in a forest, what happens to the trees will necessarily happen to the men also. It is idle to suppose that their side branches can reach full development.

The total burden of scarcity in room and wealth, society in political form usually undertakes to distribute. Apart from political rules and distinctions, men usually adopt the plan of equal sharing if they wish to preserve the peace: this is the thought-saving justice of 'nature.'[1] Social rules try to secure first the least total suffering, and then proportionate suffering according to some usable principle of distribution. But all laws, rules, understandings, assume some suffering, —an insufficiency of competitive goods, the consequent existence of unsatisfied instincts and imperfect growth.

In this respect, then, the political condition obviously

[1] Hear the anthropologist on this point: "Among the savages of the upper Orinoco, one of the most primitive of extant peoples, whatever eatable is discovered by one of a pair is immediately divided, with much care for equality of division, though there is no political authority among them," etc.

takes the form of a bargain or contract. The much maligned "social contract" has certainly no truth as a description of political origins (and was never so understood by its more distinguished expounders); but as a formal expression for a natural preference it is an entirely valid way of stating the case. Better is partial hunger "and quietness therewith" than the slim chance of a full stomach with hostility to all neighbors. Security, peace, and their corollary, "a calculable future," are worth to most men the sacrifice of the fighter's chance together with the privilege of free fighting itself: and this, to Hobbes, is the essential preference which sanctions the political state. This is, indeed, no adequate account of the two sides of the bargain. The insurance aspect of social order has been overdone in all these contract formulæ; and is still overdone in contemporary theories of the State.[2] The growth of cities shows, among other things, that to most men the hazard of a large gain is still more attractive than the assurance of a little; and the weight of preference for unsalaried over salaried occupations suggests as much. To all that Hobbes sees of value in the civil condition, we must at least add the disinterested satisfaction of social instincts and of the insistent hunger for self-knowledge. But whatever the terms of the exchange, the truth remains that we must surrender something for the sake of being social; and

[2] As in Bagehot's phrase just quoted, "a calculable future"; or Royce, *War and Insurance;* or J. Kohler, *Philosophy of Law,* "It is necessary for the progress of culture that chance be conquered" (p. 28). The conquest of chance is an important, but by no means the primary, value of social order.

so, in spite of the high polemic against the historical reality and the legal status of a social contract, no one really questions the psychological truth of its central idea.[3] The question is always pertinent: "What is the cost of organized society to its members?" and "Is such society worth the cost?"

I

For our purposes it is necessary to estimate this cost not in terms of pleasure and pain, as particular satisfactions, but in terms of instinct and will and their full development.

To Hobbes it seemed evident that our instincts are doomed to be seriously hampered, inasmuch as "the laws of Nature, as 'justice,' 'equity,' 'modesty,' 'mercy,' and in sum 'doing to others as we would be done to' . . . are contrary to our natural passions, that carry us to partiality, pride, revenge and the like."[4] Here our study of the dialectic of pugnacity comes to hand: we can state that "our natural passions" of their own motion carry us well beyond revenge, and well into the region of justice, equity, and even of mercy. This dialectic presupposes continuous social experience, and would not take place apart from

[3] The discussion of the social contract theory from Hume to the present is one of the least creditable chapters in modern scholarship. It illustrates too often how seekers of Truth can "darken counsel" by stooping to refute a position defined by themselves only. This is much easier than attempting to discover what the opponent actually meant. Even Kohler, who is everywhere substantial and wise, has allowed himself to nod on this matter (*Philosophy of Law*, p. 10, Eng. tr.).

[4] *Leviathan*, ch. xvii.

social order; but the point is, that given the social order, such modifications of behavior involve no curtailment of individual growth. The same is true of many other repressions that begin from the outside, and become adopted into the individual constitution. Could we examine here the dialectic of each several instinct we should find that none come from their social-legal baptism unaltered, or *untaught*. In general, law, which at first is contrary to the state of a person's will, *brings about the state of mind which justifies the law.* In Rousseau's judgment, it is at least possible that every human impulse should submit to its social compression, be "yielded up to the general will," and yet the individual "still obey himself alone, and remain as free as before." And to Hegel, the action of society is so fundamentally informing and liberating, that social mutilation is not so much as considered. Laws and institutions act purely to interpret to each member of the State his own deeper will.

But the rosy views of Rousseau and Hegel seem as excessive on one side as the more savage views of Hobbes on the other. While to Hobbes every social repression is a pure loss, a necessary tax on natural liberty, and none an ingredient of my own will, for Hegel every such repression is a part of my will, and none a pure loss. This latter position seems rather to describe an ideal than an actual or possible social state. If every privation incident to orderly social life, including the loss of the liberty either to judge or to avenge my own injuries,—if every such privation were just what I, with full insight, would freely impose upon

myself for the sake of more inclusive and significant
ends, it would mean, would it not, that all competitive
relations in society had been transformed or absorbed
into non-competitive relations? In so far, for example,
as the scramble for food becomes an incident of a wholly
non-competitive interest in improving industrial technique, I can truly say that social necessities are minis-
tering to the freedom of my own major desires and for
so much of a spur I may be grateful. The criterion,
then, of an entirely free social existence would be (and
this we shall call our second postulate):

> *Every competitive interest must be so trans-*
> *formed or interpreted as to be non-competi-*
> *tive, or an ingredient in a non-competitive*
> *interest.*

And we must enquire, as before, how far social arrangements facilitate, or make possible, the meeting
of this demand.

II

In the large we may say that the primary economic
needs, those for food, shelter, etc., are competitive and
always will be competitive; because the material objects which they require exist in limited quantities as
compared with the demand, especially when quality is
taken into account.

On the other hand, what we have called our necessary interests are normally non-competitive. When
you satisfy your interest in unity or rhythm or order
you help to satisfy my interest in these same objects.

For these objects are neither limited in quantity nor are they capable of being made private possession in such wise that the more you have the less there is left for me. In adding to your own wealth in these goods, you add to a common fund. Taking the 'will to live' as a typical necessary interest, it is true that there are conceivable situations in which it is "Either your life or mine,"—chiefly situations in which life hangs on some physical condition. But when I regard life as a human life, i.e., as a process of thought, a constant exchange of ideas and appreciations, the disjunction, "Either your life or mine," becomes absurd: I can have no such life unless you are there, and the more you have, the more I have also. With such goods all property runs to a common fund; and in all exchange both parties gain without losing.

Necessary interests may appear to be competitive if made to simulate the economic pattern, as when one claims a monopoly of an idea, and patents it. And there are simple devices whereby economic needs are made to appear non-competitive. They are arrangements for simulating the common fund and the process of exchange which are characteristic of the non-competitive interest. If we oblige each member of a group to get what he wants, not directly, but by way of a common fund, it is evident that he will be concerned to add as much as possible to this common fund, and so seem to have common cause with all the rest. And if we oblige members to pursue different tasks, so that each can get what he wants only by trading with somebody else, it is evident that each will be concerned to produce as much as possible for the use of the rest. But it is clear that these indirect methods of getting are artificial and must be enforced: they conceal but do not alter the competitive nature of the underlying interest.

But social life must always be a union of both types of interest. And the union is to this extent inseparable, that there are no interests, however general, which do not require the private and exclusive use of some material objects, and so far take on the economic type. The will to power will thus have competitive and non-competitive ingredients. And the fate of our second postulate will depend upon whether these competitive ingredients can be subordinated to the non-competitive ingredients.

"Power," as Hobbes has accurately pointed out, quickly becomes the representative object of pursuit, as a symbol for all economic goods. Instead of working for them, we work first for power (or for wealth, as its measure) as a means to them; then as an end in itself. In spite of the contumely heaped upon the stock "miser," this is a valuable transformation of crude instinct. "In itself," says Kohler, "the instinct for food is brutal. . . . This state of things does not change until the instinct for food is ennobled by becoming the instinct for wealth, and a certain system and order enter into the acquisition of material goods.'"[5] But this transformation still leaves the competitive quality dominant. Non-competitive relations are but simulated, as in the directer strife for existence. I can gain power

[5] *Philosophy of Law*, p. 46.

over a fish only by first offering it a service; but the tender of a meal to the fish is not an accurate index to my ultimate purpose. In human society as well, power is best gained indirectly, through proffers of service: you control me, for the most part, only by controlling what I want, or think I want. But the phrase "Ich dien" only names the indirect route through which you mount to ascendency.

Such power, in fact, is more essentially and more unremittingly competitive than any other motive, because while it is always finite in amount, it has no quantitative maximum. However much I have, another may have more; and indeed the best way for him to get more, if I have much, is by controlling *me*. Could he but be sure of this control, he would have every interest to add to my own power; the greater my power, the greater his,—just as the greater the power of a tool or machine, the greater the power of the owner. Thus the simulated identity of interests might come as close as you please to an actual identity in appearance, while remaining as far as possible from identity in actual motive.

And it is just at this point, as the quest of competitive power grows without limit, that the simulated identity may become an actual identity, and take on a genuine non-competitive character. For clearly the only way in which a finite being can ride to infinite or unlimited power is by finding that power in another being, or an unlimited number of others like himself; and the only way in which such an unlimited number of others can be brought under his control, is that they shall freely come under it because he can actually serve them. And the only way in which he can serve an unlimited number of others is by providing them something unlimited in space and time, something of the nature of *idea* rather than of matter for consumption. One must perforce enter the field of necessary interests, and of funds naturally common, in order to win an infinite ascendency. But in entering this field, not only does his own power become potentially infinite, but so also does the power of every other.

For every man has an idea, a view of things, which distinguishes him by birth from every other person; and the value of that idea, or 'point of view,' to others is his chief excuse for existence as a human being. And while the work and thought of every man do in fact leave so much less for other men to do, the sum of things to be thought and done remains infinite, so that there can be no competition for new ideas. It is rare indeed that the workers in ideas so much as fancy that another has usurped their territory and stolen away their crown; but if they fancy this, it is because they have not yet discovered their own territory. In terms of his idea, the power of each individual is potentially infinite, and non-competitive.

The total accumulated power of mankind in terms of 'ideas' (under which head we include conceptions of beauty and of utility and technique as well as of scientific law and psychological insight) we call (now somewhat diffidently) "culture." Any idea which you or I may have wins its control by entering into this growing body. And the exercise of any such power is instantly reciprocal. For to say that your idea controls me, and to say that I control your idea, are but two ways of saying the same thing. Your power is identically mine. Thus, so far as a substantial and living culture exists, the will to power of any individual may take on a non-competitive meaning.

III

But "culture" does not exist by spontaneous generation, any more than history—the mental continuity and totality of men—exists by itself. Non-competitive interests of course exist in some measure wherever two or three are gathered together. But if we seek for a non-competitive form of power which shall be substantial and compelling enough to take up into itself all the competitive forms as subordinate ingredients, we can only find it if history and culture *are created,* that is to say, if by some positive effort the race is mentally held together. It is this necessity which produces the political State. *The State is the objective condition through which a non-competitive satisfaction of the will to power becomes possible.* The State is the condition under which alone our second postulate can be satisfied. It is no psychological accident, therefore, that the first business of the will to power in the order of time has been the creation of political rule, and therewith of history and culture. By that deed, however violent, the crasser and competitive forms of this will have paved the way for their own subjugation under the more human forms.

It is not altogether surprising that men have been somewhat mystified at the degree of importance which they themselves have ascribed to political entities; nor that, becoming critical, they have often adopted, as Tolstoy, skeptical or anarchistic conclusions. For the deepest needs are the last to become completely self-conscious; and States have satisfied needs far deeper than the conscious purposes of their founders, which have apparently been for the most part of the competitive type, far deeper, too, than any economic interest. The dialectic of the will might not, of itself, have led to the creation of the State; for the State must appear as a fact to many minds at once, and not as a discovery of individual experience. But the State having been made, the human will can recognize it as that which it does in fact want: this subconscious recognition is the feeling of patriotism. It is the perception of necessary discontent with all ephemeral satisfactions, of the hunger for a permanent effect, and of the truth that the value of any human effect is measured by the dignity and scope of the tradition in which it lodges. Of themselves as units, men could not create, but only receive such a tradition: history and a culture are objects which no human being and no simultaneous group of human beings can manufacture at will. Yet without them, their own worth sinks below the human level. It is for this reason, whether they have known it or not, that they have placed the value of the existence of the State above the value of their own personal existence. To offer one's life for the State is simply to make the existence of the State one's first earthly business;

it is to take part, whether early or late, in the foundation of the political entity, without which no man's will to power can find fully human satisfaction.

Thus *all men require the State,* as a Third Being, whose power is their power, whose immortality is their immortality, whose total mind and appreciation is theirs, and of their works. It is only through the existence of such a Being that *Weltgeschichte* can in any measure become *das Weltgericht.* It is only through its existence that the race can come to complete self-knowledge, and individuals to their own through the self-knowledge of the race. It is not the will to power alone, but every instinct, that apart from the social order finds itself bewildered, not free. Its controlling canopy of meaning is feeble. Habits cannot take root and give way to habits better interpreting it. In any community, instinct may find itself opposed to custom and law; but it still perceives its own meaning, perhaps the clearer because of the opposition. Destroy, however, the custom, the permanence, the regularity, the social requirement, the force of the authoritative dictum, "This is what you want and mean,"—destroy these, and instinct gropes in emptiness, condemned to many futile hypotheses. In a choice of evils, it is better to know yourself at odds with your social order than not to know yourself at all.

The State, I say, is required by all men, as a necessary object for the will to power, and therewith for every instinct. It is the feeling of this necessity and its logic, I take it, which makes man the *zoön politikon:* this is the anatomy of his so-called political instinct.

I do not say that the State, and certainly not any specific State, is a sufficient condition for such satisfaction. For there are States enough which neither welcome ideas nor admit the logic of non-competitive power. It is the necessity, not the sufficiency, of the State which I assert; and thus a necessary preference for life within a State rather than apart from a State.

And since a preference which is necessary is unanimous, we may translate the psychological necessity, if we like, into a unanimity of decision, whether self-consciously understood and admitted or not. And herewith we have the answer to the fundamental question of the social contract. All men must prefer the State; all men are consenting to the existence of the State. And the primary unanimity necessary to the sanction of any majority is thus established.

IV

The existence of the State allows the competitive form of the will to power to assume non-competitive shape. And through this fact the transformation of the more special desires from the competitive to non-competitive forms may *begin*. The economic struggle for existence, and for better existence, becomes subordinated to what is now, not merely as a pious wish but actually, of common concern, and is interpreted by it. Thus the division of labor and the process of mutually gainful exchange cease to be purely mechanical advantages with egoistic background; they become an opportunity for individuality and unique talent and for thought-filled loyalties (Durkheim).⁶ Competition is not abolished: it cannot be dispensed with, even as an instrument of my necessary interests in self-knowledge and self-measurement. But if in any contest for material goods, I fail, while you gain, it now becomes possible for me to say, with some degree of sincerity, "I will this result," on the same principle that a sportsman, while preferring the success of his own side, may still wish, on the whole, that the best side should win. The only condition under which he or I can define our wish in this way is that the dispelling of illusions has become significant: there are real powers to be gained, and in order to gain a real power, I can heartily wish the destruction of all power of mine that is accidental and false. And whatever I gain through any such system will have a value beyond the fact that it satisfies an economic need; because it comes as a recognition of my validity, of my being on the right track, of the common consent to my enjoyment: it is interpreted in terms of my non-competitive will to power.⁷

⁶ The polyhedral limitation of man by neighboring men has long been recognized as the condition in which the awareness of his ethical qualities best springs up. "Remember," said the Stoic to himself when jostled in the crowd, "Remember what it is that you want. At such price is sold your freedom from perturbation." Remember, we might add, in the pinch of specialization, at this cost must be sold your own knowledge of your destiny. Here again, the law brings about the situation that justifies it, the distribution of tasks out of which contract can arise as an expression of personal freedom. "For human civilization is only conceivable if there is a system among mankind that assigns each man his part and sets him his task." Kohler, *Philosophy of Law*, p. 4, Eng. tr. In America we might have written, "a system which incites every man to find his part and to take up his task."

⁷ In this way I should express Hegel's meaning, in placing the stage of "Contract" in his system of right beyond the stage of "Property."

Such transformation, however, would be gradual in an ideal State,—still more so in any actual State, where the results of competition are still governed by many factors irrelevant to personal worth. Where the game retains the general character of "grab," competition will keep its predominantly exclusive quality and its primitive meaning: my gain is your loss. Hence the deformity of human nature in the State is not a myth: we can only say that it would be still more deformed apart from it, and only by its aid can it become less deformed.

CHAPTER XXIX

INSTITUTIONS AND CHANGE

IDEALS and laws are fragments of institutions: institutions are permanent clusters of ideals, customs, laws. An institution, like the law, has to meet two needs and not one only: it must be serviceable to society; it must also inform a groping individual what, according to racial experience or national experience, he wants, and hold him to that meaning. The institution of property must make clear to him the completer sense of his acquisitive and grabbing instincts. The institution of the family must interpret to him his instincts of sex and parenthood. Individuals do not always take kindly to the discipline of the institution, any more than to other discipline; nevertheless, when the postulates we have set up are complied with, the hardships of this discipline have a meaning: they are part of the normal remaking of man.

But the postulates are never complied with. The specific social arrangements we have described which tend to hold our institutions to their rightful purpose are but partially successful. We cannot say that social strains as we find them are pre-eminently informing and full of meaning. If it should be whispered of our institution of property that the results of competition and its hardships are largely without human significance, I should not know how to refute such a judgment. Hegel was never truer or more illuminating than when he said that property and contract are essential ingredients in development of personality. Yet Hegel was surely a false prophet when he said that personality has no interest in the *quantity* of property a man has, its only concern being in the fact of having some property.[1] As long as opportunity lurks in spots and is given chiefly to him that hath, as long as there are dearths of common mental food if not of other food; as long as barrenness and absence of beauty and the burning out of health destroy spiritual hunger itself; as long as man power can be reckoned as horse power, intellects and loyalties flung into the hopper as trade assets, and women and children weighed in the scales of their present efficiency without regard to any future, not to say sacred or immortal possibilities,—so long personality has a stake in the *amount* of property one has and not in the fact only. And one who calls for 'discipline,' in the sense of a hearty "I accept the social universe" and its rules, may find himself deservedly crying in the wilderness, if he blinks such residual deformations of the social order. Social unrest and undiscipline are founded on something more than untidiness of mind; they are built upon a belief that what has to be done would best be done by rebellion, overt or syndicalized.

But the worst enemy of a real grievance has always been the sham grievance; and the important thing is

---

[1] *Rechtsphilosophie*, § 49. The whole attempt to eliminate *quantity* from the realm of spirit, in which Bergson is at one with Hegel, seems to me unequivocally mistaken.

to aim our shaft at the right target. We dare not assert
that these residual deformations are wholly without
meaning for the freedom of human nature. It is a curiously distorted and unreal picture of human instinct
that appears when we imagine each craving satisfied
as it arises. Though such Utopias have often been tried,
and are the food and drink of our superficial rebellious-
ness, the thing is—I do not say practically, but intrinsically—impossible. I venture the statement that the
chief evil of most of our social hardships is not that
they exist, but that they persist beyond their time. They
play their part in a process which elicits the most
subtle and most characteristic aspects of human
nature; we can only estimate this nature rightly if we
grasp this process in its entirety.

I

A satisfied man is certainly a man whose instincts
are satisfied; but yet we cannot satisfy a man by satisfying his instincts in their severalty. History is an
immense laboratory for this experiment. The cushioning of human nature is always proceeding apace, according to the means and inventiveness of a social
order. It is accelerated by the high premiums paid to
one who finds new ways to minister to old wants, or
who finds new wants to cater to. Whoever remedies a
bump in the cushion, or what is as bad, a point of non-
support, is made wealthy; and his device swiftly runs
the gamut from luxury to necessity. Thus the self-consciousness of all tends to the level of the most epi-
curean (though there is always a privileged region of

society which receives first aid in this elimination of discomfort). The history of all this careful study of ease is everywhere the same: the more our satisfactions, the less we are satisfied.

Accordingly there is everywhere a contemporary criticism of the results of this "progress," a criticism taking many forms,—often of ascetic practice and moralizing, or of a pessimistic denunciation of life itself as an embodied illusion, a cosmic hoax. Or another alternative dominates: the active satisfactions of instinct are set up at odds with the enjoying end;[2] a gospel of active rather than passive self-sacrifice is preached, a gospel of work or of heroic *Uebermensch-lichkeit*, a call for the strenuous life, for 'energism' rather than hedonism, or even a clamor for war itself as an opportunity for venting the energies of men. The suggestions are many; but for us, one inference is clear.

The human being is *adapted to maladaptation*. This is perhaps his supreme point of fitness to survive on this planet. We are better fitted to walk over rough and rolling country than over the dead level of city pavements; a day's continuous marching over this artificially 'adapted' footing leaves us with a greater fatigue than a day's tramp across country. Endurance and patience are not in the first instance Christian virtues, or even virtues at all: they are biological qualities (closely related to the 'delayed response'), fitting us for dealing with the unfit. A dog can hold for a long time the memory of an injury, cherishing without loss the unappeased impulse of revenge. What is sporadic

2 As in Holt, *The Freudian Wish*, p. 132, etc.

in the dog, is distinguished in man, and applies to all his major passions. Man is the animal that can wait, the animal fashioned for suspended satisfaction. This power makes it possible for him to live in an uncomfortable situation while deliberately surveying it, and selecting the thrust most fitted to remove it. The extent of this power makes him in effect a divided being, who enjoys in the present knowing his enjoyment to be partial, while harboring a larger hunger, destined to indefinite deferment, yet identified most closely with himself and hence not suffered to decline.[3] The man is to be found in his *Sehnsucht,* his longing or yearning, rather than in his accomplished ends. Were it not for this capacity to retain wholeness of prospect in the midst of very fragmentary satisfaction (aided by a large power for vicarious enjoyment), it is hardly conceivable that we could tolerate, still less take as a matter of course, the actual suppressions of talent suffered in the ordinary specialization of activity, or even in the necessity (suffered by man alone) of choosing among many possibilities of action merely because the narrow time channel is overcrowded with our plans. No being is so domiciled in mutilations as man. Whatever shape institutions must take to give completest vent to the possibilities of his nature, it would certainly not be a shape which allowed him nothing to criticise or to reform. His fitness for the unfit must have its scope.

II

A completer view of the meaning of this paradox

[3] See Brown's poem, *The Roman Women.*

is gained, I believe, in what we have already learned of the structure of human happiness. The happiness of man consists in the satisfaction, not of his primary instincts in their severalty, but of his total or central will,—the will to power. And power, while it need not be competitive, can only exist where there is something to *push against,* and will be in direct proportion to such resistance.

Now the most humanly satisfying type of power, so we thought, is the power of an idea, whether in persuading other men or in shaping institutions. The exercise of any such power presupposes that in institutions there are changes to be made; the same type of maladjustment which might dispose us to pessimism may, from this standpoint, appear as a necessary condition of complete welfare. An unwitting, and hence all the more cogent, testimony to this fact may be found in the biography of pessimism, in the curious circumstance that when pessimism becomes a doctrine or propaganda, it brings with it the first stages of its own cure. And for this reason. That wherever pessimism assumes poetic or philosophic garb, it has already lifted its head above its preoccupation with instincts, and has begun a campaign in the world of ideas, if only to decorate with a cosmic frame its own sense-experiences, as did Omar Khayyam. The dissatisfied spirit has begun, in its fancy, to be a creator of other worlds, having well shattered its own to bits,—a creator of other polities, natural laws, monopolies, markets, pieties, scenes, adventures. And as within itself, the eternal Ideal plows up the field of a sodden humanity, it discovers in the career of its own condemnation of life, as a form of thought, a life that is worth clinging to. For the pessimist, it is just his pessimism and its preaching that is of value. For this is *his* edition of the will to power through ideas.

A world in which there were no institutional misfit would be a world in which such a will to power, or indeed any other, would be as nearly as possible without human occupation; it might provide a type of happiness bovine or angelic, but certainly not human.

It would be natural, but still perverse, to infer from this psychological truth the desirableness of preserving or courting or importing a degree of evil in order that human nature may gain full satisfaction. Men find, or once found, for example, a certain happiness in war: war is one way of bringing the will to power into operation against social evils, changing institutions, or at least leaving one's mark upon them; and there are occasions when because of abnormalities in political growth, social construction must take, like surgery, the paradoxical form of destruction. Yet no folly could be blinder than that of prescribing or seeking war as a remedy for the maladies of the human spirit: for no war can act as such a remedy unless it is just; and no war is just unless it is inevitable. The place of a just cause of war, or of any other evil, as a *pou sto* in the process which makes our happiness, does not logically admit it to any other place. The knight errant without a dragon or other foe may be a melancholy figure; but he must still kill the dragon when he meets him, and not coddle him along to keep an exercise for his mettle. Likewise with our social misfits: he who should counsel others, or himself, to put up with such an evil because it affords pleasing activity to contend against it, is guilty of something more than a bull. Evil has its own sources; and there is no cause for anxiety lest there should be enough of it to make permanent opportunity for the powers of all men. For a large part of evil is an incidental product of social progress itself.

III

The improvement of institutions, and social progress generally, is responsible for a certain amount of our *awareness* of misfit. For progress enhances sensitivity and desire, and both of these bring an increase of suffering.

Everyone has noticed the ineffective efforts of children to place and diagnose their own pains. They are slightly cold; they do not know that they are cold, but only that they are "uncomfortable": an older person must interpret to them their own restlessness. If we think of the child as more sensuous than the adult, we are mistaken. The adult is much more alive to sensations; he has keener discrimination and keener enjoyment. Only an adult can be an epicure, or a colorist, or a musician. The child is incapable of being "dissolute"; for nature entrusts only by degrees the more poignant experiences of sense. The fitness of the arrangement is that the appeal of sense should increase only as the policy of the self develops to judge that appeal. The adult is defined as the person who can let things *hurt,* while keeping them subordinate to his central will. On the march, knowing that water is not to be had, one is able (as the child is not) to put thirst out of mind; busy, one forgets his hunger; conversing, bodily weariness drops away. Yet the same sensations, when they get their hearing, have a definition and force proportionate to the force of the central will. Mature self-consciousness means that every impulse of a many-stringed nature has a more perfect individuality. The organism can afford to be plural because (and only so far as) it is firmly one. This is hardly a mere happy adaptation of unrelated forces: it is more likely that the added mentality and horizon are direct agents in promoting the keenness of sense-experience.[4]

A similar relation holds good between earlier and later stages of culture: the race is but gradually let down into the pit of knowledge of evil, for it is an incident of the same process which, increasing goods and their appreciation, we call progress. Primitive culture is by definition a culture preoccupied in the external struggle, hence little free to delve into itself. The same changes of occupation that have brought economic power, have brought separateness of interest and the self-consciousness that is born of contrast: herding and agriculture make occasion for setting my labor and its products against your labor and its products, bring private property with its relative soli-

---

[4] This is in accord with our view of the nature of pleasure and pain. See above, pp. 106 f. and 147, note

tude and concentration upon self, generate the schem-
ing Jacob and the thieving Hermes. Division of labor
likewise means a relative privacy in the midst of the
day's work, and promotes comparisons of value and
pains. Money, as a medium between production and
consumption, means the necessity of enquiring into
my wants before I set about purchase and enjoyment.
All these things together mean increased attention to
pain and desire; quite apart from the similar result
of gathering wealth, leisure, and the hastening of the
cushioning-process above referred to, with its inequity,
bitterness, and reflection. Those who fall behind in the
uneven social movement are hardly worse off in the
physical life than in the wealth-less stages; for the
most part they are better off—there is no new suffering except in status and pride. But old physical evils
have now become social wrongs, and hurt with a new
pain; the social difference sharpens self-awareness,
and those who lose share as equals with those who gain
in the added consciousness of the risks of fortune in
goods and evils. Thus maladjustments which were
tolerable and relatively unnoticed, because kept in the
obscure margins of the mind, become intolerable, and
begin to press upon the shapes of institutions. The
very process by which discomforts are relieved creates
the capacity for new discomfort.[5]

[5] This is the social form of that endless chain which Schopenhauer
found in the life of individual will. But it is not a treadmill. The
evils are in new places. And old issues—some of them—are permanently *settled*. We have—as the flux-philosophers tell us—a perpetual
movement, self-renewed: but it is not as they suggest a meaningless and
directionless movement.

IV

The circumstance of the origin of a part of social misfit, created as it is by growing social good, suggests that at least this part of evil is such as human nature is well fitted to cope with, and to take up into the activity of its own will to power. And this will be the case if institutions are plastic to the pressure upon them. The very misfits of the social order will be grist for human nature provided this postulate is complied with:

Whatever in institutions tends at any time to deform human nature shall be freely subject to the force of dissatisfaction naturally directed to change them.

Any residual dissatisfaction with social arrangements may, in point of fact, be regarded as a constant force acting upon these arrangements, and sure, in the course of time, to have its effect upon them. There is an old physical experiment in which one is to put into a glass vessel a mixture of shot, corn, sawdust, iron filings, etc., and place the vessel on a window stool subject to constant jarring by passing traffic. In course of time the mixed contents stratify themselves in order, with the densest at the bottom. It requires no great force, but only a constant force—if there is sufficient motion—to ensure that any tendency shall reach its goal. And so, wherever social shiftings take place, there is the opportunity for the edging forward of human nature. And as this changing and shifting has been going on for many ages, the probability is great that all the coarser and more serious maladjustments have been remedied, and that we have in our present institutions a *fit in sketch* of human nature in general.

If institutions have not always submitted themselves to this pressure, it might seem that in our Western world at any rate, where all complaint is legitimate, every idea has a hearing, and the art of representative, if not of popular, legislation has appeared, a miracle and a godsend, legislation participated in by the consumers thereof,—it might seem that all institutions, after ages of cakedness, had now finally reached a state of sufficient flux. And in truth, the chief impediment to a free human nature is now, not social unreadiness to entertain remedies that are certain to cure, but *ignorance,*—ignorance of its own desires and how to secure their satisfaction.

Legislation must, indeed, always lag behind the market-place in its part of the cushioning process; because its inventions, as distinct from the commercial kind, must be so far thought through as to take their place at once in an imposing system of ideas, The Laws, and must be suited to universal and compulsory consumption. In both cases we must get on by making multitudes of experiments and selecting from the results; but experimenting with a law must always be a graver thing than experimenting with a new breakfast food. Law-making is a most philosophic undertaking,—or should be. Otherwise it is either entangled in its own technique, and becomes a sinecure for all the self-interest and intellectual viciousness of its promoters; or else, thrown wide open to the direct popular argument from sore to salve, it loses itself in temporizing, inconsistency, and rudderless drifting. Laws can only be competently perceived through institutions, institutions through history, and history through human nature.

Nevertheless, a radical with a conscience and an intellect even moderately equal to his task has at this hour the world before him, a world desirous as never before to do justice through its institutions to all human needs. This world requires to be convinced only (1) that his remedies will remedy, and (2) that they will not at the same time destroy more than they create. And as a guarantee for this second and greater interest, it will require in him an understanding of the history of institutions which sees in them something greater than shifting arbitrariness or rough expediency or folly and oppression,—which appreciates their slow tendency to bring humanity into the full birthright of its own freedom.

V

For if society is conservative, it is so, at least in part, because it has something to conserve.

If nature could not allow the growth of sensitivity in individuals apart from their growth in will, neither can society, except at its peril, lend itself to the liberty of clamorous desire unless there is sufficient substance in men's grasp of what is necessary and common. The license that has commonly followed sudden grants of

liberty[6] is no argument against grants of liberty; but
it has its argument. It shows that men had conceived
the restraint that was over them too inimically, not
perceiving how far the social order was, in Rousseau's
phrase, compelling them to be free. It shows, then, that
the protest was, in part, inconsiderate and unjustified;
and that the conservative party was, to just that extent and no more, right in regarding the liberals as
rebels.

He who would change an institution or experiment
with it must know his own will far enough to see that
he wishes the innovation itself to be a conserved and
protected structure. The only value any experiment
can possibly have is that something may be *established*.
It is not an accident that the noisest criers for tolerance, when they have secured free way for their own
idea, have commonly shown a wish to enforce that new
idea with the old intolerance. They are but waking up
to the logic of their own ambition; which was, not that
institutions should weaken and soften or disappear,
but primarily that some particular stubborn institution should yield, and the same good force be spent on
maintaining something worthier. There is, literally
speaking, no such thing as being too conservative: but
it is terribly easy to be conservative of the wrong
objects. Hence place must be made in all our institutions for our common ignorance, our need to learn
through the free clash of convictions,—this is the valid
element in Mill's plea for social liberty, the valid

[6] See Arthur T. Hadley, *Freedom and Responsibility*, pp. 40 ff.

element in American experimentalism. The principle is, that

Conserving force shall be proportionate to certainty,—

certainty that the institution furnishes for the given society the best solution so far proposed of its own problem. This fourth postulate we must place beside the last.

CHAPTER XXX

EDUCATION

IN handing on to a new generation its notions of
what life means, of what the several instincts
mean, society is compelled to face itself, take stock of
its ideas, pass judgment upon itself. The advantage
of education, therefore, is not exclusively to the young.
Dealing with growing minds, society perforce domes-
ticates the principle of growth: for self-consciousness
is never purely complacent, least of all when its eyes
are the critical and questioning eyes of a child, a new
vital impulse, unharnessed and unbought.

It strikes us as notable—when we think how severe
is the effort of self-review, and how little satisfying—
that society has never been content simply to let its
young *grow up*. Unintentional suggestion might conceivably have been left to do its work on a gregarious
and imitative human substance. To an unknown degree
children always educate themselves, and what they thus
do is well done. But from earliest visible times, educating has been a deliberate process. Human beings clearly
like to educate: for better or worse this activity is an
especially human form of the parental instinct. It looks
at times as if the young serve simply as a stimulus to
an activity of the elders of which they, the children, become the helpless objects, an activity which tends to

increase without limit as leisure and the economic margin grow. Children create the necessity, but also the exciting opportunity, for society's effort to make vocal the sense of its ideals, customs, laws, and (ominous word) to *inculcate* them.

But though a profound human interest, analytic self-consciousness is difficult and slow of growth; and as individual self-consciousness begins in the form of memory, social self-consciousness begins in the form of history. For this reason, society has always tried to expound itself largely through the story of its own past, its folklore, epic, and myth. But with history there has been from the earliest times a demand for images of that to which history leads, images of a more completely interpreted will such as have hovered before the imaginations of dreamers, prophets, reformers. Thus in the work of educating, social self-consciousness expands until it envisages more or less darkly the entire tale of tribal destiny from its beginnings to its goal.

Because education requires this self-conscious looking before and after, a discussion of education in the midst of a book on the remaking of human nature must anticipate the end, and in some degree mirror the entire undertaking. But deliberate educational effort has its own specific part to play, more or less separable from other parts of the remaking process. Bending over the younger generation during the long years before the full impact of law and institution is allowed to reach them, transmitting its wishes through the protecting (and no doubt refracting) media of family and school, speaking at least as much through what it is as through what it tries to say for itself, society in educating is exercising a function whose purpose, like that of most natural organs, we but gradually become fully aware of. In our day education affects the technical; it becomes highly doctrinaire; it is the jousting place of all the new realisms, pragmatisms, behaviorisms, psychologisms of all brands. We need to think anew of the nature of this organic function and of its control.

I

There was a time when we might have defined education as a *continuation of the reproductive process.* Physical reproduction supplies more of the same species: social reproduction supplies more of the same tribe or nation. From the beginning of organized social life, each people has regarded its own folkways as an asset, distinctive and sacred; in imposing them upon the new brood it has supposed itself to be conferring its most signal benefit. And the newcomers, most of them, seem to have adopted this view: they have as little fancied it a hardship that the social order should impose its type upon them as that their parents should have given them their physical image. It has simply completed the definition of what they are.

We have not outgrown this conception of education. We still speak of it as a 'preparation for life,' understanding by 'life' a certain kind of life, that which marks out our own group or nation. It still seems to us the essential failure of education that our children should find themselves a misfit in 'life'; so we steer them toward the existing grooves of custom as a matter of duty—I do not say of duty to society, but of duty to the children themselves. Discussing the place of classics in Prussian schools, Kaiser Wilhelm II said (December, 1890), "It is our duty to educate young men to become young Germans, and not young Greeks or Romans." And what do other nations expect of their schools, if not to bring forth after their kind? What are the facts of our own practice?

We certainly do not put all traditions on the same level, any more than all languages or all sets of laws. But neither we nor any other modern nation limits its offering to its own type. We train our wards *to some extent* to become young Greeks, Romans, Britons, Frenchmen, Germans, Asiatics, as well as young Americans. We teach them history and geography, not indifferently, but still to a liberal distance from our own center of space and time. We pave the way to literatures other than our own. We discreetly announce the existence of other religions. Better than this, we offer them at the outset the free and primitive worlds of fairyland and legend where all desires find satisfaction. We give them poetry and drama, dealing with social orders invitingly different from the actual order, such as must set tingling any cramped or unused nerve in growing nature, and so give voice to the latent rebel in our youth, or the latent reformer. Our homes and schools habitually look out upon 'the world' not as a decorous and settled place, but as a comparatively perilous and unfinished place, calling for much courage and chivalrous opposition, requiring much change. The career of the hero who redresses an untold number of wrongs still hovers as a wholly accessible destiny before the fancies of our childhood. To this extent, we warn our successors-to-be against our own fixity, put the world before them, and set them free from our type.[1]

And to this extent, we recognize that education has two functions and not one only. It must communicate the type, and it must *provide for growth beyond the type*. It is not a mere matter of spiritual reproduction, unless we take reproduction in the wider sense as an opportunity to begin over again and do better, the locus not alone of heredity but of variation and of the origin of new species.

But why insist at all upon the reproducing of the old type? and why limit to "this extent" the scope of the liberty of choice? Why do we not display with complete equableness all views of the best way of life and say, "Now choose; think out your course for yourselves"? Instead of teaching our children our morality, why not teach them ethical science? instead of religion, metaphysical criticism? instead of our political faith, political philosophy? instead of our manners, the

[1] Admitting all the abuses of mechanical and wholesale popular schooling, I must decline to believe as the primary truth of any modern nation that "It is not in the spirit of reverence that education is conducted by States and Churches and the great institutions that are subservient to them" (Bertrand Russell, *Principles of Social Reconstruction*, p. 158; reprinted in America under the misleading title, *Why Men Fight*). I know of no society which fails to wish its children a better life than its own. And especially at this moment, in the war-ridden states of Europe a deep and pathetic tenderness toward childhood is evident, as if to say, "We have made a mess of our world: yours must be a better one." This spirit is making itself felt in thorough revisions of the plan of education in France and England.

principles of æsthetics? In short, why not make thinkers of them rather than partisans? Why not abolish the last remnant of that ancestor-worship which dwarfs the new life by binding it to the passing life?

The answer is, we have no right to aim at any smaller degree of freedom than this, *nor, for the most part, do we:* but before a completely free will can be brought into being, it is first necessary to bring into being a will. The manifest absurdity of asking a child to choose his own moral code and the rest is due not alone to the fact that he lacks the materials to choose from, but still more to the fact that he does not know what he wants. The first task of education is to *bring his full will into existence.* And this can only be done by a process so intimate that in doing it the type is inevitably transmitted. The whole meaning of education is wrapped up in this process of evoking the will; and apart from it nothing in education can be either understood or placed.

II

The will can develop only as the several instincts wake up and supply examples of the goods and evils of experience. To bring instincts into action, all that any social environment need do (and almost all it can do[2]) is to supply the right stimulus, together with an

[2] Noting in passing that the exhibition of instinctive behavior often acts by suggestion as a substitute for the direct stimulus; and in gregarious animals as an alternative stimulus. And further, just as artificial respiration may lead to actual breathing, so a mechanical repetition of instinctive behavior even under duress may sometimes work backward, as if breaking a way though an occluded channel, to set an instinctive impulse free. See above, p. 172, note.

indication of what the stimulus means. A response cannot be compelled; for whatever is compelled is not a response. No behavior to which we might drive a child would be *play:* if playthings and playing comrades fail to bring out the play in him, we are all but helpless. A response can only be *e-duced.*

If we were dealing with an organism whose instincts we did not know, the educing process would consist in exposing that organism, much as one would expose a photographic plate, to various environments to see which ones would elicit reactions. And in dealing with a new human being, always unknown, the work of educing his instincts would likewise consist in *exposing* him to those stimuli which may appeal to him,—to speech, to things graspable or ownable, to color, form, music, etc., to the goods of cleanliness, truthfulness, and the like. What powers any child has of responding to these things, whether or how far they will *take* in his case, neither he nor we can know until he has been exposed—and perhaps persistently and painfully exposed—to specific examples of these goods.

This exposure is the first work of education.

And the first peril of education is not that the child's will will be overborne, but that through no exposure or inadequate exposure to the objects that would call out his best responses, he achieves only half a will instead of a whole one, a will partly-developed and therefore feebly-initiative, casual, spiritless, uninterested. If I were to name the chief defect of contemporary education, it would not be that it turns out persons who believe and behave as their fathers did—it does not: but that it produces so many stunted wills, wills prematurely grey and incapable of greatness, not because of lack of endowment, but because they have never been searchingly exposed to what is noble, generous, and faith-provoking.

Mr. Bertrand Russell voices a common objection to immersing the defenceless younger generation in the atmosphere of the faiths religious and political that have made our nations.[3] Has he considered whether in these faiths there lies anything more than the wilful choice of an unproved theory, anything of human value such as a growing will might, for complete liberation, require exposure to? Politically guided education, he feels, is dangerous, and so it is. But I venture to say that the greatest danger of politically guided education, particularly in democracies which feel themselves obliged in their educational enterprises to cancel out against one another the divergent opinions of various parties, is that *the best places will be left blank,* because it is on the most vital matters that men most differ. The pre-war experience of France in secularized education has furnished a striking instance of the principle that in education a vacuum is equivalent to a negation. In one case as in the other, instinct is robbed of its possibility of response.

Children have rights which education is bound to respect. The first of these rights is not that they be left free to choose their way of life, i.e., to make bricks

[3] *Principles of Social Reconstruction,* chapter on Education.

without either straw or clay. Their first right is that
they be offered something positive, the best the group
has so far found. Against errors and interested propaganda the growing will has natural protection: it has
no protection against starvation, nor against the substitution of inferior food for good food. No social authority can make pain appear pleasure. No social authority can make a stimulus of something which has
no value. But it is quite possible, through crowding out
the better by the worse, to produce a generation which
thinks "push-pin as good as poetry," prefers bridge
to sunsets, or worships the golden calf.

III

But there is a radical and obvious difference between
exposing a plate to the light and exposing a human
instinct to a possible stimulus. Anybody can expose
the plate, a machine can expose it: the operation and
the stimulus are alike mechanical. But for the human
being there is many a possible stimulus which lies
partly or wholly outside the world of physics.[4] In these
regions of experience, neither a machine nor any random person can achieve an exposure.

It is true that for most of the 'units of behavior'
which men have in common with the rest of the animal
kingdom, the stimuli are strewn about in such profusion that exposure takes place with little or no need

[4] As an example, the stimulus of the 'instinct of curiosity'; see p. 81,
above. It is important to bear in mind through this discussion that the
'stimulus' of an instinct is understood to be 'the pre-perception of the end
as the meaning of the initial situation'; p. 58, above.

for social guidance. It is a commentary upon the artificiality of our urban society that a Mme. Montessori is required to remind us of the need (among other things) of sufficient and varied tactile stimuli in early years. Haphazard encounters with strings, stones, and sticks, now kept carefully 'cleaned up' and out of reach, aided by personal struggles with the more exact weapons of toilet and table, once provided most of the stimuli which we must now measure out with psychological ingenuity. Hereby we are making no doubt essential progress in self-consciousness; but for young children, country life and self-help are still the unmatched educators of their primary instincts.

But for the specifically human developments of instinct, the stimuli are commonly either non-existent or imperceptible except through the behavior of other human beings who are actively responding to them. Of these, the principle holds that *no one can expose a child to that stimulus unless he himself appreciates it*. Imagine to what experience an unmusical person might expose a child under the name of music. Consider what it is to which many a human being has been exposed under the name of mathematics. To many the true statement that number is an object of profound instinctive interest[5] would appear a mockery because, having fallen into the hands of the Philistines in the days of their initiation into the world of number, they have never so much as come into view of its peculiar beauties.

[5] As an ingredient in the satisfaction of various central instincts, see above, p. 83.

But it is especially with regard to those modes of interpreting instinct which constitute our moral and religious tradition that this principle becomes important. For no one can so much as present the meaning of an idea of this kind,—let us say of a particular way of meeting pain or injustice, a Spartan way, a Stoical way, or some other,—unless he himself finds satisfaction in that idea. And then it follows, since satisfaction and happiness are highly convincing states of mind (understanding by happiness not temperamental gaiety, but the subconscious and hence serious affirmation of life as a whole by the will as a whole),— it follows that children will tend to adopt the beliefs of those whom they instinctively recognize as happy, and of no others.

This is both a protection to children and a danger. A protection: for surely the child who has found no hero in the flesh from among the supporters of the existing order is in no danger of being overborne by that order. If a tradition can get no great believers, it will die a natural death. If the wilder people are genuinely the happier,—Bohemians, déclassées, gay outlawry in general,—it is they who will convince and be followed. If sobriety, self-restraint, all the "awful and respectable virtues" have a value, whether as necessary nuisances on the way to some great good, or as goods on their own account, they will find a following through the persons of those who are enamored of those goods, so far as such persons become known.

If the social group is simple, any genuine values it

has will be likely to find their way into new minds. One of the most marvelous examples of social conservation has been the transmission of folksong; yet if any tradition has been spontaneous and unforced, this has been. But in our modern complex and split-up societies, the chances grow large that many children are never reached by our best ideas, transmitted through an overworked and not markedly happy teaching body.[6]

In any case, what is transmitted is that intangible thing we call belief, the effective belief of the teaching surface of society. And since the type of any society is chiefly defined by its prevalent beliefs, we see why it is that the process of bringing a will into existence inevitably tends, as we said, to reproduce the type.

Perhaps it is the best of our values that lead the

[6] If the chief excellence of teachers in a parsimonious democracy is to spend much time, teach as many as possible, make neat reports showing high averages of prize-made punctuality, and 'prepare' their charges for the enjoyment of something else than what is before them, we shall produce and deserve little else than a constitutionally weary and commonplace citizenry.

The idea of 'preparation,' an indispensable workshop notion for those who consider educational systems as a whole, is a disease when it becomes prominent in the minds of the children. What children, and poets, never forget is that "Life is now! the center of the universe is here! the middle point of all time, this moment!" If children are led, for example, to read good writers in order that they may hereafter enjoy good writers, their chance is lost. The only justifiable reason for putting a good writer into their hand is that he is good and can be enjoyed then and there. I do not say understood: for children have great powers of living on a future understanding.

That the first qualification of a teacher is to be happy has perhaps never been propounded as an educational doctrine. Yet it is a fair question whether truth has been more harmed by those who are wrong but happy (if there are any such) than by those who are right but unhappy.

most perilous lives, are most easily lost or defaced in the relay of the generations: but determination and system will not save them. Ethics and religion must be removed from set courses of public instruction unless the believers are there; for mechanical teaching of these things is worse than none. Every society has, besides its rebels, who are frequently persons of great faith, many members who have dragged themselves barely to the edge of a creed; what such persons transmit is hardly that creed, but a pestilential belief in the moral painfulness of one's intellectual duty.

But given the believer, the more vigorous and affirmative his belief, the better. Life becomes worth living according to the greatness of faith, not the lack of it. If any element of a great faith proves wrong, its greatness survives as a standard to be reached by what displaces it. According to this measure will be the dimension of the wills we develop.

IV

But besides the dimension of the will, the *proportion* of the will is also a matter of importance; and to this end it is the business of education to see that none of the more general instincts or groups of instincts have an inadequate exposure.

There is in the human being, as we saw, a large power of substitution among the instincts, and this power increases as the central current of the will grows strong. Hence as children get older it becomes less and less important that all the possible 'units of behavior' should be proportionately called forth. It is a pity, to be sure, if the climbing period goes by without a fair exposure to trees, fences, staircases, shed roofs and the like; but the loss is not irremediable. If however any of the more general instincts lies long latent, as in the case of a delay in the use of language which might retard the development of sociability, the loss is more serious. Let me speak of some of the questions of proportion which present conditions of life more especially raise.

A fair balance ought to be kept between the instincts that deal with *persons* and those that deal with *things*. The small arts developed by handling, exploring, controlling, making, and owning things must furnish all the themes for the give-and-take of primitive sociability: only through the administering of such all-important privileges as those of 'hollering down our rain bar'l' or 'climbing our apple tree' can the various shades of amity and hostility be realized. The child's social life will run shallow unless his physical interests are vigorous. It is true that the deeper his roots strike into the material world and its mastery, the more occasion there is for pugnacity, the more difficult the personal problems aroused; but also, the more significant the solutions when they come. It is a mistake to try to impose a premature altruism upon these concerns in mine and thine. The two sets of impulses, competitive and non-competitive, must grow side by side and to some extent independently before they are ready to recognize their relationship. Meantime, the instincts occupied with things indicate by their strength the degree of mastery over nature we are destined to;

and the qualities developed in their exercise are the most primitive elements of 'character' and the foundation of all likeableness.[7] Thus what these instincts seem to take from social quality, they pay back again.

But between the possessive and masterful interest in things and the friendly interest in persons there is a middle term, most important in the proportioning of the will. I mean a *companionable interest in nature.* Being 'alone' has possibilities of occupation that come not merely from hands and senses but from thought and fancy. A child's fear of solitude is an evidence that his imagination has already begun to work in this direction; and what is needed in order to reassure him is not that nature should be depersonalized, but that his instinctive personifying trait should be made a resource. The growing self, if it is to acquire depth, has need of a region not intruded upon by other human personalities, not even by such as move across the stage of history and literature. While he is in this human company the initiative of his own thoughts is perpetually broken: the impulses of mental play, as sensitive as they are precious, may easily be discouraged and weakened unless an environment is found which is at once an escape and a stimulus. Our over-socialized

[7] What attracts us in another, old or young, is always the sign not of animal vitality primarily but of *validity,* the quality of spirit which is challenged and evoked in the elementary struggles with the inertia and refractoriness of physical things: resourcefulness, persistence, grit, integrity, fertility of design. Power over nature is the most summary expression of what a *spirit* ought to have, and does have in proportion to its degree of reality: it is this degree of reality which we most immediately perceive in another, and which is the foundation of likeableness.

city-bred children often lose the capacity to be 'by themselves' without intolerable tedium. Normally, however, 'nature' means much more than permission to ruminate: it is a positive educing force. For nature appears to humanity everywhere, and early to children, as (more or less cheerfully) enigmatic: it is deceptively quiescent, or it is eventful but with invisible agency; it teases out essays in interpretation. Society drives away the muse,—it 'amuses' us: but in the presence of nature the thread of our fancies is drawn at once into the living fabric of the world, making connection in the freest, and I believe not untruest, way with the spirit that dwells there. Thus the foundations are being laid for a thoughtfulness more than literal in its quality, which may ripen in one direction into scientific observation and hypothesis, in another toward merging with the poetic and animistic gropings of the race.[8] In any case, since the imagination is actively, not passively engaged, and the mental furniture is one's own, one returns to his social world a little more than before a

---

[8] In making this plea for the encouragement of an anthropomorphic imagination, I am shamelessly favoring what Professor Thorstein Veblen has called the ''self-contamination of the sense of workmanship'' (*The Instinct of Workmanship,* pp. 52 ff.), a deliberate mixing of the personal and impersonal phases of the world which it may prove difficult later on to resolve into a wholly naturalistic deadness of attitude toward the physical. I do so with my eyes open.

What and how much solitude may mean to any child cannot be told in advance: education can only effect the *exposure,* not at first without guidance, and certainly not without noting results.

Let me quote from a letter written by Sir Rabindranath Tagore to Mr. Frederic Rose, Stockton Heath, England. ''Mornings and evenings [speaking of his school in Bolpur] fifteen minutes' time is given them to sit in an open space, composing their minds for worship. We never

self. An individual *I-think* is growing which in time may have its own contribution to the *We-think* of the crowd.

But whether we thus deal with the 'I-think,' or as above with the 'I-own,' it is clear that we are at the same time dealing with the 'I-can.' The will to power, because of its central position, is being educated in all education. But this fact does not imply that the will to power needs no distinct attention. It has its own technique to acquire, and its own interpretation to find: and everything in the child's further career depends on how these problems are solved. Like all the more particular forms of instinct the will to power needs to be developed by deliberate exposure to its own kind of stimulus,—*difficulty,* and to its own type of good,— *success.*

Play, we have said, may be regarded as practice in success. The play obstacles are so chosen as to be surmountable; the play-things oppose no ultimate resistance to their owner. But that which seems the opposite of play, the set task, is needful to provide the complete stimulus for this instinct. We need not open the old debate whether the will is best trained through what one spontaneously likes or is 'interested' in or through the opposite. Kant and William James are far apart

watch them and ask questions about what they think in those times, but leave it entirely to themselves, to the spirit of the place and the time and the suggestion of the practice itself. We rely more upon the subconscious influence of Nature, of the association of the place and the daily life of worship that we live than on any conscious effort to teach them.'' The same principle in a different mood is found in John Boyle O'Reilly's poem ''At School.''

on many matters; but in this they seem to agree, that for the sake of habitual freedom from the domination of feelings it is well to do voluntarily a certain amount of what is hard or distasteful. But I presume that they would equally agree that there is little value in effort for effort's sake: there is as little to be gained from pure difficulty as from pure ease. The right stimulus for any instinct is 'the perception of the goal as the meaning of the beginning':[9] the right stimulus of the will to power is the glimmer of a possible success, which is another name for hope. The only significant difficulties, for purposes of education, are those accompanied by hope. It is thus as idle a procedure to exhort the child halted by an obstacle to "work it out for himself" as it is to do the work for him: there is no more dehumanizing state of mind than the perpetuation of directionless effort in a despairful mood. Education in such a case consists in supplying the halted mind with a method of work and *some examples of success.* There are few more beautiful miracles than that which can be wrought by leading a despairing child into a trifling success: and there are few difficulties whose principle cannot be embodied in such simple form that success is at once easy and revealing. And by increasing the difficulty by serial stages, the small will, under the cumulative excitement of repeated and mounting success, may find itself far beyond the obstacle that originally checked it.

Such use of mental momentum is a practice which I believe all instinctive teachers resort to. And it shows

[9] P. 58, above.

incidentally how false a guide 'interest' may be in education when taken as we find it. Lack of interest in any subject depends, for children, far less on the nature of the subject than on a persistent thwarting of the will to power in dealing with it; *interest accompanies any task in which a mental momentum is established.* But momentum can be gained only when difficulty can be indefinitely increased, so that the very conditions which may discourage, drive away interest, and even induce loathing of a subject, are conditions which make great interest possible when the will to power is called into lively action. We may put it down as a maxim of education, so far as interest is concerned,—*Without difficulty, no lasting interest.*

But after the education derived from play, and from the set task with its relatively prompt conclusion, the will to power has still to deal with the situation of *indefinite delay.* If it is hard to point out what instinctive satisfaction can be found in a deferred success, it would be hazardous to assert that there is no such satisfaction, when we consider that the greatest of human ends are such as are never finally achieved. The imagination, the I-think, would be cramped in any house narrower than infinity; and it is through them that the will to power can be led to its next stage of development. By the aid of imagination I can count it a success to have made *a definable approach* to a distant end; and thus increasingly long series of means that lie between initial effort and attainment can take on the meaning of continuous successes. If our view

of the State is right,[10] it is only as we become capable
of taking an interest in permanent and cumulative
objects that the will to power can subordinate its competitive to a non-competitive character and so become
thoroughly social. And it must be seasoned to delay,
before the problems with which adolescence confronts
instinct can be even fairly well met.

V

The strain upon instinct at adolescence is due largely
to the delay imposed on the impulses of acquisition
and sex. The vigorous ways of primitive food-getting
and property-getting have to recognize their transformed selves, if they can, in the devious routine of
labor and exchange. The sex-interest, under any set
of customs so far proposed, must learn to express
itself for a time in partial and sublimated forms. The
circumstance that children usually grow up in families is nature's simple and effective device for imposing
on the powerful current of sex-feeling its presumptive
meaning: every child starts life with a prejudice to the
effect that its affections will lead it sooner or later to
found a family resembling (with improvements) the
family from which it came. But when sex-interest becomes a practical personal impulse it outruns the restricted possibilities of family-founding; it meets on
every hand the unexplained check, the unexplained
inner compunction quite as much as the unexplained
social ruling. Inhibition and prohibition alike mean de-

10 P. 232, above.

lay; and the tendency of all delay is to cast the energies of impulse upward into the region of dream, romance, speculation, substitution.

Here the will to power should provide the great natural resource; and will do so if it has been linked with imagination. Delay becomes supportable if imagination gives the 'prolonged vestibule'[11] the shape of a conscious plan, with the many possible successes of approach: and for the acquisitive impulses this may at least ease the situation. But delay becomes more than tolerable, it becomes significant, if it affords leeway for the *creation of the plan itself*, enlisting the inexhaustible plan-making impulses of the youthful brain. Here the possibilities of the imaginative will to power are so great that it may assume an actual equivalence for the satisfaction of other instincts; and in particular the creative element in the sex-impulse may be largely absorbed or 'sublimated' in the new preoccupation.

For at adolescence there is at least one such task of creation which the will cannot escape, that of constructing one's philosophy. The youth finds himself, at his own estimate, for the first time an equal among equals. There is a change in the order of authority. Children have an appetite for authority corresponding to their mental unfinishedness and rapid growth; with adolescence comes a sense of competence and a disposition to be critical. The conceit of opinion in the adolescent is not empty: it is based on a readiness to assume responsibility, and on an actual assumption of respon-

11 P. 206, above.

sibility in the work of *mental world-building* if not of physical world-building. He appreciates for the first time that he has his own life to lead; he finds himself morally alone; he can no longer endure to see things through the eyes of others.

In dealing with this readiness to assume responsibility and with its accompanying conceit—the 'instinct of self-assertion' as it is called by McDougall and others—we commit some of our most serious educational blunders. We customarily put the boy into continued schooling where his powers of serious action beat the air, and we rebuke his conceit by external pressure: the first wrong brings the second after it. Continued schooling is inevitable and not necessarily unnatural; but the only fair corrective for the conceit, or rather the only right environment for this new development of instinct, is the actual responsibility it craves. Our school days and years have their intervals; and those intervals should be, at least in part, intervals of *earning a living.* The boy who passes his adolescence without knowing the feeling of doing a day's work for a day's wages is risking not only a warp in his instinctive make-up, but a shallowing of all further work in school and college, because of a loss of contact with this angle of reality at the moment when his will was ripe for it. The mental helplessness of many students who cumber the colleges of this and other lands, the dispositional snobbery and self-saving of many an over-confident and over-sexed youth sent out as 'educated' to justify once more the spirit of rebellion against the mental and moral incompetence of those who assume to lead and govern, has much of its explanation in our failure at this point. The marvel is not that such mis-shapen births occur; the marvel is that young human nature shows such magnificent self-righting qualities when its will to power is once thoroughly engaged.

But whether or not the concrete responsibility he craves is permitted him, the responsibility for mental world-building cannot be refused the adolescent, and he will take it. This is the natural moment for tearing down and rebuilding the beliefs absorbed during the era of his subordination to authority. Youth is meta-physical not because metaphysics is a youthful malady but because youth has metaphysical work to do; it has been attached to the universe through the mental veins of its authorities; now it must win an attachment of its own. The old structure of belief will not be wholly abandoned,—it may not be so much as altered; but it must be *hypothetically abandoned,* surveyed from out-side largely by the aid of the materials furnished the imagination in early years, the young Greek, the young Utopian we have implanted in the young modern. That to which one returns is then no longer another's, but one's own. Originality is not measured by the amount of change, but by the depth of this re-thinking.

It is originality of this sort, another name for 'indi-viduality,' which is chiefly at stake during adolescence. If the will to power cannot take this metaphysical direc-tion, individuality will be curtailed in its growth. If self-assertion takes the form of rebellion against re-straint of sex-impulse, individuality will be the loser not the gainer. For sex-expression is the merging of the individual in the currents of the genus; and early sex-expression signs away just the last and highest reaches of individual development. It ensures mediocrity and, by a curious paradox, conventionality of mind: nothing is so uninventive as ordinary sex-rebellion. Only deferment and sublimation can carry individual self-consciousness to its own.[12]

VI

If the instinctive life of adolescence is to be dominated by the will to power in the form of creative thinking, the impulse and power to think must be well grown; whereas originality of this sort is the rarest product of our education. The abundant well of childish curiosity which should now be brimming into the channel of explorative thought, we are commonly compelled to see running dry. Is it necessary to stand helpless before this serious failure of the attempt to educate?

The difficulty does not lie primarily in the fact that explorative thought is the most arduous way of meeting life, whether for educator or educated. It is certainly much simpler for both sides to accept classified solutions for classified situations, after the fashion of the manuals of casuistry, than to discount every actual

---

[12] There is a similar loss through hasty self-assertion in the direction of the acquisitive instincts. To win the early attention of the market it is necessary to offer something *new*. Novelty is a natural product of thought; but premature gathering of this crop has a biological reaction on the root. The normal source of the new is not direct attention to the new, but attention to *the real*; the novelty that comes as a result of the painful quest for novelty will prove in the end to be a mere variation of a conventional pattern, like the scenarios of our movies, and so in time to pall by its tawdry repetition.

hypothesis in favor of a possibly better one. But the difficulty is that with the best of will, the power of explorative thinking cannot be taught by direct effort. In attempting to communicate it, what we pass on is a solution, never the mental process that reached it. In our laboratories we undertake to teach scientific method, the method by which Galileo and his successors made their discoveries; but our typical product still lacks something that was in Galileo. Mr. Bernard Shaw has revealed to mankind the secret of Rodin's art! yet no one takes Rodin's place. The attempt to transmit originality and the attempt to transmit tradition are in the same case: if with the tradition could be given the power that created it, tradition would have few enemies. Imitation never quite imitates; education never educes the most vital power. Platonism produces no other Plato: Christianity yields no other Jesus nor Paul. If instead of trying to conserve itself, every society and every tradition put out all its efforts to make new prophets, new iconoclasts, it would still find itself conserving the husk, unless the spring of that unteachable power can be touched.

It is here that we realize most keenly that education in the last analysis must be on the part of the educator a study of *self-elimination*. It has throughout a paradoxical character. In those beginnings of independent thought which we found in the 'companionable interest in nature,' the art of exposure involved the withdrawal of society by society, a self-effacement which must gradually become complete. It is the moments of loneliness that are critical for the spontaneity of the mind:

and they can be to some extent procured for the growing self by increasing the opportunities for learning
through one's mistakes, through experiments in opposition, and through attempts at the solitary occupation
of leadership.

But self-eliminating is not a purely negative process; for explorative thought has never been a purely
disconnected fact in the universe: it has had its sources,
and the last rite of the self-eliminating art would be to
point out those sources so far as we know them. We may
at least conduct our youth to the farthest point on our
own horizon, to the point from which all that is tentative is seen as tentative, all that is small as small, all
that is human as merely human. "For each man," we
may say to them, "there is a region of consciousness
more nearly just and free than others, looking out toward absolute truth, if not seeing it. In all ages men
have sought out this region, and have found there a
promise of freedom from all residual tyrannies of custom and education; and from this source innovations
without number have made their way into social life.
What men have called their religion has been the
inertia-breaking, bond-breaking power, the mother of
much explorative thought. It has at times exercised a
tyranny of its own, and this is the most hideous of
tyrannies because it invades the region of most intimate freedom. But from it has come the power for
breaking these same shackles. There you may find or
recover the vision which nullifies all imposture of the
Established, the Entrenched, of all the self-satisfied
Toryisms, Capitalisms, Obscurantisms of the world.

And there you may find what is not less necessary for originality: unity in the midst of distraction, composure in the midst of necessary and unnecessary flux, quiet confidence in your own eyesight in presence of the Newest, the Noisiest, the Scientificalest, the Blatantest, all the brow-beating expositions of pseudo-Originality, pseudo-Progress. Your need is not for novelty for its own sake, but for truth: out of your personal relation to truth comes all the novelty that can serve you, or mankind through you. This personal relation to truth you must win for yourself; but you may be left with good hope to win it, for truth is no dead thing, but is itself a spirit.''

Society, I dare say, has never been wholly false to this self-displacing conception of education: even its most hidebound orthodoxies have produced characters capable of social and political resistance, revolution if need be. And the modes of conduct which it has attempted to transmit have been derived seldom from a direct study of its own welfare, chiefly from its own view of the dictates of this more absolute consciousness.

For this reason, in our own study of society we have given little attention to specific transformations of instinct. If anything is discoverable more adequate and final than a given stage of social transformation, it is that which social education reaches toward, and which alone can concern us, even as social beings. But our view of society as an instrument of remaking would be incomplete without some account of its negative action, its dealing with the rebel and the criminal.

CHAPTER XXXI

THE RIGHT OF REBELLION

SOCIAL pressures are not unlike physical pressures. They consist usually of a push and a pull acting in concert—a vision of good and a fear of evil. In a given society every member is subject to the same general pressure,—and though some will be nearer the fear of pain than others, all will be cognizant of, and governed by, the prevalent social punishments. For punishment is but the realization of the threat implied in all pressure; discipline and punishment are inseparable and coextensive in their domain. Whatever justifies the one, justifies the other also.

Our position has been that social pressure, and therefore punishment, is justified by the fact that it tends to realize the individual's will as it could not otherwise be realized,—i.e., in so far as our four postulates are complied with. And if there were any part of institutional life of whose value to individuals society could be absolutely certain, it would be justified (by our last postulate) in conserving that part with all possible force, i.e., in resisting with its whole force any rebellion against it.

But taking our human ignorance and need of perpetual experiment well into account, is there any part of our institutional life which can claim such wholly certain and irreplaceable value? Nothing, unless what is *necessary* to meet a necessary interest. Such a necessity we have recognized in the simple *existence* of a social order, and of a political form thereof. But we cannot argue from this necessity[1] that any given society or state is necessary; it is only that some particular state is necessary. Nevertheless, existence in such matters is a great merit; and under the conditions we have named the existing society and state are always the best,—the conditions, namely, that it is *willing to become* the best and is offering itself in good faith as agent for this becoming.

The good faith of the critic of society is tested, then, by his willingness to use society as agent for its own improvement; he is willing to criticise from within, not from without. The individual bearer of progress has always this in common with the enemy of mankind, that he attacks existing custom. But the vital difference is that the former works through such political good-will as is extant, accepting in full the obligation to replace what he rejects,—the latter rejects the obligation with the custom. The former knows that there may be one point of absolute worth in a mass of evil, namely, good faith in abetting reform. If this good faith does not exist, he might seem justified in rebellion.

But the good faith assumed in this theory is not found either in the social order or in its critics. On both sides the interest in justice is mixed with whatever malice, greed, lust, and callousness still lurks in human character. The art of social life, and of politics

[1] The logical error of Hobbes' theory of sovereignty lies here.

in particular, is to deal not with perfect beings, but with fallible and defective wills. The question is never simply, What exists? but rather, What can be made to exist? And the issue of rebellion, and of its treatment, is not simply, Does good faith exist? on one side or on the other. It is the presence or absence of *faith in a possible good faith* that decides the issue.

This issue, by its very statement, lies in regions inaccessible to observation. The last relations of individuals and societies are found in the darkness of solitary judgment. Here lies the perpetual and unavoidable opening for tragedy in history, the mutual condemnation of wills who with like rectitude are unable to reach either understanding or trust. It is idle to suppose that any legal formula can be laid down to determine when a rebellion is justified; it is equal folly to infer from the absence of such a principle that rebellion is always unjustifiable. The issue does not lie within the legal order, but it is a definite issue. Within myself I know whether I must condemn and attack the order in which I live as an order so far corrupt that no good-will of mine can hope to mend it. And my society, and my state, know likewise whether they can still have hope of me, and whether, therefore, they shall take my outbreak as a rebellion, or as a common crime.

CHAPTER XXXII

PUNISHMENT

IT is important to make this distinction between the rebel and the criminal. The rebel is he who is consciously and hopelessly hostile to the social order. The criminal is he whose deed *implies* a rebellion; but this implication is not the conscious and avowed intention of the deed—the man has simply taken what he wanted in disregard of socially declared rights.[1] The act of the State, in each case, is to make the *external status correspond with the internal status.* The rebel by his overt deed has shown himself inwardly condemning his society, and so external to it in will: society makes the exclusion visible, and as final and irrevocable as it conceives his will to be. It has not first to enquire what the rebel's rights may be; for he has rejected his rights under that order: the rebel is the lost soul, and in excluding him society is but dealing with facts, and pursuing its own duty of conservation. As for the criminal, the act of society is first to compel him to face the ignored element of rebellion implied in his behavior: he is "arrested,"—i.e., at once checked in his policy and compelled to reflect and de-

[1] To this extent all crimes come within the legal category of 'negligence.' They have, of course, the psychological character of "sin,"—the rejection of meaning,—but here the meaning in question is limited to the idea involved in the defined "rights" of the social or legal person.

cide in full consciousness of the meaning of his act. The social exhibition to the criminal of the meaning of his act is 'punishment.' Punishment is thus a hopeful policy; it argues 'faith in a possible good faith.' It exceeds the criminal's right, in so far as society might have insisted upon the implied rebellion; but it does not exceed the right of the human being regarded as changeable.

I

The converse of this proposition is also true: the only hopeful policy is a policy of punishment. It is a prevalent sentiment that the treatment of crime should aim only at the future, heal the disturbed mind, and drop all thought of retribution, which looks vengefully to the past. As if we could deal with the future of a human mind except by dealing with its maxims; and could deal with its maxims except by dealing with the deeds which those maxims have produced! It is only when we give up a person as hopeless that we cease to take issue with the decisions that reveal him; he then becomes to us, in fact, a determined Thing, and is excluded from our society as effectually as if by some magic curse we had transformed him into an automaton. By such self-contradictions false sentiment never fails to reveal its own unreality. Punishment, I repeat, is an expression of social hope—the hope of remaking or saving the man, by revealing to him in the language of deeds the meaning of his own deed. Thus the typical punishment of crime takes the form of simulating the treatment of the rebel, the rightless man: it is an exclu-

sion from society, within society,—an incarceration,—
an exclusion that may be revoked when the argument
has its effect. The argument is clearer in proportion
as the element of physical suffering is minimized. The
suffering of punishment should reveal the worth of
what the criminal has ignored: his liberty, his free
companionship and friendship, his political powers,
his ability to make and execute plans in the community
at large, his right to build continuously on an achieved
degree of power and station, however modest. Discontinuity is a sufficient argument,—if any argument is
sufficient. And if none is sufficient, the criminal is indeed the rebel; and must be so treated. The exclusion
must be as permanent as the unconvinced will.

The truth is that society cannot punish unless it can
create a "conviction." For as long as the criminal
retains the maxim of his deed, his suffering is a mere
hardship,—not an argument. The hardship becomes
punishment only in so far as he perceives and accepts
its meaning. *There can be no retribution without
reformation;* this is the true principle underlying
modern changes in the treatment of delinquency and
crime. And the same principle reveals the inherent
difficulty in the whole theory of punishment, as an in-
completely transformed exhibition of social resentment, or pugnacity. For society fails to convince, and
must always fail to convince, unless it actually has in
itself the good faith and good will of which it would
persuade him. It must be able to point beyond those
maladjustments which have borne hard on the individual, and have made society itself a partner in his

crime, to the only pure and eternal element possible in a human society, the will to correct, with his help, its own errors. But punishment, having the external shape of revenge, and administered by something less than holy wills, runs counter to this revelation and obscures it. The punishment of crime is, in form, another crime. The act of punishing always contains elements which tend to defeat its own intention. As the executioner and the warrior, though their offices were sanctified, have been counted unclean, and the hands of those that have carried out the dead: so the necessary meeting of evil seems attended with the fatality of participating in the evil.

The same motives which in the dialectic of experience drove individual expression of pugnacity from punishment to forgiveness thus have their force in public action also; but the State cannot follow the dialectic to this point. The State must punish. It may and does exercise clemency; but clemency can be effective only as following upon that conviction which is the essence of punishment, and which involves arrest and trial—or forced discontinuity of action, however brief. The State, speaking as it must to the inner intention through the medium of deeds, *has no way of distinguishing a clemency prior to all punishment from a meaningless passivity.* Further, since the criminal while possibly citizen, is also possibly rebel, the State must recognize both possibilities. The State must punish.

Further—and this aspect of the matter has not been forgotten in theories of penology, but has seldom been rightly placed—the criminal is not the only one who is to be punished for his crime. We have said that every member of a society is under the same pressure; We may now say that every member is under the same punishment. The only justification for treating the criminal by the educative method of punishment is that he is, after all, of like mind with the rest of his group; and they, in turn, are of like passions with himself. It was this which, in primitive society, made crime a common menace, calling for public, and not merely for individual purification. The theory that the gods must be propitiated was a mode of expressing an actual condition. For in all minds, and not in a few only, the goods which constitute a common culture retain their persuasiveness only by perpetual contest with the superior obviousness of the material goods and the direct ways thereto. The deed of the unpersuaded man, painted on the imagination of all who know of it, conspires with the natural gravitation of the human will. The relatively defenceless and vulnerable fabric of the necessary good has been attacked in all minds; the plague spot which appears must be taken as symptomatic. A white slaver appears in a public tribunal, and unblushingly expounds his occupation as a form of business; and as I read his testimony his 'point of view' penetrates farther than my ears, and I must take thought to revive the sources of my indignation. "When thou sawest a thief, thou consentedst with him and hast been a partaker with adulterers." The community has thus a work to do which is not limited to the person of the criminal. This work is sometimes spoken of as "deterrent,"—and so it is, but this is a partial and an after-effect; in its imme- diate force it is *punitive,*—it is the share of the entire community in the suffering and purging which belong to the thoughts of crime. It is not that the criminal is suffering for the community; it is the community which must suffer for and with him, must have its sympa- thetic share in the argument of his punishment because of its equally sympathetic share in his crime. Hence the language of the State must be stern, unmistakable, public, and awakening; the State must punish, to re- make the souls of all.

II

The Dialectic of Punishment

Dealing with crime thus involves a dilemma: it is necessary to provide crime with its argument; yet in doing so, society provides it with an unintended argu- ment against itself. Whatever is defective in the spirit of a community will show most clear in its treatment of crime, whether harsh, malicious, brutal, sentimental, or simply callous. Public resentment is never a holy reaction, unmixed with impatience, contempt, and a desire to be undisturbed in its own more decorous self- ishness. The man who is caught feels through the net the cunning eyes of the uncaught. By a deep-wrought law of nature he attracts the worst side of the social temper to himself: the pursuer of crime adopts the arts of the pursued, and becomes like him in quality and habit. It is hard to deal with evil except evilly. Even expletives of condemnation vulgarize their users:

one who employs much vituperative language becomes
assimilated to the images he habitually invokes. In condemning the vice that most tempts him, the hypocrite
has commonly found a subtle way of self-indulgence.
The extreme hostility provoked by crimes of sex is due
in part to the participation which their cognizance
imposes, and to the sense that resistance itself has
forced an unwilling consciousness upon their victims.
As administered by human beings, punishment contains a self-defeating element.

The history of criminal law shows mankind early
aware of this difficulty, and devising various ways to
meet it. Blood vengeance, which speaks in the name
of the sacred spirit of the family, is an advance upon
individual vengeance. Something exalted and heroic
may enter into it; adversaries in feud may recognize
in each other the requirements of spirit and honor.
Yet the deed of honor fails to convince the family
spirit which is its victim; it simply transfers the necessity of honor to the alternate member of the feud,
whom it has treated as an equal. Hence it fails to
punish. And it cannot punish, unless it can escape from
its simple opposition and equality into a region inclusive of both members and their passions, a region
in which it can appeal to the criminal as endowed with
a *right* not alone to judge and punish, but to close the
argument by restoring the disturbed status.

Such a region was provided, by a true social instinct,
in the ancient places of asylum, which were not merely
places secured from violence, but also places whose
sanctity could overawe the minds and passions of both

accuser and accused. And that sanctity to which the
culprit might run for protection, having shown itself
so far beneficent to him, would be more nearly convincing in its condemnation. The issue of such an interval of security, with the advantage perhaps of the
passionless judgment of the guardians of the place,
would partake of the nature of a true punishment.

But neither the interposition of asylum, nor of judgment, nor of ordeal, nor of more rational trial procedure,[2] could offer the convicted person much hope
of restoration, at least as an intact individual, if given
over at last to the mercies of his accuser. To this extent,
another device, that of payment or compensation, to
be accepted in lieu of death or mutilation, more nearly
conveyed the meaning of punishment. It also tended to
temper by reflection the passion of revenge; but this
time by a calculating reflection instead of a dominating
religious dread. The spark of valid resentment was
certain to be somewhat diluted in the desire of gain,
and most patently to the accused, whether the payment
was taken over by the accuser, or appropriated by the
common or lordly purse. The demand for a preliminary
confession and apology, while it mitigated the venality
of the transaction and made the criminal a party to
his own condemnation, hardly secured the sincerity of
the conviction.

The experience of the Greeks, embodied in their
legends, well shows the logic of the situation and

---

[2] It must be remembered that criminal procedure becomes a part of
punishment inasmuch as it determines the meaning and temper of the
punishment. It is the subject and verb of the 'sentence.'

carries the problem a step farther toward solution.
The iniquity of vengeance would appear at its height
when crime broke out within the family, and so involved the curse of repeated family crime, such a curse
as befell the ill-fated house of Atreus of Argos. Atreus,
the wronged husband (according to the version of
Æschylus), had no choice but to impose banishment
upon his brother Thyestes. But Thyestes, taking refuge
in the city sanctuary, keeps alive by his presence the
element of rancor in Atreus; so that at last the out-
raged spirit of family honor vents itself in a counter-
outrage upon the remaining spark of sacred feeling
in the outcast himself, his affection as a father betrayed
into eating the flesh of his slain children. Thus Atreus,
in punishing, injures that which in punishing he seeks
to preserve; and so with each new step in the tragic
history. Orestes alone, driven rather by the command
of Apollo than by personal bitterness to the matricide
which avenges his father, seems to have acquired an
honesty of spirit that might reconcile Clytemnestra to
her death. But the deed of vengeance is greater than
his consciousness of it; its objective impiety he cannot
overcome in an adequate sense of its divine necessity;
he, too, must be tormented by the Furies. He has not
been sufficiently inspired to convince the guilty woman,
hence his attempt at punishment is not free from guilt.
Apollo, apparently helpless, discharges his share of
responsibility by appeal to the guardian goddess of a
very human civilization, Pallas Athene. And she in
turn, finding the case "too passionate for a goddess,"
still further humanizes the solution by instituting the

court of citizens, the court of the Areopagus, whose first work will be the judgment of Orestes. Judging as men, however, they can but find both for him and against him: no act of human justice can solve the riddle and discharge the Furies from their work. It is Athene who must turn the scale,—and apparently by an arbitrary touch, whose meaning remains a mystery even in the work of Æschylus. She neither sanctions the act of Orestes nor condemns it; she regards it—so I interpret the legend—as an incident of a faulty social structure from which no perfect solutions can come. Orestes has the benefit of the historic chance that he stands on the threshold of a new order, which no merit of his could have created. And what is the principle of this new order? It is the dissolving of the family group, within which all passions are so strained that no guiltless punishment is possible, in the political community. Under the auspices of its divine protector, this community can bring a perfect passionlessness into the judgment and punishment of crime, and purge the process of the barbarism of personal impulse. The wrong done to the individual, and to the family, is sunk in the wrong done to the city-state; and the city acts by reason without wrath. The Furies are therefore freed from their mission and from their character; they become henceforth the "gracious goddesses," enshrined within the precincts of Athene's sacred hill. Punishment at the hands of the State unites the solemnity and refuge of the sanctuary with the rationality of measure. Ought it not to convince the criminal, and so solve the problem?

Our solutions are not fundamentally different from those of the Greeks; and our experience in view of these historic experiments may reveal the defect of its principle. The great success of this political process is that it *localizes the hurt,* saving the accuser from a further crime; it has shown no great power to persuade the criminal. Indeed, the impetus of the accuser's resentment is so far checked that the accused seldom feels in public custody the element of asylum which might provoke in him some sense of approval toward the auspices which judge him. Perhaps this resentment is too far impersonalized. Wherever feeling runs high, there is still a tendency to evade the circuit through the public court, and to appeal to the "unwritten law" —which means the primitive procedure—or to the duel, or to the summary process of Judge Lynch. The theory seems to be that the culprit should not be spared the sting of feeling. The practice is at odds with the theory, because conviction cannot be produced in a medium of either fear or pride. But the criticism points in the right direction: the State has cut away too much of the meaning of ancient law: it is passionless without spirit; in becoming official it has lost the co-operation of the presiding goddess. The family could not be official: hence it must give way to the State. But in losing the solemn concern of the spirit of the family in the apathetic equanimity of Pallas, that spark of feeling has been eliminated which alone can positively persuade.

The State cannot import feeling into its procedure; though in its own dignity, if it has any, it may make contact with the sources of feeling. The State must use the language of the external deed. If this deed is to become an argument, it must be interpreted by the criminal himself; and he will so interpret it only if he sees in it the deed of an august beneficence such as commands his reverence as well as his fear. He must see it as the deed of an ideal social order not wholly identical with the order in which he finds himself entangled. What the State alone cannot command must be supplied by those free elements of society which continue the motives of the ancient family bond and the place of refuge.[3] It is only through a pervading activity of a consciousness such as religion in times past has called out in men, both accuser and accused, and working in conjunction with the official procedure of the State, that a genuine punishment, and hence a genuine restoration, can be accomplished.

Thus in the negative work of punishment as in the positive work of education, society in remaking human nature seems to depend, for the last quasi-miraculous touch of efficiency without which the rest of its work has the ring of hollowness and sham, upon an agency or agencies beyond its own borders. To the quest of these ulterior agencies of remaking we must now turn.

---

[3] Attempts are made to provide this missing element by personal indulgence as a mitigation of punishment, in the hope of humoring men back into good nature. This is a false hope, not in what it adds, but in what it lets go. The test of success is that in the midst of punishment, the State itself (and not an individual warden) commands respect and good-will.

PART VI
ART AND RELIGION
Argument

In education, we said, society tries to refer each new member to a source of control beyond itself. It is bound to do this, to lead beyond itself to its own sources, if it is either to give life to individuals or to keep itself alive. It is not easy to indicate what these ultimate sources are, at a time when our minds are pervasively corrupted by the "socialization" of every interest. Truth itself, as well as art and religion, is at times, as in Instrumentalism, reduced to a function of adjustment in the midst of a continuous social process. This is a sort of topsy-turvydom in philosophy which leaves the individual helpless and without appeal from the standards which society sets for him. Liberty depends upon the fact that each person has independent access to the sources of all prescription for human nature. And our present argument is that in art and religion he finds such independent guides.

Whatever gives happiness, or complete satisfaction of the will, gives rules to life: that may be taken as an axiom. And it may be made clear that there is no such complete satisfaction in society as such. Society does provide the possibilities of success, a necessary medium for success in the life of the will to power or reality. The will cannot be satisfied without (1) a market for one's products, physical and mental; and without (2) a market for one's self, i.e., a friendly group in which one passes for something and somebody, is valued for more than he can ever bring to the public market, namely for what he is. Now these successes in the public and private social groupings are necessary, but not sufficient for the good life; they are approximate and promissory, more or less unjust and ill-founded. The will requires somewhere an absolute footing in an absolute and immediate success, or experience of power and control.

Art provides one type of absolute satisfaction of this will to reality. Art has something in common with dreams, but not much: for while dreams—some of them—satisfy desire, they fail to satisfy the dominant human passion, the will to reality. Here Freud completely falsifies the meaning of art. For what art depicts is a satisfaction found in the actual, in the presence of actual evil and resistance, and therewith a clue to the meaning of the objective world. Beauty is something so poignantly symbolic of the structure of things that we require to know it in the most perfect and immediate manner, namely by reproducing it. For what we can create, we know that we know! And in communicating this knowledge in the act of achieving it, namely, through the work of art, we enjoy an equally immediate power over the minds of other men. Thus art satisfies the will to reality.

Now the experience of art does tend to remake human nature and to govern its growth. It shows all impulses what sort of thing they want—for whatever satisfies the will-as-a-whole satisfies each fragment of the will as it were, vicariously. The artist, ideally speaking, needs nothing else; his enjoyment in creating beauty makes natural a certain asceticism in other directions; sublimates other passions. It tends to impose rules of form, of harmony, on all behavior; and to promote relations of equity in the social order. It accounts for much primitive legislation.

But the satisfaction in art has its evident limitations, in so far as it is symbolic and selective. It is only here and there that the artist finds his way to an adequate grasp of reality. It abandons all those regions of the hostile, the ugly, the disordered, the squalid, which it sees no way to reclaim. A more complete satisfaction is conceivable, that, namely, which should grasp and communicate the essence of reality as a whole in some such way as art grasps and communicates its symbolic fragments. This conception defines the place in experience which has been called religion.

Religion seeks union with an absolute being which is beyond the world, and all the goods of physical experience, but which is their source and explanation. As such, it must be in contrast with all of them, identical with none of them; and union with it must require a turning away from them. Hence in all religion there has been an element of world-rejection, of asceticism. It lends itself to the reproach of being other-worldly or anti-worldly; and in attempting to grasp all, of grasping nothing. But the place we have indicated for religion is *a real place*: the satisfaction there proposed, if it could be gained, would be a real satisfaction. For it would be the satisfaction of understanding the principle of reality, and of giving rules to all human desires by knowing their goal. Ascetic religion is only a half of religion; religion is completed in the fulfilment of human nature, naturally transformed.

CHAPTER XXXIII

VOX DEI

IN the transforming of man, society intends to civilize him, religion to save him. In these terms there is a suggestion that the work of society is more or less superficial, that of religion more radical and thorough. Man conforms his mind and habits to social requirements and becomes 'polite': he submits his soul to religion and becomes 'holy.'

But there is reason to question whether this traditional distinction can be maintained; or whether there is any legitimate distinction at all between the work of society and the work of religion on human nature. To make man a social being, to lead him out of his egoism and barbarity into the liberal interpretation of his interests afforded by civic life and its destinies, is not this to make him a religious being in the only sense of religion that has valid meaning?

In the early days of human organization, the distinction between the social and the religious could not have been drawn, not because all religion was social, but because all social requirement was religious. The setting-up of ideals, the defining of customs, the giving of laws were understood as the voice of God to the people. *Vox populi* had no other existence than in *vox Dei.* If the interests of society were at all divergent from those of religion, there was little opportunity to discover the fact: for when the ordering of life is singly and simply from above, there is no comparison of standards, and hence no rebellion in the name of a social value.

But the time was bound to come when the two rules, the sacred and the secular, should fall into contrast, if only because of their diverse methods of origin, the sacred relatively *a priori,* the secular relatively empirical and pragmatic. And when this opposition has occurred, history seems to show that the destiny of the sacred is to yield to the secular. Tabus accumulated beyond endurance; were long protected by faith and fear; but they have been swept away. Holy men fell into the way of announcing counsels of perfection such as would mutilate or destroy human nature,—the sacred books are full of such counsels: for these, practice provided an interpretation, such as all laws need; and the interpretation quietly superseded the announced ideal. The establishments and ordinances of religion became extremely costly to society, in men and time and treasure abstracted from social use, and not infrequently, too, in moral integrity: neither social utility nor social ethics would sanction many ancient forms of sacrifice. But the race has believed in its social standards as against the oracles, and these extravagances of religious requirement have dwindled or disappeared. To-day it is frequently asserted by the exponents of religion themselves that our best insight into the will of God is the verifiable welfare of society. Our religion seems to become, in effect if not in name, the religion of humanity.

Thus the question has become acute whether the reference to God is any longer significant. Is it more than an imaginative widening of the horizon under which the same acts and qualities are required, a changing of names, as from 'goodness' to 'holiness,' or from 'crime' to 'sin'? The tendency of history is unmistakable. From "The voice of God is the voice of the people" we have come to "The voice of the people is the voice of God"; and it may well be that the time has come to drop the "voice of God" as otiose, frankly acknowledging our final insight into human standards as "from below," i.e., from experience, socially transmitted. If we any longer maintain a separate place for religion in the work of transforming human instinct, the burden of proof is upon us.

I accept the burden. And I begin by pointing out an error in the logic of the argument we have just reviewed.

The course of history seemed to show that the will of God has tended to coincide with the weal of society; the inference was that the weal of society is the independent fact, and hence the only fact that need be considered. The inference is hasty. We may accept the proposition, Nothing contrary to the welfare of society can be accepted as the will of God. But the postulate that A must not clash with B does not in the least inform me what A is. I must plan my house so as not to destroy the trees on my lot: this condition does not supply me the plan of my house—would it did! Religion must not tear down social values:—this condition does not supply me with a religion. What history suggests, at most, is that the welfare of society has a negative or critical bearing on the interpretation of the religious standard. We may be *negative pragmatists* in the matter.[1] But there is not the slightest evidence, so far, that the will of God is deducible from the good of society as an independent fact.

And there is a large volume of evidence to the contrary. Let us make the questionable admission that we know and can define what social utility is; it is still true that the socially useful has never been reached by directly aiming at it, but has always come as a result of aiming at something else, as an independent object. Social cohesion, loyalty, lawfulness, are dispositions upon which every social structure depends, but which society cannot directly produce. Already in the speculations of Plato and Aristotle we find a deep anxiety as to what education, what myth, what music, what lie if need be, will be likely to generate the spirit from which socially useful behavior would naturally follow. Arguing from history, it looks rather as if there could be no social good, unless there is something more than social good, as a primary object of pursuit.

In point of fact, society has always had its religion in some form,—a principle of devotion which has pervaded the social tissue, acting more or less like an enzyme in furnishing energy and loyalty at points needing support. Law-abiding behavior could not be reached by the separate attention of each citizen to

[1] For the meaning of the phrase 'negative pragmatism' see my book, *The Meaning of God*, preface, pp. xiii f.

each law: it has to be reached for the most part through a disposition which of its own motion is "the fulfilling of the law," or the major part of the law. The man who measures each step by the law is not the good citizen: he who watches the law, the law needs to watch. There is a "spirit of the laws," something which one might call a moral substance, which shows itself in a spontaneous faith in current institutions and ideals and fellow citizens, a willingness to serve them and work with them, a spirit which society can neither give nor take away, and yet without which there is no society.[2]

I prefer to describe this spirit as a moral substance, because when we look into it more closely it is not

[2] Mr. Graham Wallas has shown, in a fascinating study, how the practical art of politics is concerned with what is instinctive and emotional, not alone with what is reasonable or reasoned. He regards it as somewhat ominous that this art betakes itself so frankly to "exploiting the irrational elements of human nature which have hitherto been the trade secret of the elderly and disillusioned" (*Human Nature in Politics*, p. 177). The chief peril, as I see it, is not that political managers will address themselves to the unreasoned, but that they will make a wrong guess as to the nature of the unreasoned sentiments they have to deal with. When one leaves the rigorous path of influencing the will of one's fellows by argument alone, everything depends on what passions one attributes to them. If with Bolingbroke (to use Mr. Wallas' illustrations) one fancies himself dealing with 'that staring, timid creature, man,' the result is likely to be supercilious and deceptive political action. But if with Disraeli one realizes that 'Man is only truly great when he acts from the passions, never irresistible but when he appeals to the imagination,' there is room at least for a generous interpretation of the unreasoned motive. Benjamin Kidd seems to have been near the ground of experience in judging that the unreasoned element in politics, in its last analysis, is a loyalty of religious character. The ebullition of national feeling at the outbreak of the war showed, especially in France, how politics in times of public stress tends to avow a lurking religious ingredient, while patriotism tends to coincide for the moment with religion.

simply a subjective temper but also a world of objects engaging each individual's interest and will in logical independence of his social entanglements; and in this world of objects we recognize the accumulated goods of both religion and art. These goods do not arise apart from social conditions, and are commonly reckoned as social products; but they appeal to the individual as an independently appreciating being, as an original self. Because this substance has always pervaded society, its real relation to society is obscured; and an attempt to define society apart from it would be felt as a mutilation of society. But this circumstance only makes stronger the contention that social good, defined apart from religion, is not self-sufficient. And I shall try to indicate a method of comparing the relative functions of each which will admit the comparison with justice to both sides.

It is characteristic of the development of human beings that the will to power tends to assume from time to time the character of some leading interest, which becomes the center of values for the whole life. This leading interest may rise to the level of a passion. In a boy's growth to maturity we can trace a series of these absorbing concerns, seldom coincident with the tasks set for him by his elders, but merging at last (generally speaking) in an 'ambition' which at some time or other struggles for supremacy with a personal affection. To these two major passions, ambition and love, correspond two major groups of institutions, those of the public order and those of the private order, as we shall name them. These together constitute 'society' in so far as society has a definable entity apart from religion and art.

Now what society does for human nature depends on *how completely it can satisfy* the individual will. A man can be said to be saved (to adopt the religious terminology for the sake of our comparison) not alone when he is reclaimed from rebellion or criminality; he is saved in so far as he is *not wasted,* in so far as the human material in him gets a chance at self-expression and utilization. In this sense the question for society is *how much of each member* it can save, not merely *how many* it can preserve from disaffection and rebellion.

Putting the question in this way, it is clear that society never does save the whole man. In general, society saves, or conserves, *as much of a man as can, at any time, find a valuation.* It saves as much as it knows how to use or esteem. The remainder is wasted. And it may easily be that the better the case any set of institutions can make out for itself as a whole, the worse the plight of that portion of human nature (if there is such a portion) which it cannot satisfy, because it does not understand.

We shall attempt to estimate what part of human nature can be thus 'saved' by the public and the private orders, at their best.

CHAPTER XXXIV

THE PUBLIC ORDER AND THE PRIVATE ORDER

POLITICAL and economic institutions we have recognized as the particular playground and home of the will to power, so far transformed that the success of one does not necessarily mean the weakness or defeat of another. These institutions may be described as the 'public order'; and in this form, the will to power may become the passion of 'ambition.' To realize his ambition an individual must market his talents, i.e., put them into a form in which they serve other men, or seem to do so. Hence just in so far as a man can be summed up in his marketable talents, he can find satisfaction in the public order.

The world grows catholic in its power of appreciation; a greater variety of talent finds its market. The man who to-day may be a poet—and make a living by it—might once have been by necessity a minstrel, a priest, or a cobbler: the public order has not always had a place for poets. Even now, the public judgment of beauty is so far uncertain, and therefore imitative, that the artist risks the fate of being either neglected or lionized; there is not as yet a firm, discriminating, and sober estimation of his worth. Apart from those who despising the public refuse to join to their art the effort to be intelligible (I am not speaking of that vulgar inversion of motive which seeks advertisement in conspicuous violence to common standards), there are presumably always a number of lost poets, prophets, philosophers "of whom the world was not worthy": in the nature of the case, their existence must be conjectural. It was not until Greek times that the man whose gift for pure science was not conjoined either with religious inspiration or an inherited fortune could find a footing: and even now, for the most part, he must unite this gift with the interest, or at least the occupation, of teaching,—usually a natural and most helpful union, sometimes a disastrous one.

Individuals may still go astray; but at least the class has come to its own. We have names for 'poet,' 'artist,' and the others; we know the type of service, and value it; almost we have conventionalized the hardship and poverty once associated with it, as a bungling penance. But what of the services for which as yet no category exists? Is it clear, *a priori,* that I must fit into any of these traditional rubrics, "doctor, lawyer, merchant, chief"? If none of these is tempting, the public order still bids me choose;—or invent and persuade. The category itself becomes something of a menace through the type it attracts, a type which may repel the finest quality in its own kind. Francis Thompson was a poet by nature, if ever there was a poet; yet not even his own self-consciousness could find its rightful certainty and pride until the many judgments and pressures of the world had harried him into a course of slow self-destruction. The marketable man is never the complete man in his uniqueness; and conversely the whole man is never marketable.

But where the public order thus largely fails, the private order wins a measure of success. The private order comprises the institution of the family with the quasi-institutions of friendship, amusement, and society in the specific sense. Here it is anything but a man's market-value that determines his survival. He is valued as much for what he cannot express as for what he can. It is the 'pilgrim soul,' unarrived, that is perceived and esteemed. The private order has its dominant passion; it attempts to satisfy the whole man by satisfying his sociability—or, more particularly, his love. The instinct we call love, whether in its special or more general forms, is manifested in a craving which relates precisely to this unexpressed, or 'subconscious' region of the will. Its language is the language of signs and symbols rather than of words; and where it adopts words, it imposes on them, through poetry, the character of symbols, with the task of carrying unreachable meanings.

This is the interpretation which society puts upon the instincts of sex and parenthood. What love wants is a mutuality of life in which each appreciates in the other what he in substance is, rather than what he does.

Thus the private order is adapted to save much that is lost in the public order. As the self of immediate expression can reveal more than is seen in the self of marketable technical expression, love does not make its judgment or its choices primarily from what it finds in the sphere of work; it looks to the self of play, of art, of bodily beauty, of manner and carriage, emotion, aspiration, religious feeling. In the economic virtues, the ability to endure hardship and to use common sense, love is not unconcerned; negatively speaking, the beloved person must not fall below the average standard of prudence, competitive spirit, persuasiveness, efficiency. For these are essential parts of the definition of a human being; they are, like the courage expected by chivalry, a test of the quality of the self of sentiment. It is for this reason that love must be 'practical,' and takes ambition itself under its control: but these things have no part in defining the principle of selection itself. The family envisages the public relations of its members within its own inclusive understanding of them; it presupposes the results of their activity there; it uses these results. But it subordinates them to what it alone can see. So far, the family is more inclusive, more satisfying to human nature, and in this sense greater than the State, together with all the professional and industrial groups or guilds within it or beyond it.

But it is also less than the State, in so far as the public order remains to it a mystery. The family is unable wholly to follow in thought the self that is valid in the public order, and estimate its achievements. The man who goes to work, goes 'out,'—and into another sphere of thoughts and standards. What the family grasps and uses of that self is its total achievement, not the method and articulation of its work. It is sometimes, in the complexer activities, unable to estimate even the moral quality of that public person; we have grown used to the picture of the crook who remains the moral hero of his family circle and perhaps of his friends also. It tends to make its own loyalties and amenities the measure of the whole character.

Hence the public order sets up counter claims; and requires that all love shall show its value for ambition or public service. It has its opinion of the over-domesticated man. The State has allowed the family its great privacy and subconscious development, less because of the satisfaction its members found there, than because of the fact, noted by Aristotle, that the strength of the private relation is a measure of the possible strength of the public interest, and that private intercourse brings certain necessary contributions to the life of the State.

The direct question: Which is your more real self, that of the public or that of the private order? most persons would find it hard to answer. It may be that the sexes differ in their natural finding of the dominating order. But for both men and women, both orders are necessary to a complete personality, and in the arrangements of life, each order, and each passion, takes its turn at hegemony. The honors are divided by alternation, and not by a disjunctive choice.

But this solution by alternation is not a solution of the psychological problem: neither order is capable of including the other,—are both together, in their alternation, capable of freeing the entire man?

CHAPTER XXXV

SOCIETY AND BEYOND SOCIETY

EVERYONE'S daily program falls into alternation between the public and the private order. This is not a matter of convenience alone: it is a psychological necessity. And the necessity is more than a need of supplementation. It is true that each order does, in the way we have described, compensate the individual person for the lacks of the other order, and forms a refuge from it. The life of the family is narrow, over-personal, and subjective, and creates a need which the public activity in some measure appeases. The public order is hard, over-impersonal, mechanical, superficial, relying overmuch on the sufficiency of analytical intelligence: it drives back to more complete and intimate realities. But the relations between the two orders are deeper than this of supplementation. For neither, without the other, can successfully do even its own part. Each to some extent presupposes the other,—a fact which is not wholly obvious, but which can be made evident by considering what each order requires.

The tendency at present is to distinguish sharply between a man's capacity for marketable service and his private life. It is in the public order that the maxim, Business is business, holds good: we ask what you can do, and if you do that well we ask no further questions,

and assume no further responsibilities. There is a great
relief and freedom in this; "toleration" wins more by
it than by any other drift of the time. Because of the
cash-nexus, with its impersonality, a man may now
sell his labor, as Arnold Toynbee pointed out, without
selling himself. Yet in all this it is not ignored, but
assumed as understood, that the *success of any man's
service depends on a state of mind which the private
order keeps alive.* I do not mean simply recreation and
rest, though this is part of it: I mean confidence, independence, and originality of mind. What any man
brings to market is something which he, as a total and
responsible agent, can perform; he brings his inventiveness and powers of discretion. The least of public
servants is expected to exercise a degree of mother-
wit. If at any moment the motive force of the public
order should be reduced to the momentum of its own
definitions, its wheels would stop.[1] It is an undefined
contribution, the life conferred on the mechanism, including the power of seeing things whole and judging
them soundly, which, on the psychical side of the account, is exhausted in the course of a day's work: and
it is this which the private order must be counted on to
restore. Success in the public order presupposes a state
of mind given by the private order.

But does success within the private order presup-
pose a state of mind given in turn by the public order?

[1] I am told that syndicalism in France and Italy knows a mode of
strike in which, instead of refusing to obey rules, all rules are literally
obeyed,—and no more: the employer, it may be the government, is
deprived of nothing it has contracted for, but only of judgment and
good-will.

What corresponds to success in the private order is simply the winning of love, i.e., being acceptable or prized as a companion. And in judging acceptability the private order is indeed likely to ask few questions about the nature of the day's work. Yet acceptability builds on that work with the same tacit understanding. Here again I do not refer to the visible or invisible "means of support" which the private order consumes: I mean, again, independence and reality of mind. Although instinctively one expects that his own liking will find response, one is always more or less aware that this response is conditional. It is not an axiom that one must have any friend at all. If such fortune comes, it has a kind of corroborative force: to be loved is a high order of *validation*.[2] And if this private world of mine does not respond, I am left curiously uncertain of myself, as if I were somehow unreal, and for that reason unable to love rightly. Love ought to be a form of the will to power; and my love has no power. I find myself willing to suffer anything, forgo anything for the sake of that acceptance: I am willing to forgo anything except just that companionship. Yet this state of mind is the symptom of false instinct. I should know, and if I were a real person would know, that the companionship I value must come as a result of first being independently real.

[2] Current speech has phrases which suggest more or less vaguely that some objective affirmation is contained in the sentiment of personal liking. Perhaps the vaguer ones are more nearly accurate, as ''There is something *to* him.'' The prestige of soldierdom in the eyes of maidenhood is of course the most conspicuous instance of the psychological principle.

Hence I cannot have it except at the price of being independent of it. I must be in truth, and not in attitude simply, "free as an Arab" of my beloved. And this independence can only come through having an object sufficiently absorbing and responsive, a valid power in the public order.

We are speaking of the logic of our commonest social attitudes, a logic which we breathe, not analyze. Its sum is this: that each order accepts and uses persons who are assumed, and must be assumed, complete and real in their lives in the other order. The alternation into which life falls means not alone that we are finding a freedom in each order not found in the other; it means also that we are *becoming* in each order what is necessary that we may have any right in the other. This is a highly effective alternation; and, so far as we can sustain ourselves in this world with becoming, rather than being, it is a self-sufficient routine, providing within itself for all its own necessities,—and also for its own growth. To this extent, society is an organism.

But the same analysis will show where the organism fails. The fact of perpetual alternation is itself ominous: it confesses not alone the constant undermining of satisfaction that Schopenhauer pointed out; it confesses the persistent crumbling of our qualification;— that qualification we must renew by returning to its source. And at its best this qualification is, as we said, mainly a hope and a becoming. Your guest appears in your circle as one who presumably has done his day's work, and has done it well. You introduce him as Mr. Blank, engineer, or as Herr Geheimrat Dr. So-and-so: he at once receives credit for all that engineers or Geheimrats are supposed to be. These categories have their function: they impose upon individuals typical characters which may fit so loosely as to amount to caricatures, but they also impose upon them ideals which they find themselves bound to serve. No sooner is it understood that M. is a 'scientist' than the imagination of his new acquaintance finishes the picture, surrounds him with records and apparatuses, adjusts the symbolic microscope to his eye, and spreads upon the pages of learned journals the announcements of his discoveries. And he, however exasperated or amused by the inept trappings of this vision, finds himself obliged to respond to the essence of the faith it represents: he sees that it is in substance an appeal to *his good faith* as a member of that social world. Whatever is vague, idly classificatory, and vain in that picture may be corrected or ignored; it still searches out what is merely empty or merely promissory in himself. He has no right in that place unless somewhere he has some stable character, founded on achievement not merely accepted as such, but real. He must bring to that social life a validation of spirit which not even the public order can furnish him, dealing as this order does partly in coin and partly in approximations and hopes. He has need of an absolute.

I conclude that in two ways the social world, at its best, fails to satisfy, and hence to release or save the human being. It fails to provide within its own resources the reality and independence which it demands, and in fact uses; it is living upon borrowed capital. And given this capital, it still fails to satisfy; because while the public order lends to the private order a scope and expression that the private order lacks, it does not provide scope and expression for just that part of the human being wherein the private order supplements the public order. What the public order fails to see is perceived and appreciated in the family,—that is true: but the family is unable to give this part its needed currency, or set it to work in the world. This residue, perhaps an infinite residue, is hence imperfectly set free.

And we may also see the conditions under which these defects could be made good. As the instinctive life of man everywhere demands an environment within which it can be active, and as the rule prevails that the most inward and hidden capacities demand and respond to the widest environment,[3] there must be an objective arena of unlimited scope for the lost powers. And this arena must be one in which a veritable and unqualified success of some sort is possible—a sufficient guarantee of reality; and such a success as might enlist a more comprehensive passion than either the public or the private order calls forth—hence a genuine independence. There must be, in brief, an *adequate and attainable object* for the human will to power.

And in two ways also, experience has attempted to supply such an arena and such an object. First, there

3 Cf. *The Philosophical Review*, May, 1916, p. 490.

are parts of the world more plastic than others, more amenable to wish and fancy; in these, men have learned to create a career both of sense and of idea, in which their desires at once chained to the real and expanding into the infinite find rest in the midst of their own motion. *Play* first opens this vista, giving, as we have said, the habit of success: and then play is transmuted into *art* as the growth of idea outruns the literal possibilities of the material. *Art* is the region which man has created for himself, wherein he can find scope for unexpressed powers, and yet win an absolute success, in testimony of his own reality. One who merely conquers a world may still wish for more worlds to conquer; but if, as artist, one has created a world, the will to power has reached an ultimate goal.

Second, *religion*, whose mission is continuous with that of art and which some conceive as a developed poetry. But religion intends to transcend the imagination, and to reveal a world which has an independent reality; herein it exceeds the scope of art. More completely than any part of the private order, religion promises to recognize all the resources of subconscious capacity: "All men ignored in me, That I was worth to God." It intends to save the entire man, without remainder; and if it can offer to this entire self the kind of scope, actuality, and permanence afforded by the State, it may fulfil its promise.

Art and religion have their own institutions, and are commonly included, as we said, among the resources of 'society.' But both appeal primarily and directly to the exploring and originative self which social inheritance, authority, and imitation can help only after it has engaged for itself with its own realities. Art and religion are always in this sense 'beyond society'; and dealing with them, the individual also (not in his private capacity) is beyond society and beyond the State.

CHAPTER XXXVI

THE WORLD OF REBIRTH

IT would be a mistake to think of religion and art as arriving late upon the scene of history, as high and last products of evolution, to take care of those fragments of human nature left unsatisfied by the social order. We would better not try to date their arrival unless we are prepared to date the rise of reason; but in any event, they arrive early: as soon as man is ready to contemplate his experience 'as a whole' they are there. They undertake to provide for the whole creature, not for remainders: and as the various social interests and institutions set up independent menages, religion and art take care of residues simply because they continue to be responsible for the whole. And while in their earliest identifiable forms they may seem simply to be playing about the horizon of consciousness like so much heat lightning, it is because the forces at work everywhere within the horizon become visible there. The rim contains all that is inside; and if the human world-picture or the scheme of human purposes has a conceptual rim, it is their work.

I say *their* work, because at first religion and art *co-operate* in providing that "objective arena" we were calling for,—an arena adequate for the whole human spirit, and so by implication for any possible lost powers. *Myth,* for example, is such a joint product,

neither pure art nor pure religion, representing a domain largely imaginary and yet partly coincident with
reality super-sensible and super-social; and in the world
of myth the human mind may be regarded as occupied
in staking out cosmic claims wherein desire and hope
can expand without limit. But myth affords a rather
meager diet for the will; and although it contains in
symbol the promise of the literal achievement of the
future, it would hardly have flourished as it did had
there not been a more concrete satisfaction behind it.
This more concrete satisfaction was found in the *direct
regulation of social life from above* by conceptions
whose origin was at once religious and æsthetic, conceptions in which every man could share as he could
share in the ideas of the sacred epic, but in this case he
could share actively, and not only as one regulated, but
also as regulator.

I am thinking of the stage in which all custom was
sacred custom and all law sacred law. And I am thinking of the fact that these bodies of regulation were
not simply, as we commonly picture them, a mould cast
over men's lives, but *a career for their wills*. As a
matter of course, the law is something which men in
general obey, for the law has power behind it; but then,
law is also something which men transmit and interpret, even if they do not make it, and so far every man
shares in the wielding of that power, whatever it may
be. Now when the power behind the law is a religious
power; when as the divine 'word' the law has *mana* in
it; when learning it has the value of communion with
the divine thinker, and sometimes confers the power

to work miracles by the sacred syllables alone, then to stand at the source of the law, whether as authors or transmitters, is to touch an instrument of unmeasured potency. There was a time when every man was expected to assume this position, though there were also specialists in the law; and to this end, every man must receive a legal education,—he must be 'initiated' into the sacred traditions of his tribe. As compared with our own, this educational process was brief, solemn, and intense; and further, it left an abiding mark. The boy emerged from it a man. It was his second birth.[1] He was coming into his social powers; but he was coming into them through first reaching a more ultimate power.

Looking upon the law as we now do, it might not be wholly easy to see in it a sphere for a passionate ambition transcending that of the social order. Still less, if we adopt the prevalent view of early law as a thing dealing chiefly with terrors, consisting for the most part of tabus, prohibitions accompanied by threats, and consistent with the theory that religion arises in the instinct of fear. But it is not alone in the Hebrew songs that we find declarations of love for and delight in the law inexplicable by any such views, yet seeming to have

[1] The conception of rebirth first appears in history in celebration of this event. In the law books of India we have the developed account of a conception already ancient. "Their first birth," says the Vasishtha Dharmasastra, speaking of the three upper castes, "is from their mother; their second from their investiture with the sacred girdle. In that second birth, the Savitri (verse of the Rig Veda) is the mother, but the teacher is said to be the father. Through that which resides above the navel his offspring is produced when he initiates Brahmanas, when he teaches them, when he causes them to offer oblations, when he makes them holy." (*Sacred Books of the East,* xiv, p. 9.)

something more than a rhetorical basis. We have to remember that this initiation concentrated into itself all the new vistas and liberties that come with the advent of maturity. The physical transition of puberty is, in warmer countries, commonly much rapider than with us; the mental liberation is felt with corresponding keenness. But the experience is not merely subjective. Law presupposes a very substantial form of human self-contemplation. The learner's eyes are opened: he looks out into a world of objects which have always been around him, but uncomprehended,—the shapes of tribal life in its cycle of generations, and the principles of its structure, not tangible and transitory but intelligible and permanent. He sees himself a responsible agent in a tribal destiny which may have had a beginning in the dawn of time but which has no terminable future. And he is an *irresistible agent* so far as he himself can give birth to thoughts such as all members of this undying community are bound to worship and obey. He finds himself emerging into the only domain in which unlimited power is possible to a finite being, the world governed by ideas. Through the weakest and dimmest part of his nature he is becoming strong, because he is becoming partner with his gods, and perceives, though faint and far-off, the principle of their omnipotence. It is thus not wholly without reason that he claims to have found in the law a moment of absolute satisfaction. His second birth as contrasted with his first may with some justification be described as "real, exempt from age and death." (Manu, S. B. E., xxv, p. 57.)

This transition is in substance the same as that which we now often speak of as *conversion*. In all ages, adolescence, recapitulating race history, finds religion betimes on the scene, offering its own career to the will in terms of a law of life that runs deeper than the law of the land. Conversion, let us note, is possible only when one can get a reflective view of human existence in its natural round, its cost in labor, thought, and pain, and its margin of aspiration. It comes to adolescence because adolescence has for the first time the data for this reflection and the capacity of full self-consciousness.[2] To be mature is to see the pleasure of life in the setting of its labors; to be adolescent is to have sufficient vigor to welcome it all. To be converted is to achieve this welcome, to catch the spirit of the world in full view of both its hardships and its allurements. It is to perceive the law of the whole process in such a light that to live by it and to promote it takes immediate precedence of every other satisfaction, and especially of love and ambition, the passions of the social order.

We may still learn something of the nature of our 'moral substance' from early forms in which this law was cast.

[2] This is just about all the truth there is in that dictum of Paulsen's that conversion presupposes the world-weariness of a blasé civilization,— with the conclusion that the Germanic peoples have never been truly converted. *Ethics*, Book I, ch. iv. He was speaking, however, of conversion to Christianity, a somewhat different matter, of which more later on. What conversion presupposes is the power of self-conscious reflection on human destiny.

CHAPTER XXXVII

THE SACRED LAW

A RANDOM page or two is sufficient to convince any reader that the flavor of the sacred law books of the world is unique, whether or not it is to his relish. As compared with any modern statute book, one is impressed by the mixture of the solemn and the trivial, and by the absence of reference either to individual rights or to social welfare as deliberate ends. The modern law is largely an embodiment of the social motives: the ancient law is largely an embodiment of that wherein religion and art differ from society in their appeal to the will. It is just this which makes it particularly valuable for our present enquiry.

As typical of what to our consciousness are the least profitable elements in the sacred law, let us take this list of the duties of a Snataka, a twice-born man who has finished his studentship:

Let him not beg from anybody, except from a king and a pupil;

Let him not dwell together with a person whose clothes are foul;

Let him not step over a stretched rope to which a calf is tied;

Let him not spit into water;

Let him eat his food facing the east; silently let him swallow the entire mouthful, taking it up with four fingers and a thumb; and let him not make a noise while eating;

Let him not dine together with his wife, else his children will be destitute of manly vigor;

Let him not ascend a tree; let him not descend into a well; let him not blow the fire with his mouth;

Let him not ascend an unsafe boat, or any unsafe conveyance;

Let him disdain assemblies and crowds;

Let him not pass between the fire and a Brahmana, nor between two fires, nor two Brahmanas;

Let him not cross a river swimming;

Let him not set out on a journey when the sun stands over the trees;

When he has risen in the last watch of the night and has recited the Veda, he shall not lie down again.

It might be straining a point to call this a mixture of the solemn and the trivial. Apart from sporadic traces of ancient tabus, it belongs to the later, meticulous stages of law-making, and the gravamen of profound human issues is lacking. The primitive decalogue, or the Twelve Tables of Rome, would give us a different proportion; but in no case would we find a basis of social utility.

Most certainly, religion was regarded as highly useful: it offered itself as a means to the "great practical ends" of life,—subsistence, tribal increase, success in war and other enterprises: any god worth the name would be of help in such matters. Religion had no scorn for utility. Yet I repeat my belief that the sacred law books of the world are closed with seven seals to those who try to see in them social instruments, however crude, for reaching social goods. Religion had ends of its own: its utility was a consequence. All the social, even the physical ends of life, once caught in the perspective of the sacred concerns, remain incidents in the profounder economy. When eating and food-getting have once become implicated in the circuits of *mana*, they never quite return to the status of simple physical satisfaction.[1] Religion undertakes not to disregard utility, nor yet to follow it, but rather to give *laws to utility*, by conferring upon all subordinate ends the quality of its own interpretation of the will to power.

What this interpretation is, early religion itself had no perfect way of expressing. When it tries to give reasons for obedience, it commonly presents its case in highly utilitarian fashion: as a system of rewards and punishments often frankly material in quality, religious law not infrequently proclaims the advantages of holiness as the best-found way to social goods (and especially to esteem) or to the joys of heaven,

[1] The same may be said of evils and wrongs as of goods. A crime does not lose its basis in physical injury, nor does the punishment of crime cast loose from the feeling of resentment; but the whole situation acquires a wider meaning when the interest of the deities is involved. Speaking of the sacred law of early Rome, Professor Henry Goudy says: "It punished murder, for it was the taking of a god-given life; the sale of a wife by her husband, for she had become his partner in all things human and divine; the lifting of a hand against a parent, for it was subversive of the first bond of society and religion,—the reverence due by a child to those to whom he owed his existence; incestuous connexions, for they defiled the altar; the false oath and the broken vow, for they were an insult to the divinities invoked; the displacement of a boundary or a landmark, not so much because the act was provocative of feud as because the march-stone itself, as the guarantee of peaceful neighborhood, was under the guardianship of the gods."

or to both. From the standpoint of a wise social philosophy it seems obvious enough that the sacred law is but making a shrewd appeal to the ingrained love of approval to drive with the developing individuality of the self-conscious animal a good social bargain; it is arranging that his egoism and vanity shall turn the social mill.

I shall not debate the matter at length. But I may point out that in the midst of the welter of banal motives, it is clear that transposing the prospect of reward to the transcendent alters its psychological quality. One who daily recites the Savitri verse during three years, untired, is assured by Manu that "he will enter after death the highest Brahman, move as free as air, and assume an ethereal form"; the pitiable bathos and inadequacy of this dazzle of supernatural potency stamp it as an attempt less to describe a literal result than to encourage an adherent germ of something different from the visible and material satisfaction. And while the esteem of the multitude seems to have been in the eyes of the Eastern saint a most impressive reward, so much so that his type names, the "princely man" of Confucius, the Aharat, etc., were names of social distinction as well as of religious attainment, the law occasionally hits upon a clear statement to the effect that it aims less to provide respect than to make men worthy of respect. "He who knows and follows the law is a righteous man: he becomes most worthy of praise in this world and after death gains heaven." Such is the opening and wholly typical appeal of the Vasishtha Dharmasastra.

II

If any evidence of the non-utilitarian basis of the sacred law were needed beyond the character of the laws themselves, it might be found, together with some positive light upon the religious end, in certain inklings of its psychological origin. The law is sometimes said to have its source (or organ of reception) in the 'soul' as distinct from the prudential reason. Now the human being, if we bring together the testimony of ancient religions, is provided with a great variety of souls. But in general, the soul is that part of a man which holds conversation with the super-sensible world: and only a being with a soul can either receive the law, whose origin is in heaven, or appreciate and be governed by it. One of the best literary instances of the soul engaged in devising and promulgating the law is found in the sayings of Ptah Hotep. For Egypt had an especially usable development of the soul-idea (and it would be hard to say how much of moral progress depends on the discovery of usable conceptions). Among the Egyptian souls there was one, the *ka*,[2] which was particularly concerned with moral and æsthetic discrimination. To "offend the *ka*" was about the same as, with us, "to offend the finer feelings"; and reverence for the *ka*

---

[2] The *ka* is defined as the immaterial self or double, having the form of the body, but being without the power of acting upon matter. Its action therefore must be wholly persuasive or advisory, and perhaps for this reason it was at the same time the object of a somewhat chivalrous regard, and a source of the degree of chivalry attained (if I may be allowed the anachronism) by the ancient Egyptians. The personal affections centered about the *ka*, and it received the chief tendance after death.

implied a careful listening to the dictates of a religiously sensitized conscience. The *ka* takes under its protection the otherwise defenceless rights of persons and occasions, even to the requirements of courtesy. For example, Ptah Hotep, not himself a priest but a wholly competent interpreter of the moral tradition of Egypt, gives instructions to his son thus:

Do not pierce the host at table with many glances: it is an abomination to the *ka* for them to be directed at him. . . .

Diminish not the time of following the heart (i.e., of recreation), for that is an abomination to the *ka*, that its moment should be disregarded. . . .

The washing of the heart shall not be repeated: it is abomination to the *ka*. . . . (The washing of the heart being words uttered to give vent to feelings angry or otherwise.)

It is the *ka* that openeth the hands of the host. . . .

It is evident that the *ka* is the guardian not alone of the uncodified obligations of loyalty, but also of the generous and outgoing impulses, and of the more intangible demands of the relation of guest to host, etc. It is clearly, too, a function which can be appealed to only with some maturity of experience. Yet it acts dogmatically; it judges the quality of an act without regard to its experienced utility; the standard of judgment seems to be at once religious and æsthetic,—an undistinguished union of the two in which now one and now the other is predominant.

This is not a type of judgment with which we are unfamiliar. For good or ill, this ancient religious legislation is the first great extension over human life of the sway of *a priori reason,*—that is to say, the assertion of thought, in advance of trial and error, that something will necessarily be found true or valuable within experience. If anything is true *a priori*, it is, of course, true for all time and in all circumstances. Accordingly, a sense of unrestricted validity enters into this legislation, and accompanies it unflinchingly into its profoundest absurdities. Questions of scope aside, it must be agreed that if the human will is to find any spot of complete mastery, it can only be possible through some such grasp of values that endure: to adapt a phrase of John Locke's, men can only be born free as they are born thus rational and prophetic. Whether we can grasp any such durable principles is a question of fact not here in debate. But it is clear that so far as a people had in common the same type of sensitivity, the same *ka*, the same necessary interests at the basis of the æsthetic judgments therein uttered, the pronouncements of any healthy *ka* would tend to be good for all others. And a prevalent respect for such utterances would tend to make people plastic toward them, and so to lend to one who spoke authentically in the name of the *ka* the power of an artist over his material. The life-forms of a social group under these conditions would become the medium for an art in which nothing desirable could be excluded as impossible, and in which everything desirable could be expected to last.

Such seems, in fact, to have been the position assumed for itself by the sacred law. And in Ptah Hotep himself I find the most ancient expression of the prophetic consciousness with regard to his own precepts. "The quality of truth," he said, "is among their excellences.

Nor shall any word that hath here been set down cease out of this land forever.''

III

In the amenity and chivalry of the Egyptian spirit it would be hard to say whether the æsthetic or the moral motive is dominant. But in the laws of Persia and of India there are frequent passages in which the æsthetic sense, the regard for decorum, the desire for purity amounting at times to inconceivable squeamishness, is in control. The list of duties of a Snataka above quoted is an example of such almost purely *æsthetic apriorism*. These alleged duties are largely dictates derived from a notion of personal dignity, a form of art which decrees what external carriage shall be taken as a symbol of an internal ascendency. To step over a stretched rope to which a calf is tied will be admitted hazardous if dignity is to be preserved; and perhaps an exceptionally holy man would need to be reminded of the contingency. Such rules would have the incidental utility of keeping countenance with the bystanders; but as is always the case in æsthetic judgments, the feelings of the bystanders have a discoverable and defensible basis. By undertaking something beyond his physical powers the holy man brings discredit both upon himself and upon his office; for nothing more quickly disproves the divine quality than an inability to recognize one's own sphere of validity and its limits. Climbing trees, swimming rivers, ascending unsafe boats and the like, are for the experimental stages of youth, not for high-caste householders with a tradition to sustain. With us, dignity is a far less vulnerable essence and so requires no such scrupulous protection; but we have had the advantage of learning from the Stoics that "freedom from perturbation" may be a purely internal accomplishment. These beginnings had their own justification.

But they were justified also in another way. The æsthetic standard has a hospitable nature and protects the early stages of many another budding ideal. To exclude the jarring and unfit is to give every voice of inner protest, from whatever source, a chance to be heard.

And after all, it is not a matter of surprise that the first efforts in law should have been innocent of the argument from effect to cause as we understand it: legislation based on social utility is not yet a fully accepted practice. The surprise is rather that, referring itself to independent principles, this ancient law should so frequently have hit upon the useful. Without declining to recognize in men only a few centuries earlier than ourselves a kindred common sense, it seems fair to judge with most recent students of the history of law that the rules regarding purity and purifications, in the midst of much that is overdrawn, have unwittingly anticipated important principles of general sanitation. Æsthetic regard for 'decency' has always been an important factor in racial health and soundness. (But let me say in passing that it seems to me an open question whether the æsthetic standard in the conduct of sex-behavior does not to this day contain more truth and meaning than the hygienic and eugenic utilities so commonly regarded as ultimate tests;—to my mind these tests fall into the logical position of 'negative pragmatism.') The significant tabus which center about the feeling that blood is a substance of mysterious potency have probably an æsthetic basis; but they have had an immense utility, as in fixing social attitudes toward murder and suicide, in the treatment of blood-kinship, in the care of women, and in the treatment of disease. A great deal of disutility has accompanied this utility and in time outweighed it. But this fact does not cancel the primary fact that the æsthetic judgment tends to find the useful long before the power of causal reasoning is sufficiently developed to find it. It must be remembered, too, that these utilities were not superficial, but the radical utilities of human life. If the struggle for existence has eliminated the groups which lacked this happy correspondence of intuition with vital expediency, the fact remains that in those that survived the intuition itself has operated as an independent organ of judgment.

Even when the causal connection is invoked in the sacred law, it is frequently a postulate of the fitness of things rather than a result of empirical observation. Certain types of behavior *ought to have* certain results; and such results are forthwith ascribed to them. Thus, upper castes may marry only upper castes; otherwise, "the degradation of the family certainly ensues, and after death, the loss of heaven." Buying a wife is an undesirable way of acquiring one, because "she who has been bought by her husband afterward unites herself with strangers." And, as in the rules already quoted, if one dines with one's wife, "his children will be destitute of manly vigor." Causality of this sort implies crediting the objective world with a structure akin to one's own principles of preference. The idea of *karma* is the most complete expression of this trait: for *karma* means that the world is at bottom a moral order in which whatever ought to result does result. Here the æsthetic apriorism gives way to an *ethical apriorism*.

IV

In the demands or supposed demands of fitness it is never easy to detect the point at which the æsthetic disappears in the ethical. The many rules which distinguish lawful from unlawful occupations, or clean from unclean foods, may have little behind them apart from the whims of feeling except historical attitudes associated with the several materials dealt with. If the Brahmana trades he must not sell stones, salt, hempen cloth, etc., through a long list; nor must he lend "like a usurer." But to this last-named rule there is an exception which introduces a new element. The Brahmana must not lend "unless he to whom he lends is exceedingly wicked, neglecting his sacred duties." There is some justification, it appears, for dealing foully with the foul if one deals with them at all. The principle of balance here is no longer primarily æsthetic, the elements of the picture are the wills of free men in noetic interplay, and appeal is made to a sentiment of *a priori* justice. Upon such a sentiment of *ethical balance* early equity was built.

The symmetry of the *lex talionis* rides rough-shod over the psychological differences of actions outwardly similar. It ignores intentions and circumstances. Its simplicity is thus specious; and with all 'natural right' it must fall under the suspicion of historically minded thinkers like Sir Henry Maine. But the psychological observer sometimes forgets that the main facts in the psychology of any situation are the facts which to the minds concerned seem objective. We dare not forget that the force of a law is in the mind that interprets it, not in the actual circumstances or motives which breed the occasion. Ideally speaking, the only real situation is the situation as felt and understood by those that take part in it; and simple minds will conceive their own deeds and interests simply. The symmetry of early law is the very quality which, by its obvious give and take, is fittest to serve as a language. The punishment which has the saving grace of fitting the crime as the perpetrator conceives it is the only punishment which has any chance of seeming right to him. He can be reconciled if at all only by a reaction which he can read at once as meaningful. The sacred law may well have had in this respect a literal 'saving grace' such as more carefully studied measures might wholly miss.

This primitive equity of balance is not incapable of progress. Any growth in understanding the nature of the act to be balanced will be echoed in the treatment; hence primitive equity, so far from being fixed, is highly variable. According to the Jewish law, if a son were to strike his father, he must be put to death (Exodus 21. 15); the code of Hammurabi prescribes that he must lose his hand. Fitness may be claimed for each rule; the deciding factor is to be found in the conception of the offence, and this conception is capable of indefinite refinement.

And I doubt whether any degree of progress will do more than perfect this refinement. The principle of equity we shall not outgrow. Deficient as the sacred law is in legal insight, it was not astray in its first principles. Indeed, its special and only proper function was the finding of first principles; and it may be well to attempt a summary of what is permanently valid in its work.

The sources of value are to be preferred above all specific values that flow from them. This is not a maxim of prudence, dictating a wise regard as for the goose that lays the golden eggs. It is rather a principle of value-experience. It shows itself not only in the recurrent demands for the honoring of the gods, the ancestors, the father and mother, but also in the claims for reverence toward the sacred law itself, and its trustees. It is sometimes thought that the law of sacrilege, containing much interested legislation and offering the best foothold for priestly corruption, is pre-eminently the outgrown element in ancient law. But this will not be the case until the sentiment of national honor, an object of vague, frequently fanatical, but essentially religious devotion, and the idea of regard for parents as a fundamental duty are outgrown. Respect for law is still deeper in the human consciousness than interest in any particular law. And no advantage could compensate any community for the vanishing of the spirit of reverence out of which all justice and all culture must come. This principle of the ancient law is still valid.

Personality is to be set above property. This might be regarded as a corollary of the above principle, if we assume that the value of property depends in any respect upon personality. That this is the case is broadly hinted in various passages of sacred law, thus: "Whatever exists in the world is the property of the Brahmana; on account of the excellence of his origin the Brahmana is, indeed, entitled to it all." (Manu, I, 100.) But apart from the somewhat over-simple theory of distributive justice here promulgated, the meaning of the principle is seen especially in three ways: the regard for the dignity of the person as worth every necessary sacrifice of utility; the indisposition to accept a compounding for personal injury by fines alone, so long as the law remained sacred law; and the attempt, in the clash of personal interests, to ignore property differences as irrelevant. When a sufficient number of differences among men have been set aside as irrelevant to the concerns of justice, the principle here stated will blossom out in the form of a theory of *equality before the law,*—in which form, the ancient principle vigorously survives. And we have had recent occasion to reaffirm the judgment that crimes against property are not to be weighed off with crimes against persons and against humanity.

In such ways as these the sacred law makes good its claim that there is a rule of life which *gives laws to utility.* It is always true, human nature being what

it is, that nothing can be useful which fails to satisfy
equity, personality, honor. So long as Russian peas-
ants believe as they have believed about methods of
agriculture, it is not a useful procedure to introduce
mechanical reapers and binders among them: dissipate
these beliefs and a new market is open to the world;
but in no case is utility freed to stand as something independent of the preferences and faiths of human
nature, whether true or false. And so long as we hold
the belief that a man is worth more than his property,
it will be impossible not alone to compensate murder
with a money-payment, but to hold slaves, or to equate
man-power with horse-power, however advantageous
the procedure from the purely economic standpoint.

Hence it is not true as Maine asserts that the influence of theocratic legislation disappears with the
advent of kings. But it is true that with the advent of
kings another type of judgment must enter as co-operative with this one.

V

The abuses and crudities of the sacred law are so
much in evidence that they almost usurp the attention
of observers; and it is necessary here to advert to them
only for the sake of due proportion. Those who regard
the connection of religion with morals as on the whole
unfortunate for morals—and there are many such—
have in mind the insistence on a blind obedience, the
diversion of thought from the experiential and social
basis of righteousness, and the tendency to condone the

humanly pernicious if the religiously correct is preserved. These are grave evils.

The nature of them might be comprehended, perhaps, in the statement that religion is prone to exaggerate its primacy into a separation. It finds a true absolute, but is apt to set it up as exclusive of the relative and pragmatic instead of including and co-operating with them. In artificial restrictions upon human intercourse, in the cultivation of mistrust and aversion toward the unbeliever, in depriving heretics of privileges and even of fair play, in inculcating an artificial terror of the beyond so great as to obscure every useful motive and so to retain intact the most preposterous customs, in hostility to novelty, the custodians of the sacred law have done incalculable harm both to mankind and to religion itself. In face of all this, it may be said that if mankind could have won its hold upon a region of absolute satisfaction only at this cost, it was worth the sacrifice.[3]

But human nature outgrows the need of any such sacrifice. Indeed, these abuses are incidents of a middle stage in the development of law, the struggle of the secular principle to secure recognition. The original tendency of the sacred law is not to reject the aid of secular principles but to make place for them. The *jus* of the Roman comitia was regarded as under divine auspices, and a natural supplement to the sacred *fas*. Likewise under the wing of theocratic law there grew

---

[3] I may remind the reader of the remark of Walter Bagehot's that at a critical point in the development of human societies it was more important that there should be *law*, than that there should be good law. It was the religious temper that made law possible.

up in many regions a body of worldly wisdom based on experience and taking the form of proverb or fable, the first humanizations of ethics, so little conscious of antagonism of principle that the sayings of Solomon could find their way into the sacred canon. The antagonism existed, however, and was bound to appear, because the *a priori* vision of the human mind cannot safely proceed much farther than first principles; the detail of the law, like the detail of the body of science, has to be built by the aid of pragmatic considerations. The rubbish of overwrought æstheticism had to give way to the pressing utilities. Religion had to learn the lesson of contenting itself with the right of giving to all second principles their final meaning. We shall have recovered the original and normal relation between the secular and the sacred when we can treat murder, adultery, perjury, breach of contract, etc., on the ground of social expediency without feeling the need to deny that they are also "abominations to the *ka*" and "to the Lord."

Meantime religion and art, relieved of social burdens to which they were only partly fitted, were free to assert to the full their specific natures. To these we now turn.

CHAPTER XXXVIII

ART AND HUMAN NATURE

UNSATISFIED wishes press in all directions, and seize on every promising object. They find the stuff of dreams and day-dreams most accessible and yielding: the imagination is the infinite space in which endless flimsy exploits occur at will, pictures and promises of the unrealized satisfaction.

But apart from their lack of substantiality, these easy private conquests have the disadvantage which always attends non-resistance. They fail to mark the distinction between a passing fancy and a profound need. They fail to leave the marks of a genuine *experience;* they arouse inadequate after-images, and so give little aid in learning what our real as opposed to our apparent wishes are. Hence in the world of dreams, taken by itself, primitive expressions of instinct flourish, interpreting power flags, and the unsatisfied will necessarily remains unsatisfied. For where every desire is appeased as it arises, or where every impulse assumes full sway, at least one large human need must be permanently repressed, the need for self-knowledge. In dreams, individual personality is at a minimum. The will to power requires a stiffer medium for even so much as a picture of its residual need.

Such a medium it can only find in that same physical world which, by hypothesis, is refusing literal satis-

faction. If the will cannot enjoy, it can still depict
enjoyment: and the effort to depict gives substance
and consistency to the dream. And as in remembering
an experience, one contemplates one's self engaged in
the experience, so in depicting enjoyment one depicts
one's self enjoying. The war dance which dramatizes
the victory not yet won is not a mere representation
of fighting and winning: it is a self-portrait of *man as
victor*. It is a real experience, and may be the basis for
progress in interpreting the will. Such physically embodied dreams are 'works of art.' The work of art is
the dream made *objective, permanent, self-conscious,
mutual*.[1]

I

The work of art is mutual or social partly because
as a physical object it cannot help being public, open
to common judgment. But it is social also because it
intends to exert a power of its own. It may or may
not be the conscious intention of the artist to announce
any new gospel regarding the human will, though he is
quite as likely to be the rebel or the prophet as to be
the spokesman of any established social order. His
art is 'beyond society' inasmuch as its source is in his

[1] The Freudian view of art is composed of an axiom and an untruth.
The axiom is that repressed wishes express themselves in art forms. For
if man makes anything at all, how should he make except in such wise
as to satisfy himself? The work of his hand will necessarily reveal any
craving, analyzed or not, which is given liberty to assert itself in that
work. The untruth is in the answer to the question, What wish is
expressed in art forms? The Freudian answer is perverse in its emphasis. The true answer is, Not any one wish, but the total wish of man,—
the will.

private dream of precisely that good which society so far fails to supply.[2] But he intends none the less through his art to speak across to the similarly unsatisfied wishes of his kind. In displaying his work, it is as if he said, "This is my wish,—Is it yours also?— Has it *man* in it?"

The satisfaction offered by art is symbolic, not actual; hence the power of art to satisfy is limited by the scope of symbol. Yet the region which art opens to the will is not one of pure fancy or illusion. As the unrealized wish is a wish for something veritable, the art which appeases it is bound to convince, not to mock. It conveys to the mind some account of reality; it is never the mere projection of the subjective longing. The tie between art and reality is seen in the path which leads from imitation to certain forms of art. Imitation is not art, but the imitation of selected parts of reality may be the beginning of art, as narration at first accurate may, by a well-known process, insensibly grow into fiction under the pressure of the idea of the happening, as one would have had it transpire. To find its subjects in a world of common experience is a necessity for an undertaking which, like art, proposes to be commonly understood; but it chooses from the world of

2 For this reason I must dissent in principle from one of the most living and fundamental of contemporary views of the function of art, that of Mr. Ralph Adams Cram. The era of individualism in art which he deplores is not a pure retrogression, it is a necessary 'awkward period' on the way to better things. Art must be democratic and win its own clientèle of free admirers; it must never again be the mere outgrowth of an authoritatively united community spirit. It must serve as one of the main paths to the future and the unborn.

actuality such parts as foreshadow a *happy solution of some problem of evil* or of resistance to will. It picks out objects or situations in which we can see or surmise the *raison d'être* of ordinary and challenging facts,—of inertia, in the repose of a majestic peak; of flesh, in the face of a girl; of human bonds, in the Madonna; of suffering itself, in tragedy and music. Bergson was essentially right in saying that the artist like the metaphysician must, through the disinterested vision of sympathy, perceive the real. The objects which art portrays are individual objects with a penumbra of universal meaning; they are objects which admit us to a perception of the way in which reality, while resisting our wishes, may yet satisfy the will.

The original intention of art may well be, not to satisfy the will, but to prefigure its satisfaction. As in mimetic dances, which are at the same time prayers, art may serve as a sort of first aid to thought, giving a more vivid grasp of the goal of desire. Such art is frequently a collective activity; collectivity heightens emotion; and heightened emotion intensifies the imaginative presentation of the objects wished for.

But the characteristic thing about art is that in this process of imaginative presentation, it discovers a secondary satisfaction which eclipses the first. The one who contemplates and enjoys a work of art may equally with the artist find his insight aided; but the artist has found the joy of authorship in an object which partakes of his own ideal. There are many objects

which can hardly be enjoyed except by physical possession: to the hungry man, a picture of food would bring
little pleasure whether painted by himself or some
other. But art, whose mission is to the unsatisfied
wishes, may safely assume that it has to do with the
hungry man only in so far as he is also a hungry soul.
The objects which it has to present are objects whose
nature is to elude physical possession. The most general name for the specific objects of art is *the beautiful;*
and the beautiful may be defined as *that which demands
to be possessed by reproduction.*

It has often been said that the contemplation of
beauty is quieting to the will; that it must be disinterested, free from the clamor for personal enjoyment.
And this is true with regard to every activity within
the private or the public order: for beauty is the
presence in a particular object of a value which cannot
be possessed by any social instinct. But the cessation of
these activities is the initiation of another. The per-
ceiver of beauty, quite unreflectively, begins the effort
to produce it out of himself, as one who has heard music
he enjoys may find himself trying to whistle it. Nothing
can be consciously reproduced unless it has been
thought through; and as the possession of beauty must
be a possession by conscious thought, the work of reproduction may be regarded as the act of taking complete possession. Art could thus be described as the
completion of the possession of the beautiful.

And so far as the element of value in beauty is a
metaphysical element, a solution in idea of some problem of evil, it is in actuality, and not in symbol only,

a finished satisfaction. The will reaches in art an absolute goal. Hence it is that art opens to some minds a career whose passion is capable of replacing all other passions. The artist has all that the metaphysician can give him, though he has it not in conceptual form. He has all that ambition and love can give him, though he has it not in the coin of actual recognition and affection. As a man he will need to possess his object *also* through the way of concepts and words, and of recognition and personal attachment; but as an artist he has already stood at the end of these paths: he has anticipated the attainment of his will. And whether or not he is 'indifferent to the public'—his immediate public— he is conscious in his achievement of the necessary and permanent persuasive power of a vital idea.

II

If this is a true account of the nature of art, we can understand its twofold effect upon human instinct. Since, in its first intention, it presents the objects of desire with added vividness, it strengthens the impulses to possess, is capable of heightening the passions, social and unsocial. Upon the spectator, the first effect of the enjoyment of art is the enlivening of his wishes, restoring a perhaps jaded faith in their achievableness and in the general worth of living. And since he has been led into a world in which success is not alone possible but actual, immersion in that world *as a spectator* might easily tend simply to heighten the rate of living, to increase eagerness and demand, while lowering patience with the restraint and postponement im-

posed by the slow processes of the social order. It is
not an accident that communities of artists and art-
lovers tend to develop occasional antinomian or Bo-
hemian traits.

But while every artist is a spectator, every spectator
is also at least an incipient artist; and to that extent
the first effect of art is superseded by the second,—
the heightened energies of action are transmuted into
energies of creativity. The full and normal effect of
art is to turn all impulses into the channel of the
creation of persuasive beauty, making this form of the
will to power their ultimate meaning.

In this rôle of interpreting instinct, the passion for
art is likely to find itself in partial opposition to the
passion of the public order. Concern for the quality
and beauty of an industrial product is not always compatible with concern for maximum quantity or exchange value: one finds in France to-day a dread of the
transformation of national life which may be imposed
by a new-born pressure for 'efficiency' as a result of
the war. With the passion of the private order there
is no such opposition. Sex-love in particular parallels
and in part fuses with the impulse of art-production;
for sex-love includes within its meaning an impulse
to take possession of the beautiful by reproducing it,
though this meaning does not rise to the same level
of consciousness as in art. And art may be regarded
as a mode of creativity, in which the will to power not
alone controls its object, but fashions its very substance and form. Hence no form of activity so completely and directly *sublimates* the awakening instinct

of sex as activity in creative imagination. Art is particularly fitted to introduce the instinct of sex to the central element of its own meaning.[3]

III

But besides the direct effect of art on instinct by interpreting it, there is another and *reflexive effect* upon the *form* of all instinct-expression.

The artist does not intentionally generalize the beauty which he finds in a particular object and deposits in another. But the meaning of beauty is universal, and cannot be confined within any one object, nor within any one medium. Beauty transfers itself, within the mind, from one medium to another; its tendency is to impose its principle upon every output of the person. It may not be true that every painter some time writes a poem. But *behavior,* the continuous product of the will, cannot escape the impress of the spread of the impulses of art. Through art the force of analogy in the mind is immensely increased. It has become a prevalent doctrine in educational theory that skill acquired in one department of knowledge is not transferable to another; and this is likely to be true if we deprive the mind of all æsthetic interest in the activity in question. But interest in beauty reaches

[3] Miss Jane Harrison relates that "an artist deeply in love with his friend's wife once said, 'If only I could paint her and get what I want from her, I could bear it.' . . . He saw that through art, through vision, through detachment, desire might be slain, and the man within him find peace." Should we not rather say that desire might thus find its own meaning, not so much through detachment as through creative possession, and the entire will of him find what it wanted? *Art and Ritual,* p. 218.

the central current of the will, and when this interest is awakened all transference of skill and discipline becomes natural. It is the nature of beauty to overflow departments and to make the man of one piece.

Hence it is that the most common impressions of physical form are translated (so naturally that we seldom think of the metaphor) into expressions of character types,—straight, crooked, upright, sharp, square, devious, etc. The words rude and refined, taken over from artisanry, summarize the series of these indirect effects of art on the expression of instinct. It would be possible to particularize these effects for each of the instincts and passions; but a few sketchy outlines must suffice.

1. Since art trains enthusiasm to the performance of definite work, it illustrates the paradox of force acquired through restraint, to the direct advantage of all social life. The subordination of dancers to the common rhythm and music is a condition of their free self-expression; and public life if it presents a more complex subordination may yet benefit by the analogy. The will to power is easily led, in simple community life, by the subtle argument of. 'harmony' into the assumption of a permanent identity of interest between the individual person and the State. This assumption, as was natural in a people so deeply steeped in beauty, was the genius of Greek social life. Increasing consciousness of individual self-interest must always come into such a scheme as a disturbing element; and once the central harmony is broken, no good-will of separate individuals could restore the identity of in-

terest. The principle is not a sufficient bond for political life, as the tragedy of Greece may show, but the appeal to a common consciousness of beauty is an aid which our bald democracies cannot afford to ignore. Public architecture, public pageantry and masque, the reverence for beauty in all public enterprises, furnish an indirect argument for public solidarity of incalculable scope.

2. In private relations, the interest in beauty has something more than decency to demand. It tends of its own accord to invite an equality between the partners, since harmony is disturbed by the weakness or suppression of one of the voices. Society in the narrower sense of the term may be regarded as human intercourse carried on under the dominance of the demand for beauty, as the most complex of the improvisatory arts. And all society creates for its own purposes a limited world from which extremes of inequality are excluded. But the standard of beauty demands no permanence in any human relationship. Art embodies its meaning within finite and framable objects; and it has no other disposition for the history of love. The tale will find its end: its passing may have its own melancholy beauty. Taken by itself the standard of art would make for temporary unions.

It is not reasonable to expect from this indirect and formal bearing of art on instinct a sufficient guidance of life. Taken alone it would subordinate the matter of behavior to its manner, preferring to believe that "All vertus be closyde in curtasy." It would insist on suavity when the situation might well demand indignation or even conflict. It has no place for the prophet, the revolutionist, the reformer; and it has but feeble contact with the more pressing problems of the 'common man.' It fits no one for dealing with the as yet unharmonizable aspects of experience.[4] Its tendency would be to seclude itself, build for itself high garden walls, and in the midst of a world small enough to be perfectly controlled, forget the ugly, the squalid, the disordered, the just causes for warfare and rebellion.

If made an exclusive object of devotion, beauty would fail at length to satisfy the capacity for maladaptation. When it so far assumes leadership in the mind as to dominate the religious consciousness, it loses its power. The gods themselves become plastic figures and lend themselves to the fabrications of myth and legend. Their severity wanes in an Olympian sunshine; and the gibe of Epicurus holds good, that these gods can no longer be supposed to wrinkle their brows in concern for human affairs. To exclude in this way the cruelty and hardness of fact from the view of an æsthetized consciousness is but to invite the day of wrath, when reality will burst down those walls and turn the unearned paradise to a place of loathing.

The real artist knows that to yield to the aristocratic impulse in the æsthetic consciousness is to cut off the sources of his own art. For beauty, let me repeat, is reality offering a glimpse of the solution of its own

---

[4] There is probably nothing to be done in the world which cannot be done with entire decorousness, ideally speaking, but for men of imperfect skill, promptitude, and invention it is sometimes necessary to choose between decorum and the demand of an occasion, between futility, even dishonor, and rudeness.

problems of evil: its soil is in experience. It must lean against its own luxury, its sensitiveness and finesse. It must return from time to time to the school of asceticism and religion.

CHAPTER XXXIX

RELIGION PER SE

AS art becomes secular and declares independence, and as law becomes civil and increasingly chary of the remnants of priestly jurisdiction, religion is left with the sphere of the supernatural as its special province. It deals with what is behind, beyond, beneath, and within the world; standing in contrast with all that is apparent, finite, and controllable by systematic thought.

When the divine element, formerly fused with science as sacred lore, with law as sacred custom and precept, and with art as sacred rite, song, and story, is thus set forth in its separate character, it seems a strangely empty essence, a mystery, a mere nothing,—for which, nevertheless, the most extravagant claims are made. When an attempt is made to describe or deal with it, it is necessary to fall back on fragments of thought, command, and symbol, and yet to deny that these contain what is intrinsically uncontainable in such vessels.

With better understanding it becomes known that these words of contrast, "behind, beyond," etc., indicate the relation of a *life* to its manifestations; as the life of an animal might be said to be behind its behavior the invisible and elusive source of its manifestations. The divine is empty as the self apart from its 'experience' is empty. The domain of religion in fact is a divine self, a Spirit which is as Subject to all finite things, persons, and arts as Object, and presumably to much else that these categories do not include. The significance of religion comes from the assumption that all the forces of the world are drawn together in foci which we call personalities or spirits; and these ultimately into one. It would be possible to deal with the whole of force, the Supreme Power, as religion proposes to deal with it only if this immense reality had its simple center, its I-am and I-will. In religion the will of man seeks union with the simple center of power which is 'beyond' and 'within' the world as the will of the world.

The extravagant claim of religion has been that union with God is itself a good, and indeed, the supreme and sufficient satisfaction of the will. But even if we can catch some hint of the metaphysical mystery of the religious domain, this claim is a new mystery. It is not obvious that union with anything is a supreme good, unless union means an alliance with the power therein vested. But religion has set its good in opposition to all other goods; it has turned its back upon the world in which the power of the gods themselves is manifested. It has renounced the world; and it has testified to the literalness of its intention by the most thorough asceticism. In its separation from art and from society, religion appears as the hostile critic of both, competing with them for the centering of human affections. Despite all this, some human beings have found in religion, as others have found in art, a career animated by a passion able to displace all others.

It is of course impossible for any one to live in the

world and maintain a complete enmity toward the goods of the world, the natural objects of his instinctive wishes. To live, hating life, even if for duty's sake one continued to eat, would be a slow suicide. There is strictly no such thing as 'thorough asceticism.' Externally, the position of the religious devotee is anomalous: he renounces society, family, the State, yet he enjoys the wealth, the friendship, the peace, provided by others. His position has therefore been called parasitic and insincere. On Kantian grounds he is immoral —so it might appear—for he cannot universalize his own maxim.

So it appears; but the appearance is mistaken. It is plausible only because one forgets that all living things have to renew their life from time to time by turning away from life, as one turns from waking to sleeping for the sake of being the more awake. If it is true that art and all social activities make use of a kind of capital whose source lies outside themselves, it would follow that one who had no other interest at heart than these would still be obliged by the nature of things alternately to pursue them and turn away from them.[1] Not alone individuals, but all art and all institutions must *save their lives by losing them*. And he that apparently renounces them all may be the one who is doing most for their conservation.[2]

[1] The theory of this necessary alternation is worked out more fully in *The Meaning of God*, chapters xxviii, xxxi, xxxii. See also R. C. Cabot, *What Men Live By*, Part IV, Worship.

[2] The argument is that there must be a distinct place in the economy of life for the cult of the absolute in its contrast with life, and if religion is the name of this place, the instinctive motive of religion

As for art, we have already seen that it depends upon
an eye for realities. The artist lives by what he can
truly see; and his eye for reality needs to be quickened
now and again, not by gazing harder into his work, but
by turning to a region in which the perception of reality
is simple and immediate. Such a region the individual
artist is likely to find in social intercourse; for the most
part, *persons* are the relatively real and relatively
available sources of all restoring of vision. But personal intercourse itself wears thin and shallow unless
it reverts to its own basis; all harks back at length to the
absolute, to religion. Whether at first or second hand,
the artist is pensioner upon the bounty of the mystic,
and not *vice versa*. The great ages of religion have preceded the great ages of art, and of science also, for
they were attending to the fertilization of the ground.

As for society and the State, it is the death of every
institution when it begins to regard itself as self-sufficient or worthy of devotion in its own right. The only
State that has a chance to survive upon this planet is
the State that knows that its power is not in itself, nor
its right. If the Sabbath was made for man, so is the
State. And the only obedience that can serve any State
well is the obedience of men who are servants of a
Greater. If religion taught men how to be independent
of the State, in an age when the State was everything,
it might well appear anti-political; and yet from the
spoils of this rebellion it has generated the modern

would be a specific craving due, whether so understood or not, to the
atrophy of social and æsthetic values, a *craving for the restoration of
creative power.*

State, the State of free individuals, which is a far greater thing. The Roman type of State *has* lost its life in trying to assert it, as such States always will— but *the State* lives—the State that has learned to subordinate its sovereign I-will to the will of God, which under certain conditions may be discerned in the will of the people.

For let us not mistake the meaning of liberalism and democracy: they do not mean that atomic individuals and their inherent rights are to be put above the community and its welfare, nor that any and every majority is right. They mean that the individual who finds and worships his God stands at the source of the community and its welfare. It is to the God-fearing individual and no other that the State must defer. And conversely, democracy without religion is neither a true nor a secure principle of social structure.

We thus recognize that religion, just in so far as it understands its own business, must insist on its contrast with all social goods, must have its asceticism and other-worldliness, *can never come in the guise of a social code*. Those who accuse Christianity, for example, of having no social code, may be bearing indirect witness to the fact that it knows the proper work of religion *per se*. Religion has no choice but to place the child in man, the total unexpressed self, above the institution; and to provide for that self a kingdom not of this world. For, after all, this Child is the strongest thing in the world, and no human interest can be strong or even safe which does not first do it reverence. The sacred law already perceived that the weak in man must control society. Religion cast loose from the law singles out this divine spark as that upon which every human value depends for its life.

It is because of this relation to *creativity* that religion, in the mere 'union with God,' has been able to satisfy the will to power in those who have understood its paradox. And for the most part asceticism, while renouncing power of one sort, has been regarded as a way to power of another sort. It has been a repression of partial expressions of the will in the interest of the whole; hence its total effect has been one of sublimation, not of repression of the will to power. In the history of religious asceticism this fact has been more or less clearly perceived: the devotees are not historically describable as men devoid of ambition; they have aimed at that supreme sort of power which works without tools, without violence, without self-assertion or competition, yet irresistibly, because all other powers are derivative or relatively unreal.

Thus in Vedantism. Brahmanism in this form abandons its interest in the deed and the law, and, as in the religion of Spinoza, empties all passion into the will to know. But the will to know is, in this form of religion, equivalent to the will to power; for, as it teaches, there is no power in the world save the power of knowledge *sub specie æternitatis,* the power of knowledge that I (and every particular being) am Brahm. This is the power that can strike off the chains of reincarnation; in it all lesser powers are believed to be included.

Buddhism still more completely and subtly defines

the goal of all passion as a passionless transparency of seeing. It attacks the self-element in all desire, demanding that the individual organism shall become the instrument of a perfect universality of indifference, to which neither existence nor yet non-existence shall appear as an object of strife. For even in the determined rejection of existence by the Brahmanic ideal a love for being lies concealed. It is evident, nevertheless, that this position is attractive to the Buddhist because of the initiation which it represents into the very moving principles of the cosmos; the love of power has not disappeared into something else, but has taken the form of an aspiration for metaphysical *status* with all the power over one's own destiny (and over other men's minds) therein implied.

Mediæval asceticism is at once less philosophic and more self-conscious. It has classified its own enemies— its tempters—with greater social insight, if not with keener psychological discrimination. It is driven to its aloofness neither by Paul nor by Plato, but by its own original self-scrutiny as we find it, for example, in Augustine. It was bound to declare war on the lust of the flesh, the lust of the eyes, and the pride of life, because of its own knowledge of the inadequacy of these goods to define the good of their own spirits. And if we may venture to interpret the recesses of the consciousness of the mediæval saints, as they made their painful and glorious *itinerarium mentis in Deum,* it was not without its own form of the will to power. Francis of Assisi has admitted us far into the mystery of sainthood in his confession of his unwillingness to find any beggar more poor than he. For he was the jealous lover of his lady Poverty; and through this devotion he claimed the devotion of others. Asceticism for these men, as for the ascetics of all ages, had the value of a *demonstration* in which the surrounding souls were necessary adjuncts. It intended to demonstrate that the religious satisfaction is an adequate substitute for all others; and therewith to announce a power of which the conquest of ordinary desire is a natural expression. To be able to endure is the badge of the entrance of the divine into the life of the flesh; it was a symptom of a metaphysical achievement which carried with it an ascendency over the spirits of men.

This ideal is sufficiently discredited; what we need to point out is that its errors are errors of insufficiency, not of a false direction. So far as human lust, greed, pugnacity, and the quest of social power were concerned, the religious ascetic has moved as one not seeing them in others, not admitting them into himself, and so not solving the problems which they raised. In the community which punished guilt he could with difficulty play his part, for the logic of pugnacity had been put behind him and forgotten. His religion had too far lost the sense of the institution and of the law to have part in their development. Hence religion in his form alone could neither leaven the community nor sustain itself; and so it largely failed of the power which was its own inward nerve and passion.

It did not entirely fail. In the forms we have mentioned, it has afforded much of the independent reality and freedom which the will needs; it has not been infertile. But worked-in as it has always been with the social life it has rejected, its organic relations thereto have been obscure, its 'moral substance' thin, and the 'objective arena' for the will to power evanescent. It is an essential part of religion, religion *per se* in its contrast with the rest of life: it is not the whole of religion. What religion may mean for the transformation of instinct must be sought in a more positive religious type.

PART VII

CHRISTIANITY

Argument

WE take Christianity as an example of religion which has no "social gospel," which is proclaimed in distinctly anti-worldly ascetic terms, —and which in the literal sense of those terms has little or no following in the world to-day,—which has had nevertheless a tremendous effect on human nature and social structures in the Western world, and which, because men do not understand how these two antithetical qualities can belong together, is little understood even by those who profess and profit by it.

Christianity rebukes pugnacity, and seems to offer a pacifistic gospel, which is variously twisted by men who desire to be Christians and yet insist on fighting. Rightly understood Christianity does not destroy but fulfills pugnacity, proposing the only course which will completely satisfy it. It lends no sanction to a meaningless nonresistance; nor does it set up an ideal for a distant future such as men to-day are not supposed to follow. It proposes to indicate for men of to-day *when* the other cheek is to be turned, and *when* it is our duty to resist evil.

Similar statements are to be made of its attitude toward sex-love and ambition. It rebukes them both, appears to suggest that it would be a better world if we could get on without either of them, and so leaves many of its followers in a morass of apologetic inconsistency. Its object, however, was not to eliminate sex-love and ambition but to define their nature, and to show the way to that complete satisfaction of the will which might find expression *either within or without* the family and the state. It proposes to indicate how men can achieve the essentially miraculous power of transforming the world about them and in so doing win their happiness.

On the psychological level, the recommendations of Christianity end in an impasse. To transform the world, or to 'save souls,' one must first be transformed oneself; and to be transformed, one must first realize his power to transform what is around him. The essence of Christianity lies not in its ethics, but in its answer to the question, how this saving of human nature is possible, an answer which is necessarily metaphysical.

What we can become depends in the last resort on what kind of world we live in. Society merely veils from us the impact of the wider cosmos. If there is, in fact, a living principle in reality, this veil is not wholly misleading; society at its best may act as a faulty symbol of the absolute. But it is only the ultimate nature of things which can determine how human nature may be, and ought to be, remade, or whether it is destined ever to be satisfied. Our destiny hangs on an issue of fact, a fit subject for religious dogma, and for individual recognition or rejection.

CHAPTER XL

WHAT CHRISTIANITY REQUIRES

MOST rules of life, secular or sacred, undertake to regulate behavior: they are addressed to the expression of instinct in action. But when original Christianity sums up its rule of life, it addresses itself to the feelings or affections. Its language is, Thou shalt love . . .; or, If any man come to me, and hate not his father . . . yea, and his own life also, he cannot be my disciple. Men are enjoined to 'abhor that which is evil,' to 'set their affections on things above.' It attacks what McDougall calls the second, or middle, region of instinct, not the third: the emotion, not the response.

The command of love to God and to neighbor is not new in Christianity: it is taken over from the code of Deuteronomy, where it occurs among many other precepts. What is new is the selective principle which lighted upon this requirement as the central and essential thing. And such a change of focus is a new moral venture; for one is committed to all the corollaries that can be drawn from one's first principle, and it is in them that its novel power and bearing will first appear.

The Sermon on the Mount may be regarded as a mass of such corollaries. Many of these sayings deal directly with expressions of pugnacity, others with the love of the sexes, others with ambition. And they retain, for the most part, the peculiarity of the first principle; their author regards himself as departing from tradition precisely in this, that the requirement is transferred from the outward appearance to the heart. Adultery is defined not in terms of conduct, but in terms of wish; murder is defined in terms of anger. And by way of hedging off the instinctive tendency to evade self-examination by relying on social approval, it is particularly enjoined that all supposed righteousness be kept hidden from the admiring eyes of men,— including oneself. It is commonly taken as characteristic of Christianity that it is concerned first of all for the 'inside of the cup.'

But there is something psychologically awry in a command to *feel*. It may be taken as evident that a person cannot at will love his neighbor, still less, his enemy. My feelings, of course, are my own, my most intimate property, and most property I can exchange or revise: but these possessions are not alienable nor directly alterable; they are closely identical with what I am, and hence appear to me as something given, inevitable. What I dislike, I dislike, and there is no help for it. Spencer accepts this fact as marking the limit of human freedom. If freedom means doing as we please, then we have freedom without limit; the trouble is (as we see when we reflect) we can do nothing else,—and we *cannot please as we please*. Hence a command to hate or to love seems, taken literally, to require the impossible.

The interpreters commonly surmount this difficulty by giving the words for feeling a practical meaning.

To love one's neighbor, it is said, has nothing to do with subjective or pathological states; we are simply called upon to perform those acts and assume those attitudes which would express good-will if we had it. We are to behave 'as if' we loved our neighbor. The rule of love is a rule of service. If I want to know what love would do in any case, the golden rule supplies complete directions without calling upon any feelings except those of natural egoism: let me think what I would want; then imaginatively reverse the situation and act accordingly, "for this is the law and the prophets." Thus the new principle becomes, like the old, a matter of conduct: the stroke of genius lies in the induction which finds the single simple principle, and establishes it in supreme control. It is through this philosophic mastery and sweep that the new righteousness exceeds the righteousness of the scribes and pharisees. Thus the law of love is interpreted pragmatically; love is as love does.

Is it possible that this pragmatic interpretation may exactly miss the characteristic thing about Christianity by pouring back into behavior that which the new idea proposed to lift out of it? Can I with any great success assume toward my neighbor a type of action in independence of my feeling? Granting the James-Lange theory of emotion its utmost, I may acquire a genial and kindly habit of mind which will serve to overcome social friction; but I should fear the moral result of a determined benevolence of bearing. Have we not seen enough of the officialized Christian manner? Certainly, in the extreme case, to force a mould of philanthropic action over a rebellious gorge could hardly claim for itself the sublime spontaneity of soul which is represented as saying in surprise, "Lord, when saw we thee an hungered and fed thee?" Strangely enough, this whole pragmatic interpretation smacks rather of Kant than of the sage of Nazareth. What if the demand of Christianity were intentionally and literally addressed to the affections?

The apparent psychological impossibility, I confess, seems to me quite in harmony with the general temper of this religion. Under the guise of extreme simplicity, it repeatedly demands the unattainable. Thus in order to enter the kingdom of heaven, one has but to become as a little child. Rebirth, or conversion, for Christianity, means a recovery of something which children have not yet lost. It might not occur to us to regard a child as a lover either of God or of man, but the child is certainly not a pragmatic servant: what can be said of him is that he has not crossed the Rubicon of that analytic and utilitarian intelligence which can think of persons as means and means only,—with all his puny self-assertion, his original sympathy with his enveloping personal world has not been broken. But we *have* crossed that Rubicon, and to recover the directness of relation of the child is not more easy than to 'love' in any other sense. It is hardly more easy than to be perfect,—and it is written, "Be ye therefore perfect."

As I understand Christianity, it needs little interpretation, for it means as nearly as possible what it says. It intends to state its requirement in terms of a complete transformation of the instincts; it is on this account that it has for us an extreme theoretical interest. We shall consider how it proposes to deal with the major passions of the private and the public orders.

CHAPTER XLI

CHRISTIANITY AND PUGNACITY

THERE is no better test of any rule of life than its way of settling accounts with pugnacity. For pugnacity is the instinctive agent of readjustment, especially of the deeper and abrupter readjustments: if human nature were so far transformed that there were no more readjustments to be made, within or without, pugnacity would of necessity disappear. The last conquest of pugnacity, before reaching the ideal state, would be the conquest of itself.

I

In society as we find it, the dialectic of experience has made a certain level of transformation of pugnacity habitual. It was only as the disposition to rush into strife was tamed that society on an ample scale became possible. And society abets this dialectic both by its rules and by making an adequate provision for all. Where there is plenty, men may be persuaded to accept their allotment in peace (so long as they have faith in the fairness of the allotment); but where there is scarcity or the suspicion of injustice, there is a tendency to revert to the primitive methods, with their risks and hopes. But the most orderly and successful society is still surcharged with pugnacious behavior in various 'moral equivalents.' Apart from competition, discussion, and various sorts of peaceful rivalry, there is the pervasive activity of the *critical judgment*. Wrath against defective persons and institutions, by being circuited through the processes of conceptual thought, is made over into an energy for their repair rather than their destruction. Criticism, armed with various weapons of peaceful efficiency, is the social ultimate in the transforming of pugnacity.

I say the social ultimate, for the injunction of Christianity, "Judge not," cannot be observed in human society. Not alone because progress depends on the perpetual work of this negative impulse, with others; but also because to be accurately judged and measured is a vital interest of every self-conscious being. He who wants power wants self-knowledge; and he who wants self-knowledge wants criticism, whether or not he likes it. It is an essential ingredient of that craving for intercourse with our kind which we sometimes dub the 'instinct of sociability' that we anticipate this mutual appraisal, "sizing up," incipient locking of horns, the Carlylian question, "Can I kill thee or canst thou kill me?"; though all such valuing and appraising implies placing in a series, a denial of absolute worth in the respect measured, reduction from an end to a means.

It is in the 'hard' public order that the activity of the critical judgment is most evident; for there the standards are most objective and definite. But the critical judgment of the private order is most searching. Here it takes a form which, for lack of a general name,

we may call *education* in its widest sense. Education, in
this sense, is not simply a deliberate transaction which
takes place between one generation and another. It occurs whenever two human beings are associated, and
without necessary intention. It is the transaction
through which, by a hundred avenues of expression, A's
total consciousness of B becomes a part of B's self-consciousness. This transaction is always selective, always
critical, and always mutual.

Ideals of education are held before us in which no
adverse criticism should appear, but all be positive and
encouraging. And so far as the expressing of our judgment is concerned, it is a principle of the greatest use
(because it is nearer the truth) to dwell on what persons
are rather than on what they are not. It is also a valuable principle to express few judgments rather than
many. But these are questions of art, not of substance:
and in regard to the substance of the social judgment,
it is vain to evade the negative element, however it is
conveyed. For the negative element is *there;* we must
be true to our own aversions. And further, we cannot
outwit the need of it in the dynamics of education: to
be conscious, sometimes acutely, of what we are steering from, is a part of our knowledge of what we are
steering to; and the elemental spurs of fear and rue
and pain are the ever present obverses of our hope
and confidence. An assumed uncondemning or wholly
beaming attitude, unless it retains the permanent possibility of instant challenge, becomes an affectation of
the godlike which departs more or less from the veritable and evokes a like departure in the addressee, rob-

bing intercourse of reality and minimizing the meaning of all language.

The most effective educating agencies known to us are free from all conscious scruples on the score of criticism. They are the spontaneous activities of those who have just emerged from some stage of relative defect, and take a corresponding intensity of interest in denouncing that stage in others. The boy who has just now learned to swim cannot sufficiently emphasize the contrast between himself and those who still flounder in the water. Without this temper and its sting, the world of boys would be robbed of its immense developing power, and, at the same time, of its attraction: it is this temper that creates around the horizon of effort a surcharged sense of the importance of just this achievement. Under this pressure the latent powers rise sufficiently high to leap the barrier: a little less concern may mean permanent failure to meet the last inch of the requirement, and hence to find what one's powers actually are. Nowhere could society afford to dispense with the zeal of recent converts, with their unsullied sense of the magnitude of their achievement. Their estimate is probably truer than ours who look on from a greater distance; for who most justly appreciates the length of a mile,—he who remembers it after a day's rest, or he who has just finished the last of twenty? We cannot always secure for our own efforts the notable spur of necessity, nor do we forever need it; but if we are deprived of the lash of a sufficiently critical social judgment, we instinctively try to replace it by invented task-masters within ourselves. And until we shall have finished our education to the extent of ceasing to be social beings, this replacement is never quite complete.

Thus society expects its members to be critical of one another, both in personal and official relations, while conscious of the dominant power of the positive social bond. The health of social movement depends on the maintenance by individual wills of a certain distance or alienation from all that invites to total acquiescence, or absolute social satisfaction.[1] Nor is there any necessary kinship between an aliveness to defect, which is the very engine of personal growth, and a cynical temper. But it remains true that the critic feels himself to some extent, and somewhere, criticised by his own criticism. It is only in the ironical mockery of a Socrates or in the denunciations of a Christ that the separative judgment loses the quality of a cry of pain. This is not the final transformation of pugnacity. We may well long for a world in which "Judge not" were possible.

II

Christianity reveals no solicitude for the necessities of the social order. Its precepts are explicit, and Tols-

---

[1] No account of the philosophy of change is complete which refers it alone to the *élan vital* with its perpetual creativity, nor yet to the Unmoved Mover that beckons all men to its absolute good. To these must be added the driving power of the standards and systems which are due to the action of human analysis and concept-making; and which by ceaselessly reminding man of what he is not, through criticism, exclusion, and negation, spur him in infinite sequence toward their own goals.

toy understood them: resist not evil, love your enemy, judge not, recompense evil with good. These precepts define not so much a transformation of pugnacity as an abolition of it, together with the whole process of social measurement and of justice itself. And so far as these commands are provided with a commentary, they seem not alone to admit but to assert an abandonment of justice. For the commentary explains that these principles are one aspect of the perfection of "your Father which is in heaven," which perfection we are summoned to make our own: and this perfection on God's part is manifest in this, that "He maketh his sun to rise on the evil and the good, and sendeth rain on the just and on the unjust." In other words, that which to some minds appears as the total moral indifference of mechanical nature is here held up as the perfection of God. What is this but to make the absence of justice, the indiscriminate treatment of good and evil, the supreme law of the spiritual world?

To argue thus is to forget that what is mechanical behavior in the inorganic realm is no longer mechanical in the realm of stimulus and response. The ocean responds neither to the blandishments nor to the threats of Xerxes; but the mechanisms of his own menials would react to the one by smiles and to the other by signs of terror. So the response of amiableness to the amiable approach, and the response of enmity to the inimical approach, while it has the semblance of justice, and the sanction of the æsthetic sacred law, is the type of a moral mechanism. And to refuse to respond in kind, while it may seem to return to the indifference of nature, *may be the precise opposite of a mechanical attitude.* The attacker expects your resistance; if you do not resist, your rejection of his challenge may enter the situation with the force of a *new idea.*

Like all surprises, the absence of resistance where resistance was expected, would necessarily arouse some new idea in the aggressor by way of reviewing the situation in his mind. His new idea, however, might be one of several: he might conclude that you were too dead to fight, or that you were too much alive to fight. Christianity depends on the possibility of putting significance into the latter idea. And the persistent refusal to criticise or to retaliate can be a sign of more life, rather than less, *only when it is a response to a greater degree of truth.* It must mean that the self which has defects or which does injury is seen to be other than the real self; and the non-resistance constitutes an appeal from the apparent self to the real self, or from the actual self to the self that may be. In this case, it is not injustice, but it is justice to the living and changeable. It is a type of justice undiscovered by the Greek, for it is based neither on equity nor on proportionality to any self that exists. Greek justice, distributive or retributive, took men statically, as they presented themselves. This type of justice refuses to take a man at his own estimate of himself; it insists on the self of a more nearly absolute estimate, the self that *must be,* and which this resolve of the non-resisting will will help to bring into being. It is a justice done for the first time to the plasticity and responsiveness of human nature toward our own wills: it is an absolute, or creative, justice.

And this is the only type of response that can finally satisfy pugnacity itself. For what pugnacity wants is not simply the destruction of evil: it wants the evil will to hate and destroy its own evil. The element of hate in fighting and punishment and criticism is directed toward making the guilty consciousness consume its own iniquity; and to this end the instinctive ferocity of gesture and grimace make for forcing the evil-doer by suggestion into a momentary abhorrence and fear of his own crime. But the evil will will not hate itself, unless it first becomes the good will: hence pugnacity is not satisfied unless the replacement of the evil by the good takes place. And when it takes place, that which was to be hated has disappeared. Hence, what pugnacity wants is to *make the man over:* it wants to create the conditions for the free self-rejection of the evil. And for this act of creation, the absolute justice of "Love your enemies" is a necessary demand.

III

Christianity intends to impose upon pugnacity the interpretation of a creative impulse. This is its final transformation. And if we have rightly discerned the meaning of these precepts, we are in a position to judge whether they intend to do away at once with social criticism, or social justice, or war. Let me mention two or three principles which will govern our decision on these questions.

1. The forgiving, or non-resisting, or enemy-loving

attitude has its entire justification in the 'new idea' which it conveys to the wrong-doer. It is a language: and the whole virtue of a language is that it is understood. The attitude itself, we saw, was outwardly indistinguishable from apathy or indifference: it must by all means distinguish itself from apathy or indifference, or it is a failure. He who so uses non-resistance that it is mistakable for passivity, weakness, cowardice, or folly, uses it unworthily; and shows thereby that he knows not what it means.

Letting myself be cheated or abused through lethargy or lack of time or courage to make an issue cannot be claimed as an exhibition of divine perfection. Unless I am, in fact, so much of a seer as to be a lover of my enemy, it is both futile and false to assume the behavior of love: we can generally rely on the enemy to give such conduct its true name. And love of this sort is seldom possible in the more transitory and impersonal relations of life: it is in the quieter contacts of man with man that this creative language has its best chance of being heard. In the dealings of a composite national mind with another composite national mind, I believe that there is a possibility of using the language of creative good-will: but the conditions are harder to realize, and the penalties for an enforcement of falsely affectionate conduct deservedly severe.

2. Not only must the user of this language consider whether he can use it honestly; he must consider also whether he has a listener. It is sometimes necessary to induce a quiescent frame of mind in the other before any language can 'get across.' There is such a thing

in the world as persistent and self-assured cynicism; and there is such a thing as determined bad-will. It is chiefly these which make wars necessary. War is not to be understood as necessarily a negation of the principle of Christianity; a just war is an attempt to create the conditions under which the opponent is *disposed to listen* to the language of the still, small voice.

3. The creative attitude is not meant to displace but to subordinate the critical attitude, and its varieties, the competitive, the punitive, the warlike attitudes.

Antagonism is not an intrinsic evil; it is an evil only when it is not included within a fundamental agreement. If it is understood that the contestants have shaken hands, they may attack each other with entire good-will. What would become of the game of chess under the rule, "If any one would take away your castle, give him your queen also"? If an abstractly devised era of good-feeling destroys the era of good chess, or of any more serious competition wherein men are fairly tested, it will not long remain an era of good feeling. Politeness may be regarded as an artful assumption of universal benevolence for the purpose of a restricted social undertaking: it does not rule out all contests, but it rules out those that would disturb the predominantly æsthetic character of the limited occasion. Just in so far as politeness oversteps its sphere, it becomes the covering of the bitterest hostility, that which fences from beneath the cloak of formal friendliness. Amenity without opposition becomes empty: even lovers weary of it. The force of the rule of love in common social interchange is directed, not to eliminating the critical judgment, but rather to making firm that prior understanding according to which we unite in the will to stand or fall by the rules of the proposed contest.

Thus, the world must have both systems. Contest is a peril to the soul; criticism cannot exist without some self-condemnation: but the salvage of human nature lies not in abandoning them, but in giving them the true setting. Religion has the office of referring men to the absolute; not the absolute which removes them from the relative, but the absolute which by establishing a point of rest within the flux of change, gives all change, with its effort and its hostilities, its total meaning.

For this reason I cannot agree with those interpreters of Christianity who say that Christianity sets up an ideal for an ideal state of society, not for the present. Christianity is never more clearly a rule for immediate adoption than in its dealing with pugnacity. It expresses the final satisfaction of the will of the fighter in the midst of every good fight.

CHAPTER XLII

CHRISTIANITY AND SEX-LOVE

NOT a few lovers of peace are now reminding us of the doctrine of non-resistance in Christianity, urging us in its name to forget the arts of war. It hardly occurs to these persons to carry the same logic into the region of sex-morality. The more consistent abstractionists, like Tolstoy, perceived that the letter of the new law is not less hostile to the family and to the State than to the use of force. If pacifism quotes Christianity, it may well learn from Tolstoy either to renounce sex-love together with physical resistance, or to find a place for both.

On the meaning and destiny of sex-love Christianity has little to say. But if we read together with the documents the tendencies that worked themselves out in the early communities, there can be no question of its preference for virginity. The monastic ideal is implicit in its standards. The sword which it brought was to divide between a man and his family as well as his possessions: "Leave all" for the sake of the new kingdom,—this injunction was meant and taken in deadly earnest, and without this intense singleness of purpose early Christianity would not have done its work in the world. It would not be untrue to the sense of Christianity to set up beside the "Judge not," i.e., Know not enmity or defect, a corresponding precept,

"Know not sex," i.e., Regard all persons as persons, and never as men or women.

We cannot say in advance that it is impossible to comply with such a precept. The life of sex, in the social order, is hardly as inevitable for the individual as is pugnacity: there are those, and their number increases, who seem to make out a complete life without it. It is true that the psychological function of the family must somehow be performed if men and women are to retain their normal balance. But it is not at all obvious that this function must be performed *by sex-love itself;* for while sex is the deepest of the hungers, it is also the most versatile in its capacity for substitution or sublimation. The Freudians are doubtless right in saying that such a need cannot safely be repressed. But we want to know *what it is that may not be repressed.* We would do well to enquire more carefully what sex-love in its own natural self-teaching, or dialectic, means.

I

It would seem the first point of wisdom in dealing with this question to be clear that the need which we call sex-love *has a meaning,* like every other instinct; and that to find this meaning requires an effort of interpretation. The use of the word 'instinct' here is likely to carry with it the greatest volume of sophistry; for it is so easy to assume and so far from the truth that we know off-hand what an instinct wants. It is impossible to read the psychological meaning of any instinct in its biological context, and more particularly the instinct of sex. The biological meaning is more likely to be found from the psychological end.

What the psychological function of sex-love is we have already vaguely outlined in describing it as the passion of the private order, corresponding to ambition in the public order. It is the life of the residual self, unexpressed in the public order. The sexes are fitted to recognize more of the subconscious and growing in one another than can ordinarily be appreciated between members of the same sex; they are drawn into a protective attitude toward whatever is groping and 'unsaved' in the other self. An extension of 'sympathy,' love appears as a premonition of a power to confer and to receive life at a profounder level than that of words and services. Thus the craving of sex on its psychological side might be roughly described as a craving for subconscious respiration.

In this respiration, the quest of power, visible as an impulse toward bringing the ineffective self into effect, is paradoxically mingled with an impulse toward complete *self-abandonment*. Passion always means the reference of the whole of life to a new focus, and hence a thoroughgoing abandonment of rival foci; but in the case of love, the distinctive joy of abandonment is prepared by a recurrent need which no one escapes. I mean the need to denounce from time to time the expression one finds, not alone in public service, but in all social activity and in the language of all conventions and of all intellectual concepts,—to denounce these not as false but as inadequate, and to break through into a region of expression which is immediate and entire, and yet a language, a communion with another self. Such a subordination of the relatively futile to a relatively adequate language, the life of sex with its symbols seems to promise. Intimacy and the symbols of intimacy, the throwing together of all concrete fortunes,—the fortunes of thought, of the plans, labors, and economies of life, and of the physical being also,—radicalism of this sort offers a prospect of complete release for that deeper will which is forever brooding over its visible career and finding it vanity and vexation of spirit,—as taken alone, it is.

This prospective release of the deeper strata of personality in the lover is due to *a discovery*—the 'stimulus' of his love—an item of knowledge, if you will; for, like all instinct, love has at its core a characteristic perception or intuition. This knowledge is, in the first place, simply his own newly awakened perception, his 'sympathetic intelligence' of what the beloved being, apart from all acquired excellences, is. This knowledge is presumably not scientifically new, except in so far as it is a knowledge of that unique individual. What makes the experience one of love is that this unique acquisition of the gift of sight with reference to that unique person is simply the lover's initiation into an old and well-known mystery. What is it, then, that he sees?

The answer, so far as it is general, may be found in asking what, after all, that being, or any other conscious being, is. And what is such a being if not a process of thoughtful and active intercourse with its own environment? To perceive such a being would be to perceive a process of dealing with the world, and thus to see *the world* through that being. What love sees does not stop short of the realities: its horizon, its stimulus, is metaphysical. The truth seems to be that the minds of men and women are so made that each, by the aid of the other, may see farther into the universe than either can see by itself or by the aid of others of its own kind. And what one seems to see in the other is largely seen *through* the other: what appears to be a quality of the individual turns out to be a quality of the world. This is not to deny these qualities of the individual, however; for the beauty and worth of a person are not separable from the world of objects into which that person habitually looks.

But whatever the content of this half-personal, half-metaphysical vision, the first impulse and meaning of love, like that of art in response to the beautiful, is to possess what it has seen by reproducing it. It undertakes to edit, portray, proclaim, give out in some way its discovery, and preferably to a worthy rather than to an unworthy audience, hence (with the characteristic inward-turning of love) commonly to the beloved person himself. Thus the will to power seems reduced and tamed to the idle form of *praise,* and spends the energy that might have moved the world in adornment, idealization, and numerous busy offices called into being not for their utility, but solely for the element of praise which they embody. But praise, it may be noted, under the guise of service, is still a subtle taking-possession, an assertion of comprehension and right. And all taking-possession in the progress of love may (with allowance for feeble terms where all terms are feeble) be described as a development of praise: with increasingly intimate care and service there is consistent enlargement of that assumed right until it ventures to include in its scope the entire gamut of the being of the beloved, from thought to immediate existence, and to render back this entire gamut as something known, comprehended, praised,—and yet with the imprint upon it of that once alien will, the consciousness of the lover and knower.

Especially in dealing with the meaning of love, the notion of 'power' threatens to become inept. For it is precisely in love that the whole conscious interest in power seems neutralized and rendered latent by the dominant interest in mutuality, in getting rid of all distance and otherness. No doubt the lover comes into a kind of incidental power or confidence toward the world at large—if he is accepted; he may even be said to taste greatness: but the greatness is conferred upon him, the power is borrowed rather than his own. Between the lovers, also, there is a wholly mutual sense of dignity which comes from the awareness of validity: with their other metaphysical knowledge, the lovers also know that between them—not in either of them—*the tribe is present;* the promise and potency of humanity as a self-continuing stream of conscious life is, if not in their keeping, still within reach of their conjuring. But what thus seems their power is not their own: it is the power of nature and of society.

But I would still say that just because of this vicariousness and latency, the will to power here notably comes to its own. For power is realized not primarily in self-assertive exertion, but rather in taking advantage of the hierarchical arrangement of the powers of the world, affecting large issues by touching their springs. The technique and strategy of love is just this, that it works back, so to speak, toward the focus of the world's forces, the tilting point of the avalanche. It touches the curve of life at the moment of its bending from the rise to the decline, where but an increment of strength suffices to work the miracle and hold life away from the gravitation of mortality. Thus, instinctively, love finds itself assuming for a brief moment the actual work of a god: it undertakes, while acting as a channel for universal life, to be an original *maker of life*.

II

These undertakings, I say, are incipient in the first impulse of love. But in carrying out its primary ambitions, love finds subjective satisfactions and pleasures, and on account of these, love, as a matter of racial and typical if not of universal experience, *suffers a fall*. The fall is that it adopts as an end the subjective joy that it has discovered. It limits its horizon; and mingling an overweight of sense in its meaning, it becomes selfish. It draws circles, creates an imaginary world of two, and thinks that all the sufficiencies of the universe are contained within it. No love begins by seeing in love primarily a natural desire; but some loves end that way, and most at some time or other tend to.

What forces love out of this circle as a rule is not abstract idealism but simply the experience of self-defeat, i.e., the natural dialectic. It finds that it cannot retain even its own narrow type of satisfaction, because it has mistaken its meaning. It is forced to break out of that circle for the very breath of life it sought there. This is a critical juncture in the adventure of love. For while love now knows beyond peradventure that it has been disappointed, it may not see clearly where the repair of its fortunes lies. One of the most inviting of hypotheses is that it has chosen the wrong individual as an object of devotion. What it thought it saw in that person is clearly not there. It may accordingly betake itself to *wandering,* as a cure for its confinement in what is subjective and poor of meaning. Fickleness is right and 'natural' in all that it denies,—it denies that *that* was satisfying. But fickleness is more than likely to be false in what it affirms. It has a negatively pragmatic value in the course of the dialectic of experience: that which does *not* work, is not the real thing.

III

It is at this point that social pressure comes to the rescue. The office of social pressure is to force disillusioned love into another inference than that of natural wandering. Its satisfaction was lost, not because its first vision was deceptive, but because it has by its own self-will obscured that first vision. What it first saw was an independent soul; and that soul has now been reduced to dependence upon itself. What one has wearied of is the limited and clinging lover, having no independent grasp on absolute reality and value, and therefore opaque to what was once visible through him. To that first spirit it could minister with pleasure, or rather, by necessity; to the present being it can bring only requests for its own satisfaction. It is not that the person has changed, but that the horizon, from which all personal worth is derived, has shrunk. The only being you can love is the being who has an independent object of worship, and that holds you out of your self-indulgence to a worship of that same object. The health and meaning of love depend on that common devotion to a common divinity. Now society insists on a part of this horizon; it reminds marriage of its responsibility to the public order; it takes hostages against too easy wandering, providing that any retreat shall be as public and as well considered as the original commitment. It thus compels a fickle impulse at least to re-examine its theory of the case, and so provides for a time the external form of loyalty, in the good hope that the pair will supply the substance thereof from their own living resources. But of itself, society cannot provide this substance, and its pressure in favor of its conventional family life, helpful to great majorities in the quest of their own individual meanings, leaves the few without a guide and empty, mere rebellious conformists, or non-conformists. Society cannot revive a dead or comatose affection; it cannot so much as explain to the arid ex-lover what it is that he wants.

Such explanation is the work of the philosopher; and Plato came nearer to fulfilling this office than most other thinkers of ancient or modern times. All love, said he, as it becomes aware of its meaning, is a demand for immortality through "creation in the medium of beauty." Ignorant love forgets that its horizon is immortality: enlightened love realizes that its meaning is only completely found when personal and family relations are left behind; it is found in that metaphysical element which all love more or less dimly reveals, in the quest and transmission by teaching of the knowledge of what is absolutely real. It is in the giving of that *second birth* of which the Brahmans taught, rather than in the giving of the first birth, that the full satisfaction of love is to be found. Thus sex-love, completely understood, has no psychological need of physical relationship nor of marriage; and Plato seems to speak in total accord with the voice of early Christianity.

But there are few to-day who accept the interpretation of Plato as complete. Nor does it seem to me complete, nor equivalent to the purport of Christianity.

IV

To reach a completer view of the meaning of love, I must recall that in that stage of the dialectic which we described as the 'fall of love,' there is a gain as well as a loss of meaning. And the element of meaning here gained is not included in Plato's interpretation.

For when, by self-indulgence, the circle of love narrows, the beloved is at times within the circle, a fellow conspirator in the limitation; and at times outside the circle. And when the eye tempered by self-interest sees the other in this external fashion, it sees him impersonally and critically. His defects are visible, not at all for the first time (for love is not blind, it is merely confident), but in the new light of a problem,— a problem which the private order must share with the public order. These defects are likely to become the object of a suffering criticism, the type of criticism which condemns the critic, but which, none the less, has its own measure of truth. In brief, the evolution of love begins to include within itself, more or less unavowedly, a segment of the development of pugnacity. And pugnacity always deals with the concrete; it is a highly contemporaneous and individualizing impulse. It does not permit the growth of love to take a Platonic direction from the more material to the more ethereal objects of contemplation. It reminds it of its highly particular historic task. Whatever its meaning, it must include all that a completely transformed pugnacity means: it must learn the art of recovering in the other the absolute self disposed to reject its own imperfection.

Love is the best agent for the instruction of pugnacity; but pugnacity, in turn, is (in some form or other) a very fit agent for the instruction of a flagging love. What it has to teach is no more than what love all along knew, namely, its own interest in the removal of defects from the beloved, its uncompromising jealousy of all such defects, its wholly sufficient power to overcome them. This is love's responsibility; but let me say that in the integrity of the natural impulse of love, it is an ingredient of love's enthusiasm. Love does not want a perfect object: it wants an object to

be made over, fit for its own power of re-creation.
The meaning of the great passion is not found primarily in bringing forth a race of new beings who
shall realize in time all that was lacking to their pro-
genitors. Its meaning, like that of religion itself, is a
claim upon present experience. It means nothing less
than the destruction of what is recognized as mortal
—I do not say in the other, but in both, and in their
mutual life—and its re-creation in the light of whatever beauty it has seen. But its impulse to destroy
that mortality and to reproduce that beauty is no
more one of abstract immortalization than is the work
of an artist: it is a very concrete and present aim.
More than this, such a transformation is what love
actually, though subconsciously, and more or less permanently, achieves.

Thus the dialectic of love reaches an interpretation
more active than Platonic and more absorbing of the
entire soul-and-body entity. Love is that region of life
which exists in giving life; and this means developing the possibilities of a mutual existence both of sense
and of idea. It is satisfied only when its power can
work in a completely historic form. It ministers to
the soul, but always by way of body and estate. Its
first impulsive certainty of power it must replace by
a more conscious and responsible certainty. But if the
interest in life-giving sinks into tolerance and habitual
modus vivendi, love is hibernating or dead. It is better
that it should remain consciously critical. For love is
by necessity aggressive and originative.

V

Christianity sets itself at the goal of this dialectical development, careless as always of the relations of the goal to the usual social process. It sets an absolute standard for the relations of men and women; but it hardly suggests that this standard is to be reached through any such course of experience as we have depicted, still less through the ascent of the Platonic ladder. Its teaching may be stated somewhat as follows:

1. By assuming, as Christianity does, the non-necessity of marriage for complete satisfaction of the will, it teaches by implication that love is capable of complete 'sublimation.' But it is noteworthy that in the typical transformation of love adopted by Christianity, the element of physical 'ministration' is never lost. It is through the washing of feet, the tendance of the injured, the breaking of the box of ointment (not in any sense a useful social service), the cup of cold water, that the repressed wish finds an outlet. As a matter of history, the notable trend of Christian energies into philanthropic efforts during the first few centuries is the manifestation of a humanitarian passion sufficiently profound to drain the entire life of affection into its channel; and philanthropy is not Platonism.

But it is likewise characteristic of Christianity that the personal ministration was never allowed to shrink to the level of purely objective and useful service. The cup of cold water is given 'in the name' of something believed to be of cosmic importance and imperative upon the completer will of the person served. The situation is given its own horizon of meaning, unobtrusively in the main, by a sign, by the wearing of a uniform, or by nothing visible at all; but the purpose is never relinquished of remaking the mind while remaking the body. Love, to Christianity as to Plato, means the will to confer immortality. And apart from that intent, the legacy of 'charity' imposed upon our present social order begins to appear as a wretched substitute for justice, and a mockery of all honest love. The justification, and the only justification, of charity is its metaphysical import. The future lies rather with the useless gift, the box of ointment, i.e., with the increasingly adequate sublimation of love in art, the disinterested, but yet physical, tendance of the immortal in man.

Philanthropy and the production of beauty, both creative activities, are the two chief social equivalents of sex-love. But Christianity proposes them as complete equivalents only when they are elements in its own form of the religious life. This form is one which involves a concrete union of 'ministry' with *worship,* and an alternation between the two. In the usual treatment of the subject by psychologists of religion it is commonly assumed that the ministry is the substantial, and worship the insubstantial, idle, and perhaps harmful element. But without worship, both philanthropy and art merge too completely with the public order. Worship is the recollection of the spirit and the renewal of that consciousness of meaning which is to be carried into the administration. It is an effort to shake off the dust and illusion of a partly secularized consciousness, and to recover a sense (not a 'mere idea') of the quality of value, of beauty perhaps, in the ultimate reality of the world. It has no other object than that same metaphysical truth that love catches glimpses of—this objective truth is the primary bond of identity between them. And if worship attains its end, it is the realization of what love through its symbols perpetually seeks.

Thus we confirm the existence of an analogy of the life of religion with the life of sex, which has been much dwelt upon of late as though it were a new discovery. But what it means is a very ancient insight; and that insight is not that religion is nearly identical with sex, but that sex, as it finds its own meaning, approaches identity with religion. The same is obviously true of patriotism, and only less obviously true of ambition and of every other positive human impulse; but the relationship is particularly direct in the case of sex-love, first because of its occasionally clear and confessed metaphysical horizon, and second because of the natural rhythm or alternation in its life, akin to that of religion just pointed out.

A right understanding of this truth has distinct social importance at present, when marriage as a career is increasingly a matter for deliberate choice or rejection, and still the absence of marriage is felt as a loss of selfhood. The right understanding seems to me to be contained in this simple proposition: that the only thing about a human will that needs to be satisfied is the *whole will;* and that religion is the satisfaction of the whole will, the will to power in its inclusive form. Apart from this fact, one can understand that it might become a social theorem claiming psychological support that no substitution for the life of sex is possible, and that the social evil or evils are necessarily always with us. With this fact, the consideration of any desirable social changes is at once freed from the false and intrusive note of 'necessity.' It may be remarked in passing that particularly in this matter what we imagine to be necessary is the chief agent in creating a necessity; and conversely a presumption of non-necessity, supported by a psychological understanding of the principle of 'interpretation,' may well be the first step to emancipation.

2. But the absolute which Christianity prescribes in this field, like its other absolutes, intends to live with the relative, not to displace it. The final meaning of sex-love is one which is to be held within marriage, and within all the other relations of men and women. There are a few religions (think of the religion of Schopenhauer, of the Shakers, of Tolstoy's later days) that have attempted to exclude the life of sex; but Christianity is not among them. The possibility of sublimation which it asserts is such as to set individuals free to choose their own destiny, celibate or not, as otherwise they would hardly be free. It is certainly not such as to prescribe either type of destiny.

In the relations of men and women, what Christianity explicitly demands is not defined in terms of any given type of behavior; it is the meaning it is concerned with. It is a question of how one "looketh upon a woman." And the sense of its legislation seems to be this: that any behavior is right behavior which is consistent with looking upon her as a person having a destiny of her own to work out, a possibility of immortality which depends in part upon your own attitude. Any behavior is right which is consistent with this: no social constraint need deflect the conduct of one who sees always as far as the "pilgrim soul" in the person of his neighbor. But an attempt to bring this meaning into the relationship will quickly exclude many varieties of behavior. There is more room for self-deception here than in most other regions of behavior in declaring freedom from particular social rules for the sake of an alleged general meaning or spirit. But the meaning proposed by Christianity supplies a test with a cutting edge if one is disposed to use it. All of love is right when it takes for its meaning the giving of life, i.e., such life as can satisfy a human will.

CHAPTER XLIII

CHRISTIANITY AND AMBITION

EARLY Christianity had no overt hostility to the regular business of State life. It paid its taxes and its debts, observed the civil laws, baptized centurions and magistrates without expecting them to abandon their callings, and on occasion appealed to Cæsar. As to the public *corvées,* it proposed that if any man, i.e., an officer, compel you to go with him one mile, the proper spirit would pay a double stint.

Yet it would be vain to read into these occasional signs of acquiescence any adoption of the purposes of the public order. Whatever are the ordinary objects of ambition,—precedence, wealth, office, public power, —they are relegated with an almost contemptuous gesture to the unimportant: "for after all these things do the Gentiles seek."

A new ambition, however, enters upon the heels of the old. The spiritual life of the universe has its own structure, its own focus, and as it were its own court and order of nobility. And for him who would be first in that realm there is a maxim: let him be servant of all. Ambition is recognized, and in the same breath annulled. It is by lighting on the existing paradoxes of the will (not by inventing them) that Christianity was able to carry the art of life beyond the Greek level.

Ambition faced with this reversal of its natural aim

is compelled to undergo a metamorphosis and acquire a more stable meaning.

But does the change amount to anything more than translating into another world the essential aims of the present? A longer aim may easily reverse a present policy. Treasures are to be laid up, as usual, but in a safer place. One is to become cosmically intelligent and therefore cosmically prudent. A motive in which one detects strands of instinctive self-assertion and instinctive fear, stirred by perceiving the perishableness of all finite goods, is to lead men to seek in an imperishable good the absolute security of the soul. I am not among those who find prudence an objectionable virtue; nor who reject the interest in personal survival as unseemly in a mortal. One who loves life at all is forever becoming more deeply involved in it; and the self-conscious lover of life cannot otherwise than will his own continuous existence. To desire the saving of one's soul in this sense is a necessary desire;[1] and under these circumstances, it is no high merit to remain indifferent regarding ways and means.

But prudence is not the noblest of the virtues, nor the last word of Christianity. Buddhism had long ago detected the moral danger of an indulgent heaven-quest, and had sought to make ambition commit suicide in a selflessness without desire. It sought dispassion; and it sought it by the way of compassion, because

[1] A fact which is not altered by the results of any questionnaire, especially of a questionnaire circulated among the more sophisticated and self-challenging members of the community, as in the enquiry by Professor James H. Leuba, reported in *The Belief in God and Immortality*.

thereby the root of individuality was best killed. But it is no easy task to destroy in oneself all desire, or all the *skandhas* that attach to individual existence; and if one enters upon and persists in this noble and arduous 'eightfold path,' it must be through some powerful impulsion. In truth, *ambition is the essence of religion.* There is always possible to men a life of least resistance, taking oneself and the world as one finds them, accepting the horizon of nature. If one repudiates this and takes upon himself the pains of a Buddha, it is through some deep-laid passion, which the goal of Buddhism, as defined to our Western ears, hardly explains. If religion destroys ambition, it destroys itself.

The solution of Christianity perceives this principle. It recognizes as does Buddhism the faultiness of heaven-seeking; but it seeks to remedy that fault by proceeding in the opposite direction,—by carrying ambition to the limit of its own meaning, giving a final answer to the question, *What does ambition want?*

The dialectic of experience has shown us from many angles how the quest for power tends to revise its aim; how the pursuit of power-over becomes the pursuit of power-for. As power must have its object, it is so far dependent upon the existence of the object, and must seek its welfare. At the limit, the exercise of power is indistinguishable from service; it consists in giving or in adding to the being of another. Christianity places itself at this point and defines, as the goal of the transformation of ambition, *the conferring of spiritual life.* The compassion which in Buddhism is the corrective of the self-centered bent of the will is present here also, but with a different meaning. The compassion of Buddha looks on the world of men as caught in the error of individuality and its consequent suffering, and in releasing them wins its own release. The compassion of Christianity looks on a world of men as lacking individuality and hence unable to meet suffering, and in confirming their selfhood confirms its own.

Ambition in this form is the most characteristic product of Christianity in the field of behavior. It is the passion for the historic spread of the new community, or in more personal form, the "passion for souls." Nothing is more dominant in the early history of this cult than the willingness to suffer, to be despised, to endure all things, if by any means some could be persuaded to become members of the community, the kingdom of heaven in the guise of a militant church on earth.

In this transformation, ambition does not lose the other-worldly sweep of the transcendental prudence we were speaking of. It is still laying hold on that other world, but with more radical power than is implied in simply attaining future status there. It is indeed far more ambitious. It lays hold on that world with the intent of so much present mastery of its quality and principle as to weave them into the fabric of human history.

This passion for souls we have described as the final transformation of the ambition of the public order; but it is evidently more than that. It is the same form of will as that which gave the final meaning to human love, the will to confer immortal life. It is likewise the last transformation of pugnacity, the will to displace evil with good. It is, in truth, *the point in which the meanings of all instincts converge.* It is the positive meaning given by Christianity to the human will as a whole. 'Saving one's soul,' so far as psychology can deal with the matter, is the achieving of this passion. 'Conversion,' or the second-birth, means the translation of natural impulses into terms of this form of the will to power. It is this change which gave Wordsworth his maturity in that moment when he became a 'dedicated spirit.' It is visible, in more or less veiled form, in the final insights of Goethe's Faust, of Browning's Paracelsus. But it is in more literal and potent fashion the force behind the careers of Jesus and Paul, and, apart from their unfinished metaphysics, of Buddha and of Socrates. And it is more or less obscurely the motive of all our more honorable efforts in education, social reform, and other expressions of parental instinct.

The fact that these several instincts come together in this meaning is circumstantial evidence that the meaning is a true interpretation and final for them all. And as tested by experience, it has been a successful interpretation. It has become for many men an absorbing and satisfying purpose. And from the standpoint of those who look on and estimate the results in terms of character, there is little disposition to question that in those men who have most embodied this passion human nature has touched its highest points.

But unless the direction of this passion had been concrete and historical, it would not have been successful in winning ascendency in a human will. It is successful only because and so far as it retains all that respect for the circumstances of the physical and social being that we saw to be characteristic of affection and of pugnacity. The community with which it concerns itself is never merely an invisible church of all the loyal, such as Professor Royce had in mind as the "beloved community." It is this; but it is also an institution among institutions, having its own work in the world and its own aims. It is among other institutions somewhat as the State is among them, while in its purposes it includes them and reflects upon all of them. Its purpose is to hold out precisely this interpretation of their wills to all men as being the adequate interpretation; to bring all plans and goods into subordination to this; and thus, while nominally undermining all other institutions, to pave the way for the most subtle of common understandings, the interracial and international understandings which are crystallizing in the shape of a world culture and an international law. Thus Christianity becomes a corporate body having an ambition of its own: it becomes a propaganda, breaks across the provincial boundaries of its origin, and aspires to universality. Like Buddhism it is by its own principle a missionary religion. And if by being 'true' we mean among other things being awake to the nature of one's business in this world, we may say that no religion is a true religion which does not in this way aspire to be corporate and universal.

For the most part, it is the Catholic Church, rather than the Protestant Church, which has kept to the concrete view of its undertaking: it has more consistently approached the soul through its physical and social entanglements. Protestantism has been more intellectual and abstract. But there are not a few men in whom both types are united, as in the work of Livingstone, or in that of Dr. Grenfell, in whom the medical mission and the community mission are combined. All tendencies at present make for this concreter conception of the undertaking in which, when it completely understands itself, all human ambition culminates.

CHAPTER XLIV

THE CRUX OF CHRISTIANITY

IT must be said, however, that the growing concreteness in the form of missionary effort among Protestants is not due wholly to a deepening perception of the meaning of the enterprise. It is due in part to a sort of embarrassment in the intellectual preaching of religion as propaganda. The mission begins to be regarded rather as an educational or philanthropic than as a religious undertaking, as it were a gift of culture, sustained mainly by the desire to be serviceable in a pioneering way. The attitude of the prophet or evangelist, keenly conscious of the vital import of religious differences, is felt to be less natural of late, as if the human spirit had entered upon a new phase of self-consciousness.

The causes of this change are many, but among them I believe we may recognize an element of diffidence in assuming the rôle of the propagator of religion, as if that rôle were somehow *presumptuous*. And is not this the case?

Is it not true that this entire interpretation of instinct as a will to power, and of the will to power as a will to save souls, or to re-create or reform or educate mankind, has in it more than a trace of presumption? What it amounts to seems to be this, that if the complete salvation of an individual will requires the transformation of all its instincts into the will to save others, we must be *saved by saving;* and it is very doubtful whether in our unsaved condition we have any right to suppose ourselves competent to save. We might as well assume the right to forgive sins. For when in our current criticism we recognize sin, and when we subordinate this criticism (as we thought we should) to a spirit of creative justice, what is this but an attempt to displace a will defined by us as evil by a good will likewise of our own definition? But can we be certain either that that evil is really evil, or that which seems good to us is absolutely good?

An attitude in which one detects himself subtly usurping the functions of Deity, while wholly vigorous and unblushing in the activities of an earlier generation, has become all but impossible to a large part of our contemporary self-consciousness. There is an evident disinclination to walk out very far on any venture of moral judgment, through a sense that this judgment is most likely to mislead when it is most conscious. There is a preference to acknowledge quite frankly the tendencies of the less ethically effortful self, to confess one's egoism, one's ambitions, one's enjoyment of praise, to let one's tempers, dislikes, and affections have their say, because after all one must be sincere and what one is does the talking in any case. In all speculations about what human beings finally want, our formulæ are likely to do violence to hidden impulses while they satisfy the obvious ones. And this moral self-propagation which we have reached as the best meaning of the will seems to do violence to an intuitive hesitation to regard one's moral self as ever quite worthy of being propagated.

We have not, however, been asserting that our ideal is practicable; we have been asserting that it is what Christianity demands, and that if it could be attained it would satisfy the will. The difficulty we have just encountered affords additional evidence that our interpretation of Christian requirements is the true one. For original Christianity encountered precisely the same criticism of its aims, namely, that they are presumptuous. Was it not this very charge that led to the crucifixion, and from the point of view of the judges perhaps justly so? For did not this man profess to forgive sins, and in other ways make himself equal with God? And did he not hand over the keys of heaven and hell to his followers? He professed to save others, and it was a pointed gibe, regarded as equivalent to a refutation, that he could not save himself. In political translation, the offence of the man was in his pretended kingship, the true substance of which was his self-asserted mastery over the souls of men. Historically speaking, the crux of Christianity is its element of presumption.

For the same reason Christianity aroused the antagonism of the Roman State, hospitable to nearly every foreign cult. For the Christian community regarded itself in a wholly unique and arrogant light: it presumed to provide a salvation which made salvation in the State unnecessary, and supreme devotion to the State impossible. It claimed to be a kingdom in which the whole world could, and eventually would, find refuge. It compelled choices, and announced a competition for allegiance, whereas other religions were content with combined loyalties. In brief, it assumed to be right, to possess the Way; and the pretence of divine right implied in its passion for souls was as little palatable to Rome as it is to the ethical diffidence of the present hour.

There would be little or no fault to find with the standard set up by Christianity, if it were only reserved from being professed and administered by human beings. Religion can hardly do less, perhaps, than demand the complete transformation of instinct; and the definition of the goal of human nature is not refuted by the feeling that no human being is quite qualified to adopt it. And further (if we are right) it is not Christianity alone, but the dialectic of our own experience, that leads to the requirement we have stated. The only thing we can justly demand of Christianity, if it makes itself responsible for this ideal, is an answer to the question, How is this transformation possible?

CHAPTER XLV

THE THEORY OF PARTICIPATION

USAGE has identified the word Christianity with a type of disposition,—one whose main ingredient is a sentiment of human charity, embedded in a metaphysical faith and hope. And when scholars began to address themselves to the question, What is the essence of Christianity? many of them accepted this usage and assumed that the essence in question is to be sought in some standard for human character such as we have been considering.

But if this assumption were true it would be hard to find a sufficient reason why the ideal in question should be called by the special name of Christianity. For quite apart from the historic fact that many elements of the Christian ideal have been found in other places and traditions, there is no good reason why the ideal in its general form should not become a common possession of psychology. So far as it is the outcome of the dialectic of experience, which is the same everywhere, it must in time become such a common possession, enriched indeed by the various historic modes of approach and expression, but the better domesticated in the human family for being, in substance, free from any special channel of communication.[1]

---

[1] It has been said, as by Professor G. B. Foster, that the characteristic thing about Christianity is not its statable ideal, but the embodiment

It is not in any set of moral precepts, nor in any view of the transformation of instinct, that the essence of Christianity is to be found, but rather in its answer to the question, How is this transformation possible? Or, to put the question in Kantian form, How is ethical experience possible? Every religion makes its demands; but its special obligation, as a religion, is to show *how these demands may be met*. The religion is to be identified not by its ethics but by its theory of salvation and by its actual provision for saving human individuals in their historic context.

The necessity for such a theory lies in the fact that, as we have seen, the demands themselves involve a practical dilemma. This dilemma, the fundamental problem of Christianity, we may restate somewhat formally as follows. We cannot satisfy our wills, nor the demands upon them, without adopting the attitude of creative artist toward our *milieu*. This attitude, however, for human beings, is presumption. It is such an attitude as only a divine being would be fully justified in taking. As for us, no demand could be more reasonable than that we should first cast the beam out of our own eye, before undertaking to give light to others. But the difficulty is that we can only get rid of the beam through this very undertaking. To be dis-

of this ideal in a person. And it is certainly true that such embodiment makes any type of disposition more available and impressive than any possible theoretical statement could be. But what this personality *means* to men is in any case a universal, and one which the founder of Christianity tried to state as well as to exemplify; and any such universal meaning must be capable of theoretic statement and verification, and so, in the end, be detached from the accident of its historic emergence.

posed to save others, we must first be saved ourselves;
yet to be saved ourselves we must be disposed to save
others. On the ground of the moral order alone there
is no way out of this circle.

But Christianity proposes a way out. It relieves the
individual at once of the burden of supposing that it
is through any merit or power of his own that he can
save others; the power is conferred upon him by way
of a loan. It is nothing inherent in us that is to do the
work, but something in which we *participate*. What
this means may appear through analogies from the field
of knowledge.

One who knows an object becomes to some degree a
partaker in the qualities of the object. Knowledge has
for its special business the reaching across from self
to what is not-self, and making that not-self, so far
as its qualities can be appreciated, an appurtenance
of the self. What I know of any real object is never
the object in full, but a selection of my own: I know
as much of it as I can 'take in,'—the phrase is accurate.
Any quality which I appreciate enough to remember
and name has already begun to be a permanent source
of change in me; but even if I merely gaze on an object,
all that I succeed in taking in is at that moment an
element in my being. What we call an 'idea' is a quality
of an object in so far as it has become a property of a
self. Participation of this kind[2] is particularly natural
and direct in the case of personal qualities and values.

---

[2] In the Platonic theory of participation, it is the object that participates in the ideas. According to the view here proposed it is the
self which through the idea participates in the object, without enquiring

I may witness an heroic deed and be no hero nor become one: but if I appreciate its heroism I become at least momentarily a partaker of its quality. The psychology of masses and of political movements frequently exhibits this principle, which is more fundamental than that of imitation. Mazzini gave Italy an army of heroes; but their valor was not at first an intrinsic quality of themselves. It was a quality of their leader, and became theirs through their knowledge of him. With another leader it might well have remained not alone latent, but non-existent. Much of the hope of democracy lies in the fact that no set of psychological tests can ever tell what any man or body of men is capable of. All men rise to the level of their leaders in so far as they understand them and believe in them.[3]

Through this participation of the self in its object there arises the paradox that the same act of appreciation which confers greatness upon a self reveals to that self its habitual littleness. It was Socrates who burned into our memories the truth that the beginning of wisdom may be the knowledge of our ignorance. But in another form this same truth has been the common possession of all the mystics. For their insistence upon the inadequacy of concepts and definitions is an-

whether the object itself has an original or a communicated being. Ideas in this sense are not conceived as eternal patterns but as living processes of osmosis between self and not-self.

[3] It is this factor of belief, with the implied act of affirmation, that marks the distinction between the effect of knowing the good and knowing the evil qualities of things. There is a degree of participation involved in the knowledge of evil, even for scientific purposes. But the non-consent that goes with such knowledge, if deep enough to remain in subconsciousness with it, limits the area of its remaking of the self.

other way of saying that a true knowledge of reality
makes all prior ideas appear as so many limitations or
negations. Likewise in the world of the will: if one finds
and appreciates anything holy in the world, the participation in that holiness it at the same time a destruction of moral conceit. And this, I believe, explains the
emphasis of Christianity upon humility. Humility is
not a virtue; but it is a condition without which the kind
of virtue demanded by Christianity is not possible: it is
an infallible result of perceiving in any adequate way
what kind of will it is that is needed to do a man's work
in the world. It is a result of beginning to participate in
that will.

Now to possess goodness in this participatory
fashion is not to be good, but only to *begin* being good.
But as long as the appreciation is alive (and this is
vital to the whole matter) the incipent possession of
goodness may do the work of goodness itself. *What
the man sees becomes the working part of the man.* This
principle explains and justifies the tendency which we
found general in society of taking men on the basis of
their hopes rather than of their achievements: what
men reach out to will do some part of its proper work
through them, if not by them. This is especially true of
those who labor, as poets do, to bring to earth an insight which is still marginal and vague to themselves.
The men who dimly perceived "Liberty, Equality, Fraternity," had their effect in spite of the haziness of
their vision: this effect was certainly not due to the
haze, nor much helped by it, but neither was it delayed
until their insight was perfectly defined. There is some

ground for thinking that no idea is wholly definite until it is dead. Those books and writers appear greatest to us who make connections with the surmises of our minds, because they have been able to give substance to the surmises of their own: we can only on this ground understand the effect, not alone of most of the great seers and of most of the bibles, but of many a writer within the period of the world's "enlightenment," of Bunyan, of Locke, of Kant, of William James. In this there is no glorification of an obscure idea because it is obscure; for the only justification any idea can have is that it makes connection with objects as they are. But it suggests that waiting for finished neatness may have something unduly cautious about it. The appreciations we have should begin their active march when those appreciations arise as convictions within the mind. There is an element of vanity in waiting until we think we are all that we admire before we allow ourselves to communicate our admiration. To know that we work less through what we are than through what we worship is a great economy of pride.

And it is also an economy of time. For to wait for fitness would mean in most cases to wait till the end of eternity. The only indispensable fitness is the capacity for appreciating or reverencing the object—as the greatness of a Boswell or a Tolstoy lies less in personal force than in what we are pleased to call immense "objectivity"—and this capacity for reverence is often greatest in the newest or remotest initiate. This is at least part of the meaning of the doctrine of the Incarnation. The perfect dwells in the imperfect *now,* in so

far as the imperfect takes the perfect for an object, and
it does now the work of the perfect.

Thus, the fact of participation makes it possible to
act as gods without presumption. With every element
of self-assertion in the work of education, or propa-
gating a national type of mind, or laboring for any
causes such as involve persuading men, or loyally holding to instead of turning away from some one whose
fault has become patent, or with whatever other form
of saving human nature, comes in the same instant its
antidote: "Yet not I, but whatever I have found visibly
divine in the world, worketh in me." If the reader has
found himself irked by our constant (and admittedly
faulty) use of the phrase 'will to power,' the sting of
that term is now finally drawn. There is power in the
world, and such power as I must wield if I am to find
what I mean by living; but that power, even if it resides
in me for a moment, is very little mine. Far from a testimony to my ability if I accomplish something with it,
it is a comment on my culpable lack of faith if I fail to
work miracles with it.

But while this principle furnishes a partial answer
to our question, How is this transformation possible?
it is not a complete answer. For to participate in the
nature of God, it is, by this principle, first necessary
to see God. And it is only those who are already pure
in heart that can see God. Participation would remove
imperfection, or begin the removal; but the imperfection obscures my vision, and so bars effective participation.

This dilemma is not one that we can banish by ignoring it, or living complacently with it in our ordinary will-to-muddle-through. We have said that ambition is the stuff of which religion is made; it is, if you like, the instinct to do one's living *well*. It is characteristic of animal life to live in accommodations, and piece out by 'vitality' the inconsistencies of ideas: it is characteristic of religion to seek out all rankling roots of dissatisfaction and clash of meaning, to drive latent problems out from cover rather than cloak them, to declare relentless hostility to our animal and 'vital' ease.[4] It is religion that compels us to face this logical *impasse*.

Nor can we escape the difficulty by placing the vision of God, as Plato does, at the end of a long ascent in the dialectic ladder, with a fine gradation in the stages of the journey. For at each stage the dilemma, in principle, recurs. The next step in approaching the vision of the Good, wherever you now stand, requires as its

---

[4] One of the most unfortunate results of letting 'life' take care of this particular puzzle is the adoption of a properly humble attitude toward all enterprises which might imply faith in one's own type of mind, i.e., faith in one's faith. This type of humility is seldom socially obnoxious, because it is for the most part amiable; it is not often observed that by its irresponsibility it is the dry rot of all democracy. When it appears in excess, we recognize in Uriah Heep the epitome of all that Nietzsche properly hates, and mankind with him. But whether or not in excess, the moral and logical fault is the same. To take humility as the essence of Christianity is to mistake its symptom for its essence, and to fancy that because the poor in spirit are blessed, one can become poor in spirit at will. The true relation of things is that the pure in heart catch a glimpse of God, and they who see God become humble. All other humility is hypocrisy. And the problem then recurs, How can the imperfect mind see God? This problem is not escaped by letting it heal over.

precondition that very purity which is its own natural result, and which the relatively impure will cannot put on for itself. The question is the ancient one, How can a man know God?

CHAPTER XLVI

THE DIVINE AGGRESSION

LET me resume the logic of our situation in terms of an experience common in principle. In recent years playwrights have once more ventured to bring upon the stage the miracle-working divine character; and the reception accorded such plays as "The Servant in the House," "The Passing of the Third Floor Back," shows that human nature is ready to recognize and respond to its natural destiny. What one sees there one admits without parley as the strongest thing in the world; and further, in so far as one is moved by it, one is for the moment participating in that type of power. Suppose that the conviction were deep enough to disarm the habitual playgoer's defences, and to persist into the life of the next day. It would meet certain obstacles which the playwright had not included in the difficulties, let us say, of the Servant in the House. For in the first place this Servant is steadily in the right, and knows himself for what he is; but when criticism must both be given and received, the rôle of the divine can with difficulty be sustained. This is one of the embarrassments I should encounter.

But looking deeper, I should find the fundamental difficulty to be this: that I do not, as a fact, care enough for either God or men to play this part with success. I certainly do not see them in a light that compels my

complete affection. This is due to the fact that, being
what I am, I find in my dealings with the world
hindrance, deprivation, pain, to an extent that leaves
me highly unreconciled and at heart protesting. Being
what I am, I say,—because it may well be that if my
instincts were completely transformed I should judge
things differently. If I could love God, I might overcome or understand deprivation and suffering; and
if I could accept deprivation and suffering I might
love God. But as it is, I remain a critic of the divine
economy and hence of God himself; and the vision
that might transform me is closed to me. It is the
unresolved problem of evil that stands in the way of
the saving of my soul. I am unable to see the divine
as an object of admiration, not to say adoration. God,
if there is a God, is a blunderer, or a malicious play-
maker, or finite and helpless, or callous, or blind. Such
is the summary value-judgment that without consult-
ing any deliberate thought of mine my instincts, in
their present state, are incessantly reaffirming.

And apart from what our lips or our theories tell us,
this is perhaps the commonest of commonplace attitudes toward the universe. The socialized human being
looks with a natural skepticism upon any proposition
to the effect that there is a wholly good God. So far
as we can see into the structure of the world, it is a
place in which our instincts are not alone unsatisfied,
but unsatisfiable. If religion has been blind to this
situation, religion might as well quit the stage.

But religion is not blind to this situation; it is the
first to announce that there is nothing in the world

of men and nature, as we naturally see it, that can justly claim a complete allegiance. It sides completely with our civilized skepticism on this point; and it not only admits, but asserts, that of ourselves we cannot see things in any other way. It adds, simply, that what we cannot do for ourselves another must do for us; our reconciliation with reality must be brought to us from outside. The salvation of a soul requires a divine intervention.

II

The idea of salvation from outside is offensive to our sentiment of moral independence. It is offensive, however, chiefly when we think of righteousness as a course of right action or decision such as every man must effect for himself, rather than as a state of right valuing such as no man by solitary effort can reach. Experience should throw some light on what men need and can use in 'working out their salvation.' The experience of India is especially worth considering, because it is in India that the greatest religions of self-help, Brahmanism and early Buddhism, have run their course. It is not without meaning that while on the soil of India Brahmanism has declined and Buddhism has largely disappeared in favor of religions teaching divine help and human dependence, both have taken on as it were departments of supernatural aid foreign to their original logic.[1] And farther west,

[1] Professor J. E. Carpenter quotes a modern Hindu prayer which shows well the spirit of the predominant piety of Hinduism,—the bhakti-piety, which seeks an influx of divine power such as endows the soul with mastery over its earthly nature not essentially different from the

from the sixth century B.C. onward, the spread of the
private mysteries whose purport was to bring the
initiate through various sacraments into effective
union with a god who had suffered and was disposed
to redeem his soul, may be read in the same light. The
vogue and earnestness of many of these mysteries
certainly imply a development of individual self-consciousness and cosmic anxiety such as the corporate
national religions were no longer able wholly to ap-
pease; the race was then beginning to recognize in
a groping fashion that the self, so far as society could
help it to its own, was inadequately helped and in much
danger of being lost; it had begun to define the problem which religion in its distinction from the national
life had to solve. And we may regard Christianity as
one of the latest of the solutions of this problem, containing the kernel of all the other mysteries, and sur-
viving them because it was fit to survive. Read in this

mana of aboriginal and eternal human piety except in its primarily
moral impact: ''O Lord of the Universe, O All-Consciousness, presiding
Deity of all, Vishnu, at thy bidding and to please thee alone I rise this
morning and enter on the discharge of my daily duties. I know what
is righteous, yet I feel no attraction for it; I know what is not righteous,
yet I have no repulsion from it. O Lord of the senses, O Thou seated
in the heart, may I do thy commands as ordered by thee in my conscience.'' (*Comparative Religion*, p. 158.) The Krishna of the
Bhagavad-Gita may be regarded as the Brahmanical form of the divine-
human deliverer from passion and all earthly attachments. And Buddhism has produced such conceptions as that of Avalokiteçvara, who
made a vow not to accept his own release until the demons themselves
as well as all men should be enlightened and saved, the Amithâbha
Buddha ''of boundless Light,'' who, carried to China and Japan, becomes the holy Amida, by whose exertions alone new hearts are conferred
upon men.

way, religious experience gives strong support to the view that salvation from outside is needed.

But we may also read all this, as Professor Gilbert Murray is inclined to read it, as a symptom of political disintegration and a colossal and widespread "failure of nerve." The facts of history never yield a conclusive principle for their own judgment. For such a principle we must look to psychology,—that is, to our own knowledge of ourselves.

And certainly the idea of salvation from outside is not without psychological support, or, for that matter, biological support. For life itself, so far as experience yet shows, always comes from outside, from prior life, as something conferred, not acquired.[2] It is not out of natural order that certain parts or ingredients of life should come in the same way, as by a mental epigenesis. Such an addition from without can frequently be verified in the transition from one level of value to another, at times when a person seems unable to accomplish that transition for himself. For example, I am told to cheer up and take things with a grain of humor. But how is humor possible to me, if as a fact I am morose? Probably it is not possible by any solemn effort I may make for it; but there are persons whose entrance can make it possible, and all but force it upon me. Or, how is confidence possible, if as a fact I am afraid? It is not possible, and my efforts to reassure

[2] Fichte, for whom the moral will is the supreme reality, tried to explain the emergence of a personal self into existence as an act of its own freedom; but not even Fichte's ingenuity succeeded in giving the hypothesis a footing.

myself, by confessing my fears, confirm them. But I
can do a great deal to 'take' heart at the summons of
one who has it, or even at the memory of a voice that
is charged with it. These processes may be processes
of participation; but they are frequently of a more
active sort on the part of the other mind, like an in-
tentional and aggressive *imposing* of a state of mind
upon me.[3] They appeal to the consent of the self-to-be
rather than to the consent of the present self, though
unless something in that present self gave consent the
state could not be imposed.

These facts imply that the self is not a closed monad
in its moral life any more than in its mental and
physical life. Just as there is a mental hunger for new
data to be ingested into our mental substance, a hunger
which we sometimes call 'curiosity,' and sometimes
the 'empirical attitude' of mind, so there is a moral
appetite which has as yet no name, but which makes
a part of our social appetite. For in social intercourse
we receive here and there not alone new data, but new
inductions already well grown, new ideas ready to
transplant and mature, new attitudes toward experience as a whole,—almost, one might say, new selfhood.
We remain ourselves in all this, because we choose
what we admit; but we become as it were the spirit of a
living society of included selves, receiving constant
accessions not alone by germination from within but
also by adoption from without. It is because of this
openness of mind on their part that our neighbors, if

---

[3] This process is doubtless akin to suggestion, but it is more direct
and avowed to the subject than suggestion is.

we were competent, might be saved by us (as we have all along assumed); and it is by this same openness of mind that we, if there were a competent other, might be saved. The question, How is love to God or to men possible if as a fact I do not have it? would be answered if there were, as the moving spirit of the world, an aggressive lover able and disposed to break in upon my temper of critical egoism and win my response. This would seem to be a necessary, if not a sufficient, condition of 'salvation'; and thus far psychology lends support to our reading of the history of religion, namely, that in the development of the private mystery, religion was finding its way to a knowledge of the actual needs of men. How Christianity proposes to meet those needs we may state in our own way.

III

Plato and Aristotle represented God as that absolute good which, unmoving and changeless in itself, the soul pursues and longs for. To Christianity, it is the soul that is pursued; and God is forever restless, in quest of what to him is lost. The God of the Christian is one who invades the earth in order to bring men to themselves: to every soul of man he "stands at the door and knocks." He does not forgo the power of silent attraction found in the non-assertive Tao of Lao Tze, or in Brahm, or in the Unmoved Mover of the Greek; but it is as one who has known finitude and is 'lifted up from the the earth' that he will draw all men unto him. He disguises himself, takes the form of a servant; he comes to his own and his own know him not; he is despised and rejected and done to death. And all this is the foil and background of his great joy. For he has his moment when to some mind, more honest than usual to its own need, there comes a pre-sentiment of recognition, and the awed question, Who art thou, Lord?—to which he answers, I am he whom thou persecutest.

No assertion could be more empty than the Christian saying that God is love, if that love were simply a subjective disposition on the part of a being forever inactive and unseen. If God exists as a good-will, that will must do its work in the world of time and event as a will to power not wholly unlike our own, and so coming to itself, as we must, through the saving of others. Christianity is right in holding that such a God, if he exists, must somehow appear in the temporal order. And it seems to me that it is also right in say-ing that he must suffer; and not alone with us (as any god must who knows what is going on) but also for us, and *at our hands.* For the 'hardening of our hearts,' i.e., their alienation from reality, due to our preoccupa-tion with our own suffering, could hardly be overcome except by seeing that in the actual mesh of our own experience the brunt of our selfishness has fallen upon *him,* and that he, in this sense, bears our sin in his own body. It is such a god, active in history and suffer-ing there, that Christianity declares as the most im-portant fact about the world we live in.

To believe in such a god would give history a mean-ing over and above any visible or experimental mean-ing it may have: it would have to be read as the drama of God's life, his making and remaking of men. His concern for them would have to be thought as literal and individual as they themselves are literal and individual. Love, as Royce has said, individuates its object; but it is equally true that it individuates its subject: it takes an individual to be a lover. And every human being, if these things are true, must be able to discover as the sense of his entire experience a direct address of the absolute being to him, as if the world were made for him alone. The universe becomes suddenly, not egocentric, but multi-centric. Just as in infinite space the center of reference may be assumed in any point; so in history, as Christianity must see it, the center of the universe is everywhere that the divine interest finds a person. "Whoever you are, now I place my hand upon you that you be my poem": this is the point of tangency between Whitman's semi-pagan genius and the spirit of Christian history. Without excluding a movement in history toward a goal or toward many goals, there is in this picture no meager one-way teleology, but loss and supreme attainment are everywhere. It is not unlike the world of the child, who has not yet learned to doubt that all things exist for his sake; and to the end it requires something of the spirit of a child to enter the world of Christianity. The strain on belief is at a maximum; and this religion does nothing to relieve it.

Judicious heads, having seen much of the world's actual indifference, might incline to ease the burden of so much faith by reducing God's alleged love to a general disposition, a kindly wish and effort toward a far-off good available to the ultimate denizens of time. A finite or mildly benevolent power, struggling as a sort of *élan* of life against the perpetual resistance of matter, and like a cosmic council of war so lost in vast designs that the private fades before its view into the mass, seems much more probable to those whose metaphysics is a distillation of the mixed essences of experience. But probability has no place in metaphysics; and the probable God is a very unlikely God, in the sense that he solves no problems. Whether the world we live in is or is not the world of Christianity is *a question of fact*.

CHAPTER XLVII

THE LAST FACT

I DOUBT whether philosophy can affirm the existence of this fact. It can show that if such a fact
were extant our dilemma would be solved. It can show,
further, that certain characters of the world are in
harmony with such a fact. Thus, the dialectic of experience, as we look back upon it, may be understood as a
part of the strategy of "The Hound of Heaven." The
world is so devised that "All things betray thee, who
betrayest me": the will, apparently driven by dissatisfaction in its own false definitions of good, may to a
deeper knowledge be seen as driven by the wind of a
god's desire. And as for all the irregularly distributed
individual deprivation, it is at least conceivable that it
is part of the individual appeal of that same god:

> All which I took from thee, I did but take
> Not for thy harms, but just that thou
> Mightst seek it in my arms. . . .
> I am he whom thou seekest.

But the power of so understanding the dialectic, or
so interpreting evil, is retrospective. The force which
could lift the mind into a position from which this
reading seems *the truth* does not lie in the dialectic
itself. It must come as a positive datum, something

itself personally experienced or 'revealed.' It is here that religion takes the issue out of the hands of philosophy.

For religion in its historical forms is empirical: it appeals to the realistic temper: it deals with facts. Its function is not to prove God but to announce God. For this reason, its doctrine is stated as *dogma;* and the fundamental dogma of religion is *Ecce Deus,* Behold, *This* is God. Such a dogma certainly appeals to the reason of every man, for it can mean nothing to any one except in so far as he is capable of understanding his own needs; but beyond that, it appeals to his power to *recognize what he needs in what is real.* Recognition is an act of the mind which thought can lead up to, but never quite enforce. Hence religion calls upon every man for an individual and ultimate "I believe," which means, "I recognize this to be the fact," or, more simply, "I see."

. .

In the last resort, it is by his own vision that every man must live:—when we call a man an individual, we are thinking of the solitude of his ultimate relation to reality. He must live by what he, for himself, can recognize; and his power of recognizing is an integral part of his instinctive equipment.

For as hunger may be trusted, for the most part, to recognize what will serve as food, so all instinct may be trusted to recognize what it needs in the world, if what it needs is there. Animal instinct will recognize its needed physical facts, human instinct its needed physical and metaphysical facts,—if they exist.

. .

Conversely, whatever beliefs, or metaphysical findings, men have lived by are to some extent corroborated (certainly not by 'general consent,' but) by the circumstance that they have formed part of the vital circuit of human instinct, have been the feeders and shapers of instinct. The more durable of these beliefs are not wholly illusory: *"l'action ne saurait se mouvoir dans l'irréel."*

But in the composition of these working beliefs, fiction and mere hopefulness may mingle with positive metaphysical finding in unknown proportion. The mystic in man, the original seer of ultimate things, learns but slowly to discriminate between his perceptions and his dreams. The critic in man, the judgment based on experience and self-conscious reason, rises but slowly to the task of releasing what is significant and true in dogma from what is irrelevant and false,—condemning sometimes too little, quite as frequently too much.

. .

The individual, then, who realizes that his metaphysical questions are questions of life and death for instinct and will, can give no exclusive credence either to the mystic in himself or to the critic; he will require them to act in co-operation. He will be satisfied neither with pragmatic beliefs, chosen for their promise of

satisfaction (ghosts of human desires offered as substantial food to these same desires), nor with true general ideas (entities which taken alone make no difference and do no work).

He will realize that his instinctive appetite for knowledge is an honorable appetite. It is in the existing world
that instinct must grow and work out its meaning; and
the existing world is distinguishable both from pragmatic dreams and from true general ideas: it is a union
of general ideas with matter of fact in a living fabric
of historical movement and change. It is to this living
mesh that mystic and critic must direct their vision.
Whatever is real and significant for instinct must in
some way exist in the active surface of history,—some
of it no doubt *built into history* at various points of
the working edge of time in such wise that we could
not now unbuild it if we would.

As an inseparable part of the question, What sort of
world is it that we live in? he will thus be driven to
enquire, What sort of world *have we been living in?*
What have been the metaphysical foundations, real or
supposed real, for those qualities, those instinct-shapes,
which characterize our present human type?

. .

The qualities which have made and are making our
contemporary civilization are not qualities of intellect
more than qualities of character: they are such qualities as integrity, reliability, legality, practical force,
love of liberty. At the root of them is a capacity for

facing and absorbing the increasing pain which is incident to increasing contact with objective reality. To surrender ourselves without flinching to the findings of natural science is something we have had to learn by painfully slow degrees; to accept the unflattering position of man in the Copernican world and in the evolutionary scheme; to regard and burrow deeper into the human mind as an object in nature; to submit to the hardship involved in making a social order on the principle of a thoroughly objective impersonal justice, —all this has required the 'virtue' of Rome together with a sympathy and sensitiveness to what is not-ourselves that has not come from Rome. Our civilization is one which has once for all put away vested interest in illusions, and has dared to stand naked before the last facts so far as it could find them. In this there is much of the plain 'grit' such as Joseph Conrad loves to celebrate: but grit is not necessarily attentive to the weak, the incipient, the minute, the growing,—and it is here that our peculiar strength and promise lies. It is a union of strength and tenderness which has brought us to the best we have so far found.

The strength that we have is not the strength of physical instinct; nor has it ever been for mankind 'pure' grit. In former times, with the zest of original pugnacity and the conviction of mounting passion, men could throw themselves without reserve into the issues of battle; and battle became for them a quasi-religious orgy in which the spirit of the fathers and of the tribe drew near almost to touching and filled the frame with unwonted power. Grit and enthusiasm went together.

And now without the aid of primitive feeling or hope of individual glory men of more sensitive mould go simply to a mill of war whose portent of possible suffering is incomparably more intense. What do these men stand on? Not on any consciousness of the heroic, but on the plain sense of what is necessary; and they profess thereby a faith of some kind that facing what is necessary is better than muffling the head in a lying dream. Effectively and actually men care more for reality than ever before, and behind that confidence lies some kind of creed, or let me say, some kind of contact with the spirit of the world.

Neither is the tenderness we have the tenderness of physical instinct. We tend, we teach, we legislate, we try our hand at justice and reform. We do this not from any pure outflow of kindness: we do it with a certain joy of power which is at the same time fully awake to the defect of our performance. The parent who deals with his son and the publicist whose thought becomes the rule for millions are well aware in these days of the human equation in their judgments. We are democratic: no authorities among us dare set up as absolute. They live, we all live, at the requirement of the movement of things over a gap unbridged by our own competence. Earlier men acted thus instinctively, with the confident affection and protectiveness of the animal parent or leader. But if we act thus it is because, while self-doubts emerge and continue to emerge, they have seemed to receive from the world we live in assurances that satisfy, as if at least the kindlier enterprises of living were, or might be, a partnership with power more

intimately attuned than our own to the inner facts of
history, capable of reaching its goal in the midst of our
inadequacies.

. .

If the spirit of the world is actually such as to justify
to the growingly self-conscious being this kind of confidence and sensitiveness, we should doubtless, as with
all pervasive utilities, better recognize the ingredient
which does this work if it were experimentally withdrawn.

And as it happens, such aid to vision is not wholly
lacking at this moment. A calamity having the force
of a ghastly experiment occurs, vivisection of this
vaunted Western life, with all its sources, material and
otherwise, putting a harsh end to all mere momentums
of belief, to all complacencies, sanctimonies, and infallible prescriptions, to all sleepy tugging at dry paps.
How much can you do without and still live?—this
searching experimental question war presses home to
soul and body, abolishing stroke by stroke gross quantities of wealth, gross quantities also of life, beauty,
happiness, personal and public. But with all these aboli-
tions spreads another,—the swift and easy abolition
of that supposed 'sanctity of human life' together with
other sanctities formerly potent: this, too, we are called
upon to do without if we can, or perhaps rather to see
it for what it was,—a glamour of some sort, a conspiracy to hold high the level of self-esteem, mutual palaver
of polite society, valid enough so long as no serious

business is on, no occasion for telling one another cold
truth.

Cold truth being now in order, we measure humanity
in the mass as so much force, resistance, morale; feed
it into the hopper by regiments, brigades. A comrade,
a friend, changes in an instant into débris, so much
wreckage to be cleared away. Once more we see man
in terms of his yield: *er ist was er isst;* and that will of
his, that morale and mentality, is a bit of equipment,
an *appareil,* working best when nearest the ground, fit
for short flights, better avoiding long ones and certainly all infinite flights. 'Infinite value'? Infinite
conceit!

When this sentiment about human value is thus un-
sentimentally challenged, we perceive that it has had
much to do with sustaining those qualities of confidence
and tenderness which we thought distinctive of our
civilization. It is not itself a metaphysical belief, but
a by-product of such a belief, doubtless the belief of
which we are in search, and whose character we may
now dimly make out.

. .

There is an instinct in us as yet unnamed by psychology, perhaps the deepest instinct of all: it is the *total
infantile response to the maternal impulse.* This instinct knows what kind of metaphysic it needs, namely,
a world maternal not in part only, but altogether. What
has happened, then, is obvious, is it not? That benevolent god with a trillion equally dear children, that pic-

ture of world-familydom, or of world-shepherdhood, that impossible Absolute engaged in countless simultaneous 'seeking and saving' enterprises,—all of this is but the poetry of childhood, valid there in fact, and holding over into the more sheltered corners of mature hopefulness, lingering to comfort minds that insist on being comforted, minds incapable of genuine maturity,—or perhaps even to protect certain subjectivities and prides, personal, racial, genealogical, remnants of stale human provinciality liking to believe itself the chosen strain. This persistent metaphysics of the motherhood of history or grandmotherliness of history,—is it not the most palpable of pragmatic fictions, or instinct-beliefs? And if so, it can no longer serve us, *having been found out.*

. .

But what becomes, then, of these contemporary qualities of justified strength and tenderness? They do not disappear; they are merely replaced by more elemental editions of themselves, suited rather to a world aloof, preoccupied, or indifferent than to a parental world.

If 'justified confidence' is unavailable, there is always a well of instinctive confidence to fall back upon, the simplest, least-borrowed thing in human nature, least needing to be justified,—the now admittedly *pure* grit of man at bay in a world neither his own nor anyone's; confidence original, titanic, defiant; confidence *ueberhaupt.* There is an attitude needing no meta-

physics, an attitude, well so-called, which few are incapable of striking if necessary. We can always act
as if men, or some men, were worth while, and had
rights, ourselves included. For the human life authentically valued by an absolute valuer, substitute the instinctive self-valuation of the human animal, particularly the masculine animal; and for the deference due
to beings objectively worthy of reverence, substitute
the warmth of a maternal sympathy spreading from
the center outward as the vital economy permits. Give
these well-founded sentiments an artificial extension by
the device called the State; so that a degree of parenthood enters into an entire community in its relations
to its own members,—competing and warring from
time to time with similar sentiments of parenthood on
the part of other communities; and as there is no real
parent, parenthood may be said to exist just so far as
it can forcibly make itself valid in the world.

This is the alternative into which we may seem driven
by the disillusionments, the down-crashing of all current sentiments, in this day of reckoning. And in that
case history, having reached its summit, turns downward.

. .

Let it be clearly understood that this reversal of
direction is involved in the proposed change. For
animal confidence can no longer sustain a fully human
effort as we have come to understand it, not even a
human war.

The flame of war can leap into life among common people only because of the presence there of a metaphysical outlook that seems to make a number of things, including human life, objectively valuable and 'sacred.' If the aims of war, or the activities of war, contradict this belief; or if self-consciousness in the midst of the carnage is driven to press its questions, Do I matter? Does any deed or thought of mine matter? Does any other deed or thought or interest or life matter? Does the 'cause' itself finally matter, or the nation and all its wars, holy or unholy?—the spirit inevitably seeps out of the fighting. It is possible for fighting to undermine one's sense of the only things worth fighting for.

And what is true of war is true to an even greater degree of the long upbuilding effort of the creative arts. If 'progress' must bring disillusionment and the harsh daylight of a denying realism, progress is destined to devour its own children.

Values, human values, can survive only if, reaching out toward a metaphysical condition which their dream-shapes foreshadow, they *find it*. They need reality to climb on; they need a reality they *can* climb on. They want an independent source of standards, a mooring outside of nature, such as we surmised at the beginning of our study. Their own *poussée vitale* droops, half-grown, unless it meets an equivalent *attrait vital* streaming into its environment from some pole outside itself.

. .

And thus this experiment, this world-surgery, begins

to make so much unmistakable: That what human nature has been responding to is not its own instinctive self-esteem, codified in institutions, or uncodified, but a valuation believed real and objective, supposedly hailing from beyond nature, authoritatively requiring of man that self-honor and that honor of his kind which his own impulse achieves but fitfully and from the center outward.

And this valuation, be it noted, has appeared to him not as a proclaimed theorem regarding human value in the abstract, but as actual *valuedness,* i.e., valuation acted upon in multitudes of deeds, struggles for human rights and guarantees thereof, sacrifices and martyrdoms without number; in all of which an authentic divine will and activity were supposed discernible by those having eyes to see. To many of these human doers their own deeds appeared to be utterances not alone of their private wills but also of the ultimate will of the world. In brief, we of this age have been living on an aggressive valuation, built into history, and supposed whether wisely or not to transmit an absolute judgment.

. .

And not strangely, mankind seems to have counted most on the costliest of such deeds, the most deliberately defiant of the natural appearance. As at this moment, so it has always been: it is the negation by the brute forces of the world, the negation and contempt of what humanity has held most precious, which has split opinion into its concealed extremes.

For it is just such negation which creates the opportunity for deeds most audaciously experimental, deeds of self-immolation of which the onlooker must say that they embody either the wisdom of the gods, or else infra-human unwisdom. It is upon the great *experimental sacrifices* of history that men have climbed to their positive metaphysical insights; or to what they have taken to be such, be it only their passionate assertions that such sacrifices, such blottings out of man's evident best, cannot have been folly, and shall not have been vain.

. .

It is not for us, here, to assert or deny, either passionately or otherwise; but as students of human nature and its destiny to state deliberately the connections of cause and consequence, and face our alternatives. Our metaphysical finding, our last fact, may be such as to release and encourage the growth of instinctive meaning, warming out its inner logic and wider linkages; it may be (as with Schopenhauer) such as to wither and repel it; it may be no finding at all, but an enigmatic silence of a non-committal world which denies only by refusing to affirm. In no case is it indifferent.

Absence of belief that the world as a whole has an active individual concern for the creatures it has produced need neither destroy happiness nor the morality of compassion. Life would always be worth living and worth living well, so long as free from the major tor-

Cooper Union Library

ments. Instinct has its satisfactions in an uninterpreted or partly interpreted condition: it will reach some accommodation to the world that is. Nothing would necessarily be destroyed or lost from the good life which some at least of the human race now know and many hope for,—nothing except the higher reaches of curiosity and sympathy, and the wisdom of developing them. It is only the enthusiasts for a far-off good, for an endlessly progressive humanity, for a profound and logical love of life, that would be cut off; it is only the martyrs that have played the fool; only to saints and sages the world has lied.

THE END

APPENDIX I

THE DILEMMA IN THE CONCEPTION OF INSTINCT, AS APPLIED TO HUMAN PSYCHOLOGY[1]

1. The common use of the term instinct is not embarrassed by the fact that its meaning is hybrid. It means a mode of *behavior* and it means a mode of *interest;* and for ordinary purposes the mixture of physical ingredients with mental ingredients makes no trouble and requires no explanation.

But when a technical definition is sought mixtures are no longer satisfactory; a concept must have a fixable character, not a dual personality. Yet the effort to reach a "clear and distinct idea" of instinct commonly results in a dilemma. When the definition does justice to all that instinct means in physical terms, it fails to fit what instinct means in mental terms; and *vice versa.* When either side is securely nailed down, the other warps up and refuses to fall into the plane. The definer is tempted to ignore one or the other aspect of the conception; but this way of escape cannot be successful in human psychology, for reasons hereafter to be stated.

2. If the meaning of a conception could be determined by its history, there would be little doubt about the definition of instinct. For the native haunts of the idea of instinct are in behavior, animal behavior. The epoch is not far past when the animals had all the in-

[1] Reprinted (with slight changes) from *The Journal of Abnormal Psychology and Social Psychology,* June-September, 1921

stincts, and had nothing else to go by, while man had all
the reason, and had no instincts to help his reason out.
This is far from being the case to-day; but it remains
true that the conception of instinct is more at home in
the place of its birth than elsewhere. It is quite possible
to give a definition of instinct which takes care of all
the items usually dubbed instinctive in animal behavior
and excludes the rest. The following composite photo-
graph of various such definitions shows their tendency
to converge:

An instinct is an innate behavior pattern, common to
all members of a species or of a sex of a species, leading
from a situation marked by a specific signal or 'stimulus' through a fairly regular and more or less complex
series of operations to an end favorable to the survival
of the individual or of the species. Its most useful
marks or criteria are adaptiveness, and untaught skill
in the use of specific organs.

3. If, however, we try to approach a definition of
instinct from the side of our own experience, we find
it awkward. Try to enumerate the items of your own
stream of consciousness that you regard as instinctive,
and the reason for this will become clear.

Unless we are exceptionally instructed or sophisticated individuals, we do not label our instincts by that
name while we are using them. When we are angry, it
seems to us the reverse of an irrational course of conduct: it seems rather the reaction of reason itself to the
irrational behavior of others,—we know nothing of an
'instinct of pugnacity' in such a moment. Or if we find
ourselves disinclined to take a high dive while social im-

pulses favor the performance and reason reassures, we as a rule make no conscious avowal, even to ourselves, of an 'instinct' of fear. The grounds for action or inaction appear to us objective; we rationalize them: and in this process the instinctive factor is transmuted, or is apparent chiefly to others.

The salient mark, from our own standpoint, of those events which psychology comes to call instinctive, is simply *interest,*—positive or negative interest. Instincts stand out from the rest of our mental life chiefly because of their emotional accompaniments and a sense of power or ease that goes with the action. In the vernacular, the domain of instinct is simply the domain of the "things one *takes to* naturally,"—satisfactions which life discovers and which neither offer nor need any explanation.

4. The recognition of instincts in ourselves is greatly aided by the rôle played by the non-rational in the *social context* of our lives. There are the common interests which obviously help us to understand one another without elaborate explanations, to work and play together, to build intricate social arrangements on safe calculations of what human beings will want and do, and to be amused at the familiar-strange ways of the whole human tribe.

It is this quasi-cynical interest (characteristic of all psychology) which a man takes first in his fellows and later in himself, that accounts for the inescapable attachment of the conception of instinct to the mind, where naturally it is a stranger.

5. In its use, in the mental field, we have a striking

instance of the disposition of mature human self-consciousness to make a mythology of itself, and to fill
itself full of hidden mechanisms which it conceives as
springing perpetual surprises upon its unsuspecting
person. Mankind dearly loves a little machine which it
can substitute for itself when it tries to think about
itself. And if the machine has trap doors, which conceal
a subterranean chamber full of dynamos and secret
springs, and guarded by a jealous, sycophantish, and
otherwise stagely-villainous censor engaged in tyranni-
cal repressions, the mythology acquires all the fascination of a detective story.

If consciousness is the place where appearance and
reality coincide, everybody should be a natural authority upon his own states of mind. But no one who has
taught any subject with a strain of psychology in it
can have failed to notice the almost complete docility
with which most students will accept doctrines about
what they are made of, and their almost eager readiness to believe themselves full of 'complexes,' and other
phantasms of the living.

Now it would be absurd to say that these mechanisms,
which evidently hail from the world of physical behavior, throw no light upon our conscious selves. Consciousness has its self-luminous regions; but it is not
all self-luminous: and in those regions where it admits
of light being thrown upon it, nothing else promises so
much light as just these curious machines. But it is
necessary to be clear that all such behavioristic elements are *imported,*—not found in the natural output
of introspection,—if we would see the nature of the

difficulty of the conception of instinct on its mental side.

6. This difficulty will become more apparent if we consider the importance of the work which instinct, in human psychology, is called upon to do.

When we study instinct in animals, we are first attracted by the amazing tricks which lead to results so much superior to most works of conscious device. Then we learn that instinct is engaged not primarily in doing tricks, but in governing the whole normal round of animal life, its breeding, food-getting, migrating, etc.,— broad categories which describe equally well the natural round of human life.

It is at this stage that we are likely to import the conception into human psychology; for instinct in man is not of the trick-working order but rather of the order of interests which govern the broad life-cycle. And the classic list of human instincts as 'love, hunger and self-defence' expresses well the meaning of the conception at this stage.

In popular and literary use, the conception will probably adhere to this meaning. When Goethe wanted to express the quasi-cynical, Solomonian view of human life (Solomon, the first psychologist whose works have come down to us), he did so in the lines which I will venture to render as follows:

Why all this ado under the sun, this labor and turmoil of men?—

They are striving to nourish themselves, to bring children to birth and to nourish them:—

No one achieves a jot more, torment himself as he may.

The whole sum of human biography and history is told in terms of these three great impulses or interests, and on the basis of introspection, these major interests are simply *there*. An interest explains all the actions that men carry out for its sake; it does not explain itself. And it may reasonably be held not only that an interest needs no explanation but that it is incapable of explanation. Value is the only self-explaining thing in the world: and interest is value conceived as present to a conscious and active being.

But when values are referred to instincts, the conception of instinct seems to offer some explanation of those values. It implies that our interests are *not* self-explanatory; that we are not content to take them simply as ultimate facts. And it proposes to explain them by referring them to something very different from value, namely to the behavior-machines we were speaking of. It is here that the difficulty becomes acute.

I am not referring at present to the fundamental difficulty involved in the proposal to get light on the character of an interest by conceiving it as a mode of motion. All explanation proceeds by referring a thing to something else. And it is especially evident that if instinct is to explain interest, it can do so only on condition that instinct itself is defined in non-mental terms. For if instinct were defined by its conscious aspect alone, then to say that the original interests of human life are due to instincts would be a circle: for instinct, as a mental fact, can only be defined by the facts of interest.

But the difficulty is this; that if we avoid the circle

by defining interest in terms of the behavior mechanisms, there is a serious gap between those items of conduct which can fairly be referred to the mechanisms, and that large area of conduct which is governed by the major interests of which we have been speaking.

7. In the first place, the great interest-trends of human life are highly general, and the behavior mechanisms in proportion as they are strictly conceived appear highly specific.

If you carefully limit the conception of instinct to operations which mechanical conceptions (with a reasonable margin of hope) allow you to explain, you naturally begin with reflexes, and pass on to chain-reflexes and more highly compounded forms; but you end by leaving out just those major trends which make the conception psychologically important. You provide explanations for movements of manipulation, but not for curiosity; for separate movements of grasping, masticating, swallowing, locomotion, but not for a 'food-getting instinct'; for blushing, sex-play, copulation, but not for courting, sex-love, domesticity: for grasping, reaching, pulling, but not for 'construction.'

It is natural enough for the stricter scientific conscience to seek relief from this situation by roundly denying that love, hunger, self-defence, construction, curiosity, etc., are instincts at all: asserting that the only legitimate instincts are those units of behavior for which a definite stimulus and definite response can be determined, while the more general categories are instincts only for literary men and philosophers. And this is a perfectly reasonable attitude; for, we repeat, the concept of instinct is primarly a behavior-concept; and the right to define it lies with the physiologist.

But to accept this position is to take away the conception from those uses for which it was brought into human psychology; to restrain it from offering explanation for that round of life and its major values for which it was first invoked;—in brief, to confine its use in human psychology to the comparatively trivial.

8. In the second place, the great interest-trends are doubtful in their identification and in their boundaries. They were certain to fall under scientific suspicion, if only because every writer gave a different list, and because between the lists there was enormous divergence in the number of items. If some mentioned three, others (as William James) enumerated between thirty and forty.

Is there, or is there not, an instinct of fear, or of imitation, of self-preservation, of curiosity, of constructiveness? Is there an instinct for each phrenological bump? The explanatory promise of the conception is so alluring that writers are tempted to coin an instinct for any fairly persistent trait of mankind which they wish to signalize. There is said to be a moral instinct, an æsthetic instinct, a religious instinct, a political instinct, or even (as one writer asserts) an Anglo-American instinct for parliamentary government.

There is no wonder that the technician is deterred from launching out on seas peopled by such monsters as some of these. And yet, if all such traits are omitted, in favor of the demonstrably congenital stimulus-response arrangements, the major part of human nature remains untouched. "The theory of instinct becomes comparatively trivial when they are omitted, yet it has always been muddled when they are included."[2]

The hard alternative would seem to be that between behavioristic clarity with inadequacy, and introspective adequacy with muddle.

9. But there are at least two conceivable ways of bettering this alternative.

In spite of the disposition of the concept, when defined in mental terms, to break away from all scientific restraint and sobriety, it may still be possible to introduce usable criteria which will limit the play of pure fancy and tame the concept to scientific uses. This is the way adopted by Dr. William McDougall.

Or, we may tie to physiological clarity, and try to enlarge the mechanical resources in such wise as to cover more adequately the field of human conduct as we know it.

This second path, that of contemporary behaviorism, Dr. McDougall regards as hopeless, not alone because the major impulses are so far out of the reach of present explanatory devices, but because, in his view, physiological explanations fail to account for the very simplest types of animal behavior.

The present status of the question, then, might be stated in some such way as this: Any student of human nature to-day must make up his mind,

a. Whether physiology can explain *anything* in behavior;

2 P. 86 above.

b. Whether there is reason to hope that it may explain *everything* in behavior;

c. Whether the introspective account of instinct can be made fit for scientific use.

In following sections, I wish to discuss these issues, beginning with an enquiry into the reasons which lead Dr. McDougall to think that the physiological route has no outlet.

II

10. Dr. McDougall finds two defects in physiological theory of behavior which are not accidental and remediable, but constitutional.

First, its inability to account for persistence of effort toward an end *with endless variability of the means* employed. A machine may be regarded as making toward an end; but it makes for that end either by a rigidly fixed course of intermediate steps, as in case of the locomotive on its track, or else, as in case of the self-steering torpedo, by a course having a very limited range of variation. The visible criterion of conscious action, according to William James, is the pursuit of ends with the choice of means; and this is a criterion of conscious action only because, as McDougall believes, such action cannot be mechanically accounted for.

Second, its inability to account for responses which are responses to *meanings,*—not to any assignable sense stimulus or group of sense stimuli. Wherever you can discover a recurrent set of sense-elements in the initial situation, you can believe in the possibility of mechanical explanation. But where, as in the case of the crying of a child, the expressive reaction may be provoked by situations of a thousand sorts from physical pain to the mere fancy of neglect or reproof, where you can safely defy any one to allege a constant sensation or group of sensations in these initial situations, in brief, where the only invariable antecedent is a 'meaning,' the very attempt at mechanical explanation becomes absurd.[3]

Let us consider these two difficulties in turn.

11. First, can there be a physiological explanation of the pursuit of ends with unlimited or very large variability in the choice of means?

It may be admitted at once that the explanation of instinctive behavior by the chain-reflex pattern has definitely broken down, for all such cases. The most obviously instinctive behavior, such as nest building in birds, is too irregular in its progress, permits too many interludes and *divertissements,* alarums and excursions. A chain-reflex should have an invariable order: process A should always come before process B, because its conclusion is necessary to set process B in motion. If by accident process B is set off first, it will never go back to A, but will proceed mechanically to C and D. If, per contra, there appears to be a degree of liberty, so that ABC may be performed as well in the order BAC, or even CBA, the chain-reflex needs some outside assistance, such as would be supplied by a mental picture of the whole result to be achieved.

Further, any chain is likely to be interrupted or im-

[3] Cf. *Body and Mind,* ch. xix, esp. p. 264 f.

peded; in which case, a proper chain has little power of substituting a new link for the unworkable link. If, as in most complex instinctive processes, intermediate steps may be carried out in many ways, one has to fancy the chain endowed with a supervisory official capable of perceiving the equivalence of the substituted links to the original links *for the purpose of the end in view*. Naturally, an intelligent chain can explain intelligent action; but in mechanical explanations we have always to be on guard against a generous disposition to lend some of our own mentality to the machine for the sake of helping it over the critical phases of its operation.

12. That type of mechanism, then, does certainly fail to explain instinct. And I dwell upon this point, because I believe that wherever we find vitalism to-day, it depends upon a criticism of physiological explanations which is in principle essentially the same.

Why, for example, does Driesch require an entelechy to understand how an embryo slashed at random can develop into a typical adult? Is it not because, being forced to work with different means, it yet arrives at the same end?

Why does Bergson, thinking of organic evolution, appeal for explanation to a vital principle? Is it not because independent series of organic forms, having different beginnings and different intermediaries, nevertheless converge to similar results? In the processes which eventuate in the eye of the pecten and the eye of the vertebrate, Bergson can only see a single experimental impulse operating with widely variant means.

In a word, in all these cases it is *guidance* that requires explanation and it is precisely guidance which mechanical agencies are judged incapable of giving.

13. But if the mechanical explanation of guidance has its difficulties, it will not do to assume that the vitalistic explanation is free from them.

Any principle of explanation which refers physical conduct to an entity of mental order seems to save the biological postulate that all organs (and hence consciousness) must be of some use, but it does so at the expense of the postulate that all physical events have physical explanations.

If one were forced to choose in this lamentable way between postulates of equal dignity, one choice might be as defensible as the other. But it is more than doubtful whether vitalism, in sacrificing one principle, actually saves the other.

For if consciousness is to be of any use at all in carrying on life, it cannot be limited to those residues of conduct which mechanics at any time threatens to leave unexplained. Consciousness must explain all of conscious behavior or none. The only principle that accords in the least with introspection is this: that whatever my body as a whole does, *I do*,—not a fraction of it, but the whole of it. We cannot separate out the 'guidance' from the rest of behavior in that way. If I go down to breakfast, that event is not to be described as a process carried out by certain hunger-mechanisms inciting certain locomotor mechanisms, while I, the conscious self, simply steer the event at the turns of the stairs and in the unexpected encounters with other living entities. It will not do to bring in consciousness to account for *remainders*.

Putting this principle into positive form, it means that if consciousness has any explaining power at all its scope *includes that of mechanism:* whatever mechanism does consciousness may do also,—so that no extension of the field of mechanical explanation would press upon or invade the field ascribed to conscious action. And conversely, no proof that guidance, or any other feature of behavior, is incapable of mechanical explanation would serve to insert consciousness more firmly in the biological realm.

14. And I am inclined to think that the proof that "guidance cannot be explained" has not been given, and indeed cannot be given. Unless I am mistaken this alleged gap in explanation is already in a fair way to be filled.

The very effective use now being made of the conception of appetite, or appetence, as a factor in instinctive action by Professor Wallace Craig, when supplemented by the studies of my colleague Professor R. B. Perry looking toward a behavioristic view of purpose, seem to me to leave the physiological view of instinctive behavior in a hopeful condition.[4]

Craig defines appetite (or as he now prefers to say, 'appetence') as a state of agitation which continues as

[4] Wallace Craig, Appetites and aversions as constituents of instincts, *Biological Bulletin*, February, 1918.

R. B. Perry, Purpose as tendency and adaptation, *Philosophical Review*, September, 1917; A behavioristic view of purpose, *The Journal of Philosophy*, Feb. 17, 1921.

long as a certain stimulus is absent; aversion as a state of agitation which continues as long as a certain stimulus is present. In the case of the appetite, the agitation is adapted to set in motion 'seeking behavior' which tends to lead the animal, under ordinary circumstances, to the appeted stimulus, whereupon the reaction appropriate to that stimulus follows, and the organism returns to a state of comparative repose or equilibrium. Meanwhile, the channels which that stimulus is to set into action are in a curious condition, a condition different both from activity and from inactivity, and which can best be designated, perhaps, by the word 'readiness.' It is in this 'readiness' that we may now, according to Professor Perry's analysis, find the physiological secret of 'guidance.'

15. Readiness is evidently a present condition, if it is anything at all: and yet it refers definitely to a future contingency. To be thirsty is to be at the present time in a condition such that the sight of a vessel with the proper liquid in it will set off appropriate seizing, lifting, and drinking reactions.

This present condition involves a certain muscular set as well as a certain set in the nervous tissues. Offer some one a cork ball painted like a cannon ball, and observe what is involved in his 'readiness' to lift a heavy weight. So far as the nervous condition is concerned, the readiness may be conceived to involve a lowered synaptic resistance, and an incipient innervation of a group of reflexes, of which the 'consummatory reaction' is the last in order.

This 'last in order'—in the above case, the drinking

reaction—is *now* last in some spatial order, as it will be the remotest in temporal order,—much as the batter now last in a series of batters sitting in a row will be the latest to come to bat, or as the ball now in the bottom of a Roman candle will be the latest in time to emerge.

But if the readiness of this final member is the *cause* of the readiness of the preceding members of the series, there is a physiological meaning for the relation expressed by saying that these preceding members exist 'for the sake of' that final event. And this final event, or rather the readiness of its channels, may in turn be said to 'select' the activities which lead up to it.

And if one of the selected preliminary operations proves unavailable when the time comes, the same mechanism will be capable of selecting a substitute. If the readiness to drink spreads into adjoining channels until it takes the mental form of a plan for getting a drink and then an actual beginning of operations upon the plan, the failure of any part of the plan, as through a missing cup, will simply divert into other channels the readiness which, so to speak, *radiates from the channels of the consummatory reaction*. This peculiar disturbance tends to affect in some degree all channels which in the (generalized) experience of the animal have led up to the final event; and if one of them is stopped, others become more ready, until one of them supplies the bridge between the existing situation and the appeted end.[5]

---

[5] This conception of multiple readiness is used to explain another type of selection by Joseph Peterson. ''Completeness of Response as an Explanation Principle in Learning,'' *Psychological Review*, 1916, 153-162.

In all this, there is no pretence that the mechanism of end-seeking or of selecting is actually understood: we merely suggest that there are prospects, and that it is too early to say *a priori* that the phenomena of guidance can have no physiological expression.

16. The second barrier to physiological explanations of behavior is found by McDougall in the fact that many responses—and the most important ones—are responses not to sense stimuli, but to meanings. Let me recall two or three of McDougall's illustrations of this difficulty.

First, the telegram illustration. Compare two telegrams,—Our son is dead,—Your son is dead. Slight difference of sense-stimulus; enormous difference of response. The response is not to the sense-stimulus, but to its 'meaning.'

Second, curiosity in presence of the novel. Curiosity has various other possible occasions, and novelty various other possible results: but let it be admitted that novelty has a tendency in growing human organisms to excite the behavior characteristic of curiosity. The logical consequences of such an admission are highly interesting. Assume that a stimulus may be defined as a sensation or set of sensations which will set off a given reaction *each time it recurs.* That which is novel or strange is defined as that which has not previously occurred, and which, when it occurs again, will no longer be novel. If novelty, then, is a stimulus to any instinct, it is a stimulus which *negates the very definition of a stimulus* above given. The recurrence of novelty contradicts the recurrence of sensation-groups. Further, the novel is relative to the experience of the individual: that which is strange to A is not strange to B. Hence there can be no set of sense-stimuli which can be universally counted upon to arouse curiosity. Novelty is uniform only as a meaning, never as an object.

Such instances (and we may recall also the crying reaction above mentioned) put beyond question the proposition that what occasions the reaction is, in a large part of behavior, no assignable set of sensations, but a meaning.[6] Indeed, the case for response to meaning is so clear, when stated, that Schneider's now somewhat ancient classification of impulses into sensation-impulses, perception-impulses, and idea-impulses, seems to have been accepted by William James without hesitation:

> To crouch from cold is a sensation-impulse; to turn and follow, if we see people running one way, is a perception impulse; to cast about for cover, if it begins to blow and rain, is an imagination impulse.[7]

17. But does the fact that idea-impulses exist prove that in such cases the event is not physiological? Not unless we commit ourselves to the view that having an idea or a meaning is a mental fact to which no event in the brain corresponds. But surely it would be at least as difficult to prove that there is no brain event corresponding to meaning as to prove that there is no brain

[6] 'Meaning' is here to be understood in the sense of the general idea, not in the sense of simple reference from particular to particular, as occurs in any case of conditioned reflex or other forms of the transfer of stimulus through learning.

[7] *Psychology*, II, p. 385.

event corresponding to guidance. Admitting to the full that "meaning is the essential link in each case between the series of physical impressions and the series of physical effects"—and I believe this to be a true and important observation—admitting that in the case of the crying reaction, "the only invariable antecedent of the expression of distress seems to be disagreeable feeling,"[8] is it not contrary to all probabilities to suppose that such a meaning as a 'disagreeable feeling' is not well represented in a complex of physiological states? It is not necessary that the stimulus should be limited to congeries of sensations in order that it may be physiological. I am obliged to judge, therefore, that upon scrutiny this second barrier likewise disappears.

18. We see no reason, then, to set limits to the possible progress of physiological explanations of instinct, —always with the usual understanding that no such explanations presume to identity with the thing explained, still less to displace it. McDougall is, in fact, more concerned to maintain the positive doctrine that instinct is conative in character than the negative thesis that it is incapable of physiological explanation. He has himself suggested a possible explanation in terms of energy.[9]

But we must here point out that when we save the day for the physiological explanation of idea-impulses, or responses to meaning, by insisting that there may be a physiological basis for meaning in some central process characteristically different from sensation-

[8] *Body and Mind*, p. 266.
[9] *American Journal of Insanity*, 1913, p. 866.

process, we involve the physiologist in a serious admission as to the psychological value of his explanations, and hence of his entire conception of instinct.

For the situation we have reached is this. Either the physiologist must admit that there may be centrally initiated reactions (corresponding to the responses to meaning) or he must abandon his case. But if he admits such centrally initiated responses, he admits at the same time that our knowledge of the physiology must be derived primarily from our introspective knowledge of the corresponding experience, not our knowledge of the experience from the corresponding physiology. He hands over the conception of instinct, at the point of its most important development, to the student of the mind on its own ground. Certain consequences of this admission we have to trace in our final section.

III

19. The conclusion we have so far reached may be stated summarily as follows: We can save the possibility of a physiological explanation of instinct, but at the cost of much of its usefulness.

In the phenomena of 'guidance' and 'response to meaning' there is no demonstrably impassable barrier to the physiological theory of behavior. But neither of these phenomena will be made a whit clearer by the discovery that a mechanical process can be imagined which might run along with them. Here it can hardly be said that the explanation helps to understand the event: it is rather the event that sets the pace for a limping and highly speculative power of explanation.

The possibility of extending the behavioristic picture of instinct into these regions is highly important for the general theory of the relation of body and mind: but for actual investigation, that picture is useful only where we can identify in physical terms the stimulus or initial situation and the response. Where either stimulus, or response, or final situation must be identified with hypothetical conditions of indemonstrable processes in accessible nervous centers, any advance of knowledge must be gained from other sources—presumably from introspection—and our conception of instinct will perforce take on a mental ingredient.

Let me now make this general conclusion more concrete by pointing out how various further facts about instinct likewise carry us into this region of central factors. These facts concern chiefly the ways in which our instincts are connected with one another,—matters of great difficulty, but of the first importance and of endless interest. My contention will be that the empirical facts cannot be brought into their rightful order without an appeal to introspection.

20. Consider first a group of facts which we might label *the instinctive regulation of instinct*.

Our instincts do not simply 'go off' like a piece of fireworks when the fuse is lighted: they are subject to certain adjustments in their working,—adjustments which are so universal and typical that they are themselves usually regarded as instinctive, and might be called instincts of the second order, or reflexive instincts.

Play is an excellent example. Play would perhaps not exist unless there were more primitive instincts needing preliminary exercise, and showing a budding readiness before their day of maturity. Among the stimuli of play, then, we must reckon this 'readiness,'— a central condition. And all instincts which take part in play are kept under the constant control of meanings which can only be referred to central processes,— the make-believe or feigning idea, for example. In feigning, the normal stimulus of an instinct may be absent, and some substituted sense-object may assume that character, as when in bayonet practice a soldier sets up an excelsior dummy and imputes to it the character of enemy-ergo-stimulus-to-pugnacity; or the veritable stimulus may be present and the course of the reaction may be held in check by the feigning attitude. This is especially the case in the feigned hostilities of social games.

Analogous to this instinctive control of instinct in play—and often fusing with it—is control of instinct by *social dispositions*. Craig has observed a characteristic restraint of pugnacity in the domestic quarrels of pigeons:

The male is always restrained in his attacks upon his mate. Indeed, the male shows restraint even when quarreling with neighbors outside his own family: for if they are birds with which he is familiar, he fights them with less fury than he would show to an utter stranger. Many other examples could be given of what I must call the pigeon's sense of rights and duties.[10]

10 *American Journal of Sociology*, July, 1908, p. 98.

One of the most striking of these instinctive regulators of instinct, however, is *pugnacity* itself, which in the above instances was a regulated reaction, not a regulator. For as McDougall has excellently pointed out, pugnacity is excited by a hindrance to the operation of other instincts, notably of acquisition and of sex; and its function seems to be that of bringing an access of energy to their pursuit.

In discussing 'guidance' we have already noted that an impeded nervous current has resources for finding some substitute path, or even for adopting some alternative object of appetence. But pugnacious behavior is marked by the rejection of these outlets: it insists on its object and on its path, and bends its effort to the removal of the obstacle or the competitor. What could be the physiological sign for preferring the pugnacious resource to either of the others?

21. The differentia of the pugnacity-arousing situation must lie in something corresponding to an unusual mental reluctance to give up this particular object of appetence, or this path, for some other object or path, together with a recognition of possible *removableness* in the obstacle or competitor. It seems to be a function, in part, of the energy of appetence; as if the circumstance of choosing a particular object of pursuit and of beginning that pursuit had made the value of that object more imperative, sometimes carrying the appetence over a threshold beyond which the resource of substitution in case of check is no longer admissible. Beyond this threshold, the determination of energy is

toward a subordinate or auxiliary appetence, that of removing the obstacle.

But the pugnacity-differentia is also a function of the presumptive removableness of the obstacle, as may be seen by noting the relation of pugnacity to two other of these instinctive regulators of instinct,—namely, *fear* and *curiosity.*

The place of the instinct of fear (or of flight with emotion of fear) is a moot point among psychologists; with a strong tendency to deny the existence of a single instinct of fear, and to refer the various responses commonly included under that head to a number of different 'fears.' It must be said, however, that the search for a common element among these different fears has not been prosecuted with especial vigor, partly because physiology has no clear way of dealing with logically common elements, and partly because the variety of fear-provoking situations is so great, varying all the way from the specific stimuli of sudden loud noises, threatening animal expressions, etc., to certain states of imagination induced by solitude, darkness, and the uncanny generally.

But there seems to be a key to all this variety when we consider the very close physiological kinship between pugnacity and fear, which suggests that if pugnacity regulates other instincts, fear may furnish a complementary regulation. With this in mind, we discover that most of the fear-provoking situations are fairly described as *situations in which our primary instincts cannot act,* or do not fit us for acting. We have no instinctive equipment enabling us to live in water,

or abysses of air: in darkness, instinctive adjustments
are largely hindered, especially adjustments to sudden
and stealthy movements, etc. All fear is, in this sense,
a reaction to the uncanny. And fear, in this common
character, is an instinctive disposition tending to remove the organism from environments in which other
instincts cannot act to an environment in which they
can act.

Pugnacity and fear, then, both respond to the thwarting of instinct; but pugnacity responds to a type of
thwarting which is remediable (typically due to a competitor, hence to a kindred and commensurable force),
while fear responds to a type of thwarting which is
irremediable.

Both of these reactions in their typical forms are
vigorous, and imply cognitive *certainty* regarding both
the unpropitiousness of the environment and the question of its remediableness. But both, again, shade into
a common region of uncertainty, in which the animal
halts between fear and fight. In this case, and in the
similar hesitation whether to treat the environment
as propitious or as unpropitious there comes into play,
in the more highly developed organisms, a further
regulatory instinct,—*curiosity.*

During growth, curiosity has a slightly different
regulatory rôle. At this time curiosity changes its direction as the major instincts develop: thus, when a boy's
constructive disposition begins to appear, a curious
interest in analysis, dissection, etc., accompanies it.
That same condition of *incipient readiness* which
stimulates play seems to stimulate also a curiosity to

which play itself lends effective aid. One might conceive these incipient instincts as chronically hesitant in the human being, qualified as he is by the very nonfixity of his instincts to live in an environment which changes from generation to generation, and for the same reason required to establish his own specifications of stimulus and response: curiosity has obvious uses in the growing stage of such a creature. But it remains as an auxiliary to all instincts, especially to such pairs of instincts as branch out in opposite directions from a common situation, as do fear and pugnacity, and so give rise to recurrent passes of uncertainty.

Thus, the primary instincts are provided with a remarkable structure of instinctive regulation, in which the stimuli for the instincts of the second order, the regulators, are *finely differentiated conditions of the central nervous current*. Some of these secondary instincts, perhaps all of them, have also specific sense-stimuli of their own; but in human psychology, their most important function is in this subtle regulation of other instincts, which we can only explain by appealing to central stimuli.

22. Consider, secondly, the relation between general instinctive tendencies and specific mechanisms. As we have just noted in the case of fear, the physiologically verifiable sequences are relatively specific, and appear as various fears rather than as a single instinct. Until it is seen that central conditions may act as stimuli, physiologists are reluctant to recognize a biological fact corresponding to the logical

common character of different fears. And the same is true of all those general tendencies which we saw as making up the broad round of life.[11]

But since the conception of appetence has given us a physiological picture of the subordination of means to end, and the conception of a stimulus has widened beyond the sense-group order to include central processes, such as might correspond to highly general ideas, there can be no reason for further hesitation to recognize the broad categories as genuinely instinctive,—if there is sufficient reason *for* doing so.

That there is sufficient reason for recognizing many of these general instincts I have already indicated in my book on *Human Nature and Its Remaking* (see especially the tabular 'Survey,' p. 56); though I found myself at that time (1918) in much doubt about several of these categories, and printed a question mark after them. This was true particularly of two very general instincts which I then called the instinct to physical activity and to physical inactivity. These would correspond roughly to the two types of reaction, expansive and contractive, from which Schneider in his genetic speculations conceived the

---

[11] It is to be noted that the most specific units of behavior, such as the infant's grasping reaction, are logically general in the sense that *any* object of the class defined by the stimulus-description will set them off. The difference between grasping and hunting or food-getting, between vocalization and sociability, etc., is not that the former is particular and the latter general, but that the latter (food-getting) unifies into one sequence a variety of units of behavior, subordinating these units both as means to an end and as the less general to the more general. This logical and teleological integration of behavior elements must certainly not be forthwith assumed to exist as a physiological integration.

rest to be derived. But I was inclined to regard them as genuine biological entities rather because there appeared to be definite units of behavior belonging to each:—yawning, stretching, rubbing eyes, listening, stalking, as fragments of a process of passing from rest to action,—and corresponding postures and actions belonging to the transition from action to repose, sleep, and even death.

Since that time my attention has been called to certain studies of Szymanski[12] describing readiness, alertness, rest, sleep, etc., as variations of attention: and attention in turn as a setting of the organism in respect to the reception of stimuli. This description of attention would make it a process regulative of instinct, but not itself an instinctive process. Szymanski proceeds, however, to distinguish positive and negative attention, sleep being a negative state of attention; and to point out that in the sleeping attitude each species protects its most important sense-organ,—insects, for instance, protecting their antennæ. Adjustments of this sort appear to be as definitely instinctive as any of the more noted units of behavior and the appetence toward rest or action is certainly as definite as the appetence of hunger: I am inclined, therefore, to regard these two tendencies as instincts highly general, and also reflexive, as having functions regulative of other instincts.

And while it must be, in each case, a question of fact

[12] Published in Pflüger's *Archiv*, 1918, under the title "Allgemeine Betrachtungen über das Verhalten der Tiere. (1) Körperstellungen als Ausdruck innerer Zustände der Tiere." Reviewed in *Psychological Bulletin*, June, 1920.

which of our general categories are merely logical clas-
sifications and which are actual dispositions, the case
in principle for the reality of the general instincts
seems to me made out.

23. But thirdly, the same conditions which lead us
to recognize the integration of units of behavior under
various general instincts will lead us to recognize a
further integration which (I will not say unifies, but)
tends to unify the entire life of instinct.

Even from the view of the most mechanical conception of instinct, the simple enumeration of instincts in
a list never tells the whole truth about them. Apart from
the integrations and regulatory devices above discussed, it is a commonplace that in instinctive behavior
an organism typically acts as a whole; and this means,
physiologically, that the highest centers at any moment
active are involved in the circuit of the instinctive process. In mature animals, the processes in these centers
have achieved a momentum of their own, a trend of
attention, so that the stimulus for any instinct has a
certain resistance to overcome before it can gain right
of way: the number of stimuli that secure no hearing
at all is indefinitely greater than the number that gain
the saddle. In the mature human being, this trend of
attention has become a *dominant appetence,* exercising
functions of 'selection' and 'consent' upon candidate-
stimuli in much the same way as we found particular
appetences exercising 'guidance.' This dominant appetence is an essential part of what is termed 'will':
and conversely, wherever it is pertinent to use the term
'will,' there the instinctive behavior of the animal is

subject throughout to the guidance of a dominant appetence, which resembles a *most general instinct,*—the persistent but unspecified craving, or ambition, or wish of the entire creature.

24. But what is the object of this elusive appetence or craving which strives toward a rough unity of instinct, and seems to gather definiteness and assurance with evolution and with individual growth? Can physiology give us instruction on this point?

We should be able to learn something about it from current theories of the *physiological basis of pleasure.* For quite apart from hedonistic assumptions, the connection between pleasure and successful instinct process is certainly close; and any one who would choose the term 'value' as a name for the common object of instinct on its mental side would be inclined to agree that the object of any most general instinct or appetence would be a most general value, qualitatively akin to pleasure.

Now it certainly cannot be said that there is any school-doctrine among behaviorists about the nature of pleasure. But we occasionally find it stated, and more often assumed, that a certain ease, or fluency, or facility of response is pleasurable, or is pleasure itself,—a behavioristic version of Aristotle's observation. "Pleasure," says Peterson in the monograph above referred to, "is a subjective indication that the response is along the line of least resistance." Pleasure is not an agent; it does nothing; it does not 'stamp in' the successful reaction after a series of unsuccessful trials: pleasure is simply the character or form of the successful act itself. A tendency toward the pleasurable would be a tendency toward a certain *mode of nervous process* in the centers, a particularly fluent or frictionless operation of the mechanism.

Now, there is nothing physiologically improbable in the view that nervous processes show a definite disposition to assume a specific form as the most favorable form for their action: in view of the physical analogies of stream-flow, etc., it would be rather physically improbable that there should *not* be a disposition of that sort. It is clear, however, that the idea of a disposition which is due to the *nature of the nervous process itself,* and not to any canalizing of the path through which it must pass, threatens to provoke some radical change in our view of mental dispositions, and so of instinct. Just this is implied in the theory of pleasure here mentioned. A similar view is implied in Professor Woodworth's contention that all mechanisms have their own drive.

For while Woodworth seems to hold that the driving power lies in some peculiar concatenation of nervous elements which deserve the name of mechanisms, the real force of his argument appears to be that 'drive' is a character of the nervous excitation itself wherever found (which would certainly follow from the proposition that the nervous process is a flow of energy of some sort); and that mechanisms merely aid this excitation to take on certain auspicious forms rather than others.

This may be shown to advantage by considering the criticism which McDougall has made of Woodworth's theory in a recent issue of *Mind*.[13] It would follow from Woodworth's view that there could be a love of music, apart from any instinct for music, if there were mechanisms congenital or acquired favoring skill in music. McDougall is inclined to deny to the interest in music any such independent status, referring it rather to affiliations with the instinct-drives, with "ambition, vanity, the desire to excel, emulation, the desire to please parents or teachers, the desire to understand, the desire to fit themselves for a career, the desire to overcome difficulties, the vague desire to give expression to various emotions." He further points out that a talent for music is no single thing, but highly composite: "it implies superiority in such functions as tone-discrimination, appreciation of rhythm, of time, of tone-relations. . . . But can we suppose that such a function as tone-discrimination depends on a 'mechanism' that has an intrinsic drive? Do we ever find any one absorbed in the exercise of such a function for its own sake?" The questions are absolutely pertinent: the answers, I believe, can be made definite.

We certainly do find persons absorbed in such functions as tone-discrimination, for their own sake. Has McDougall forgotten those who choose to be piano-tuners? Certainly, there are few sources of enjoyment more general in the human family than this of making discriminations,—as also of drawing analogies, or applying general ideas and names to particular cases. But "can we suppose that such functions depend on

13 Vol. xxix, N. S., No. 115, pp. 278 ff.

mechanisms having their intrinsic drives?'' That is the damaging question for Woodworth's theory, and it is quite as damaging for McDougall's view: for it is equally hard to think that such functions and satisfactions depend on the instincts which McDougall has in mind.

Consider, for instance, that ''appreciation of rhythm'' which according to McDougall forms part of the talent for music. This is an appreciation, or value, so general in the human species as to lead some writers to ascribe it to a special instinct. But it is certainly not an instinct of the stimulus-response pattern; and it is not a disposition that can boast of extended animal ancestry. Studies of rhythmic behavior in animals render it doubtful whether any animal but man enjoys rhythm. The commonly observed rhythms in animal activity, as the swinging of birds on perches, the chirping of crickets, synchronous flapping of wings in flight in flocks, are more probably explained on other grounds.[14] And the presumption thus raised against the view that this interest in man can be referred to an inherited mechanism is strengthened by the fact that the interest seems rather waxing than waning in the race. But the facts fall naturally into place if we assume that the mode of central nervous action which accompanies the observing or executing of rhythm is *intrinsically satisfying*. If this value is to be referred to an instinct, it must be to a type of instinct whose stimulus and goal are alike central, one which would have

[14] W. Craig, On the ability of animals to keep time with an external rhythm, *Journal of Animal Behavior*, Nov.-Dec., 1917.

to be described in terms of an unknown (but presumably propitious) type of nervous process.

And the same, I believe, would prove to be true of the other interests included in the 'talent for music,' as for most of the characteristic human interests. It will be found, I venture to predict, that Woodworth is right in dissociating their 'drive' from any primitive instincts, and that McDougall is equally right in his distrust of 'mechanisms' with intrinsic drives of their own. As physiological psychology reaches clearness in its accounts of the basis of valuation, it will turn its attention away from the now prevalent pictures of paths, synapses, connections, etc., toward pictures of the different forms which the nervous current is capable of assuming. The most general appetence of the human being will appear as a disposition toward some special mode or form of the central flow.

25. But if this is the case, it may also be predicted that for our chief data regarding this region of instinct, and regarding the most important relations among the instincts, both we and physiological psychology itself will have to depend on introspection. Especially the great business of unifying the instincts into a more or less serviceable will requires the achievement of a dominant value-trend which we shall always understand better from the way it appears in consciousness than from the way in which physiology may explain it. The theory of values can never be made a corollary of the theory of instincts.

On the contrary: the theory of instincts cannot be finished until it becomes, in its major part, a corollary of the theory of values. In dealing with the unity and connections of instincts, the theory of instinct must change its base.

For the unity of instinct is primarily a condition of selfhood. Our chief item of certainty on this subject is that a man is not in a fully human position toward his own conduct until he is prepared to justify what he does. To justify what he does means to give a 'reason' for it: and this means, to refer it to a value. But to refer conduct to value—not alone in case of sporadic dashes for this and that good, but also in cases of conflicting impulses and of deliberate plans and policies— requires a standard of value, single, and more stable than the competing impulses themselves.

I certainly do not say that any one achieves conscious possession of a single and changeless value-standard. But I do say that human life implies growth in that direction, through the repeated process of referring particular conflicts to 'reasonable' solutions. A large part of life is left unrationalized by the avoidance of conflict and the evasion of thought: the day's program allows inconsistent goods to be pursued at different times, and the life of instinct remains pluralistic and experimental,—fortunately so. But however we evade or distrust the exercise of that most dreaded effort we call reason, there is no pair of goods which we would not submit to the comparing process if we had to. And so we live in partial pluralism, but on the assumption of a *discoverable unity* of all values, and so of all instincts. And a discoverable unity is, of course, an actual unity, though partly subconscious.

It is not, however, unrecognizable; and if some philosopher undertakes to give it a name, we can reasonably discuss whether the name is a fit one: for that unity itself exists nowhere if not as a working-fact in our own active experience. If Schopenhauer calls it the will to live, or Nietzsche the will to power, or Freud one kind of libido and Jung another kind, we can estimate the justice and adequacy of those descriptions. For my own part, I believe that no description will be found wholly satisfactory. But I have elsewhere given my reasons for preferring 'the will to power' to either of the others mentioned. It is a phase that has possibilities beyond those that Nietzsche found in it. There is a clearly ascertainable truth in the statements that in all our major instincts we show phases of a will to mastery, —in pugnacity, in curiosity, in sociability in all its forms—self-assertion, self-abasement, sex-love itself, —even in fear. And so far as life is occupied in finding out what it is that we want, that process may be described as a process of interpreting this will to power that is in us, getting rid of its crudity and barbarism, putting its competitive and physical elements into their place. This phrase tells enough truth about the nature of the unity of instinct to make it useful in the present stage of theory.

26. Admitting the 'will to power,' then, as a rough description for the common and uniting element of instinct,—always ready to yield to a better, we may set up a working definition of instinct for human psychology in some such terms as these:

An instinct is any specific form of the will-to-power

which reaches its end by the use of innate motor mechanisms, common to the species.

This is a hybrid definition. It imports elements of physiology to discriminate entities within the field of consciousness. It has that type of hybridism which distresses the radical behaviorist beyond measure. It falls fairly within the field of Perry's remark that "wherever (introspective) accounts of the motor-affective life preserve anything distinctive and peculiar, they incorporate something of the movement and action of the physical organism."[15]

But to this remark, which is intended to be critical, our first reply is a challenge to avoid hybridism and keep usefulness in your conception if you can. Our entire discussion has been an argument to the effect that this cannot be done by the behaviorist any more than by the introspectionist.

Secondly, however, the hybridism which we adopt if we begin with consciousness is only apparent, whereas the hybridism to which we are forced if we begin with physiology is both real and misleading.

In spite of all efforts at theoretical purism, the behaviorist is obliged to patch up the elements of his mechanisms with mental cohesives. Future reference, selection, memory, hesitation, effort, are never successfully reduced to—though they may be symbolized by—the characteristics of nervous interplay with the world.

But if we begin with conscious experience, the facts of physiology are not ultimately alien entities: on

15 *The Journal of Philosophy*, Feb. 17, 1921, p. 89.

purely mental grounds we should require the experience of nature, and all the bodily machinery that action
within a world of nature signifies. In other words, we
can derive the whole set of behavior phenomena in
principle from the demands of consciousness: but we
cannot in turn derive the fact, nor the need, of conscious
life from the principles of the bodily organism and its
world.

We have, then, in our conception of instinct to make
a choice between two positions, one of which is consistent in the midst of its apparent hybridism, the other
of which is either in the presence of an ultimate and
confessed mystery or else presents us with a helpless
and unfinishable torso of a man.

APPENDIX II

THE SOURCE OF OBLIGATION

IN our account of sin there is a missing element. It is the missing element, but the implied element, in all psychology, namely, the outer world. We have described the moral undertaking as a struggle within self-consciousness, the effort of a self to pull itself together, as it were, from the midst of a mass of would-be independent impulses,—to find its own meaning and to make every instinct share in that meaning. Sin we described simply as the deliberate suppression of meaning, the treason of self-consciousness to its own most vital effort. In all this the outer world has been in abeyance; but it has not been forgotten. An "impulse" is but an abbreviated name for an "impulse to this or that action, and for the sake of this or that objective good." All psychological terms are just such abbreviations, naming a relation to reality from the inner end. Our term, the will to power, carries the external reference on its face. And so, while we have spoken of obligation as the debt of a partial impulse to a total will, a relation wholly within the mind, we have not been unmindful of the corresponding relation in the world of objects, that between a partial good and a total good.

But if this total good, the object of my total will, is thought of simply as my own good, we have not

reached the center of the idea of 'obligation.' Obligation descends upon me from a region beyond anything
that I can call mine; it has its source in the interest
of some being other than myself in my conduct. My
duty is the inner angle of that other being's right. The
nature of sin may be understood on the ground of psychology, but the degree of importance attached to sin
and righteousness cannot be understood without a
study of the external source of obligation.

I

The most natural, and popular, view of the case is
that I owe obligation primarily to my neighbor: any
and every other man is the repository of some right in
relation to me. The essence of wrong is the disregard
of these rights; and sin, on its practical side, is therefore simply selfishness. Or if 'selfishness' is too limited
a term—too *naïve* possibly, or merely indulgent or
passive—then join with it 'self-will,' which may be as
vigorous and determined as you please. Sin is wilful,
unfriendly, or unsocial conduct.

This view covers most of the ground, if we can think
of the moral aspect of behavior in terms of areas. Most
sins are unsocial acts. In most cases, the wider thought-
system which I ought to consider is one which takes in
more of the minds of other persons. This is a good rule
of thumb, especially for the public phases of moral
questions. But our question is not whether most sinful
acts are unsocial acts: it is whether any act is sinful
because it is unsocial or unneighborly.

If you define a world with two wills in it, and with an insufficient supply of goods and consequent unsatisfied wants, it is not obvious that either will ought to give way to the other, or that each should do so. So long as they are two wills, related in such wise that the altruism of one is the egoism of the other, the idea of obligation cannot be extracted from the situation. I cannot find it in the simple fact of my neighbor's existence nor of his want.

Nor am I convinced, though I may be overawed, when you multiply and organize and perpetuate this needy neighbor, and call it society, or the State. Professor E. A. Ross represents a large body of opinion when he makes the egoism of society the proper object of my altruism and self-sacrifice.[1] But who is this social ego, that I should thus indulge it? I am inclined by many natural impulses to accept suggestions from a social group and to deal sympathetically with its members; but this is something short of accepting the group as a final authority for my deference. The moral quality of the behavior of Socrates or of John Brown is not decided by the circumstance that it both antagonized and

[1] *Social Control*, p. 67. Professor Ross would scorn the idea that he has dealings with the absolute; yet I must accuse him of setting up an absolute in the form of this social ego. And many others to-day who think that 'absolute' is a bad word, calling themselves pragmatists, and saying that right must be relative to the stage of social progress and to the social good at any stage, are in the same position. For whatever thing is stated as the thing to which other things are relative, is by definition their absolute. The pragmatic moralists, for the most part, have simply chosen a social absolute instead of some other. Their question should be not whether there is an absolute in morals, but whether they have the right one.

tended to dissolve the society in which it appeared. If you answer, in view of these examples, that it is not what men actually want, but what they rightfully want, that is authoritative over me, you abandon the case. If another mind, single or collective, is a source of obligation only when it desires what it ought to desire, the implication is that I have an 'ought' only when the other mind has an 'ought,' and we are as far from the source of obligation as before.

This is not a mere logical quibble: like all good logic, it is but the briefest expression of what experience, at great length, teaches. That I have an 'ought' to another only when the other has an 'ought' also, is quite plainly a result of experience. We do not find ourselves moved by respect toward others on the ground of their existence, their force or their prowess, but only as they themselves show respect to something beyond. Need itself would not move us if need were arrogant rather than earnest. It is pure futility to attempt deriving the sentiment of reverence from any mixture of fear, awe, self-abnegation, etc.:[2] reverence goes to the reverent, and to no others. This is the main part of the answer to the occasional anxious question, What can be done for the sobering of an irreverent younger generation?: the secular-minded person, society, State, receives and deserves slight deference; it is man at worship who alone becomes worshipful, and no pedagogical finesse can outleap this principle. Whenever men defer to each other, admit duties to the other's

2 McDougall, *Social Psychology*, p. 132.

rights, it will be found that there is a twofold deference:
each is deferring to a third entity, dimly discerned as
a mutual object of respect, and not to the other as individual. Is it not in some such relatively abstract *third*
that we find the real source of obligation? Such is the
view of Kant, who defines right not in terms of society,
but in terms of a *law*, which is over all alike.

II

In setting up a *law* as the supreme object of respect,
Kant seems almost to abandon the outer world and to
leave the individual alone once more with the workings
of his own reason. This law is occupied entirely with
what we have called the "meaning" of an action. Every
decision, thinks Kant, is made upon some general principle or "maxim": this is my reason, or excuse, for
the act,—it is what the act means to me. The requirement of duty is simply that I shall be willing to stand by
these meanings, when I think of them as being universally adopted. "Admit into your conduct only such
meaning as you would willingly see universal"—such
is the essence of Kant's law.

To apply this law, I must use both imagination and
logic. I must imagine my motive made universal; I must
conceive every act as conveying a tacit recommendation
of its 'maxim' for general use: and I must consider
whether, in all logic, I can stand by it. Like a marksman,
the moral being has a 'picture' to which it is imperative
he should adjust his sight,—that of perfect consistency
of policy throughout a rational universe. When his act

presents him this picture, he may release it,—it is right. This picture, and nothing more concrete, is the object of his obligation.

One must use imagination, I say, to apply Kant's law, yet it would be highly unjust to represent this law as a purely imaginary object of devotion. The tendency of our maxims, or meanings, to propagate themselves is real enough. Acts, we say, tend to establish habits,—a very crude bit of psycho-physics and only half true. For no one can tell from the mechanics of an act *what* habit it tends to establish. I give a penny to a beggar: what habit does this leave behind? If I give it from pity, one habit; if for display, another habit; if for getting rid of the beggar, a third. Everything depends on the meaning: it is this alone that universalizes itself. Self-propagation of maxims both within and without an individual life is no mere fancy; and sin, from Kant's point of view, appears as the refusal to accept the very real legislative responsibility of an act for its maxim.

It must be admitted, too, that Kant's theory agrees closely with moral experience. When men refrain from breaches of the peace, or of contract, is it not because they perceive quite beyond any actual consequences that that kind of principle will not do for general use? And if they go out of their way for mutual aid, or for the service of a nation, is there not, behind the personal or patriotic sympathies invoked, a sense that the principle of refusal means ruin to a certain spiritual structure which has been an object of unspoken faith? What one instinctively holds to, and tries to preserve, is not

'society,' as an eating and breeding entity (otherwise
our minds would be attuned as pragmatically as our
language often sounds); it is the world as a place of
consistent, thoughtful meanings, the home of universal
law.

The error of Kant's idea is not that his law is too
formal and empty, nor that it is too vigorous and un-
bending. These two criticisms may be left to cancel one
another; for a law so abstract as to command nothing
at all can hardly be so rigid as to allow no room for
individuality and growth. Kant's law stands near to
that critical point which a perfect test of right and
wrong must hold: it is abstract enough to free the mind
from all tyranny of concrete absolutes (as the ten com-
mandments); it is not so abstract as to be devoid of
meaning.

The trouble with the Kantian theory is that the law
in question is just a test or *criterion* of right and
wrong; it is not itself the source of obligation. A *criterion* must be abstract—it would be absurd to criticise a thermometer as a test of fever because a thermometer is not itself a temperature. But no abstraction
can be a source of obligation. Kant's notable utterance
of reverence for the moral law involves attributing to
that law a substantial reality, like that of the "starry
heavens," and more so. It is only because the law was
to Kant the point of contact between experience and a
world metaphysical, 'intelligible,' and total that it
could seem to command the allegiance of practical
reason.

III

The source of obligation must be something that unites the living reality of fellow men and society with the totality and finality of the Kantian law. If we have no conception at hand which promises at once to unite these characters, the schoolmen certainly had, and we may still learn something from them.

Thomas Aquinas was already familiar with the idea that the moral law should be followed for the sake of the moral law; and he had already pronounced this view, in so many words, to be unmoral.[3] For the law exists only for the sake of a goal or destiny of human life,—our real obligation is to that destiny.[4] We have a particular interest in the views of St. Thomas, since he has stated his idea of obligation in connection with a theory of instinct.

The lower animals, he thinks, are governed by instinct, and especially by a fundamental life-instinct which controls all lesser instincts. In man there is something which corresponds to this central life-instinct, indicating to him his destiny: it is his '*synderesis.*' It is defined as a desire or longing which presents to us our total possible good in the form of an anticipatory vision.[5] Its claim upon our duty lies in part in the fact that it presents to us our possible blessedness; it commands us to live according to reason, but that

---

[3] *Summa*, I, d. 1, q. 2, a. 1, ad. 3.

[4] *Summa*, I, 2, q. 71, a. 6, ad. 3.

[5] "Inchoatio boni"; in another phrase, "desiderium naturale, voluntas ut natura."

means to St. Thomas, using the behavior which reason shows as means to blessedness.

Sin, from this view, is a rejection of one's own blessedness; but it is sin because that rejection concerns another than ourselves, namely, the appointer of destiny, the real being. The interest of God in our realization of our destiny is not simply that of one who has devised that destiny; it is the interest of one who is to participate in it. For blessedness, according to Aquinas, is found in union with God: such union is at the same time a fulfilment of God's will and of our own.

I am not concerned here to discuss the accuracy of these metaphysical ideas: I only wish to point out that our moral experience gives much weight to this account of the source of obligation. Unless the universe has a central and unified life in which our destinies are involved, and which gives these destinies a higher importance than they can have for our own finite vision, the notion of obligation loses the degree of dignity which we, in fact, ascribe to it. When we speak of the rights of man and the duties of man, the respect we accord them is measured by our belief that they belong to man as a metaphysical entity, a ward of the universe. The work these "rights" have done in history may testify to the truth of this statement.

And our interest in our destiny is at the same time, as Aquinas says, an interest in a possible blessedness; though not simply in a far-off divine event. For the destiny of the human will is to co-operate, in some degree of present awareness, with the central power of the world; and so far to perceive in present expe-

rience the quality of "union with God." In their complete meaning, our human actions are not only law-
giving in an ideal world,—they are creative in an actual, but unfinished world. Acting as artists and origi-
nators, every deed may be more than a conformity to
a rule, or a subsumption under a preconceived good:
it may be also an invention, a new fact. It may assume
in its own degree a will to power which is not interpreted adequately as a suggesting of maxims for general use, but rather as a contribution through our
thought to the spiritual substance of the world. Thus
to conceive each deed is the best privilege of human
nature. Our obligation in its ultimate interpretation,
to achieve such blessedness. And from the same position we reach the completest expression of what we are
to understand by sin.

If right action is action so interpreted that I assume
the place of creator to my own destiny and that of
others, wrong action appears as a false assumption of
this same place. But the false claim to be doing the
work of a god in the world is precisely what the Greeks
called 'υβρις and the Romans *superba;* and we, with
hardly equivalent force, presumption. Inasmuch as it
is not usual for us to conceive our deeds consciously
sub specie æternitatis, at least not one by one, this may
appear as a somewhat imaginative extension of the
meaning of sin. Nevertheless, with the right of interpreting which we have no choice but to use, the ordinary
courage of men who daily face their own destiny as an
entire metaphysical fact involves just this will to stand
in loco Dei to the circumstances with which they deal

Inasmuch as they are human they, in turn, have no choice but to see things whole, and as nearly as possible as they are. What an act conveys in meaning is not the work of a special conscious judgment: it is, as we have said, the sense imposed upon it by its total context. And thus, whether we will or not, our acts have for us a metaphysical meaning. But there is this difference between the Greek conception and our own. To the Greeks the sin of arrogance, 'υβρις consisted in forgetting to think as mortals; and its punishment was like the punishment of Babel, a dizziness, bewilderment, madness, such as must come to those who are out of their own element. To us, sin consists equally in forgetting to think as gods. It was Aristotle who, in replying to the charge that philosophical thought was itself arrogant, uttered the proud word, "Let us live, then, as if divinity (immortality) were our share." We would add only: This is man's native element. It is his destiny so to live. His sin is to neglect that destiny—or to assume it unworthily.

We have here, too, perhaps the best illustration of the principle we have noted from time to time; that of the descriptive identity of sin and virtue. In the higher reaches of self-consciousness, the difficulty of decision often lies here. If any one assumes a position of moral leadership, and therefore of moral solitude, he cannot wholly avoid fearing his own audacity; hence the conflict which we know to have taken place in the minds of such men as Mazzini, Luther, Lincoln,—the conflict of determining the narrow margin between the true and the false presumption. The reported temptation of Jesus seems to be a symbolical account of an inner struggle such as could occur only to one who had gone far on the way to a great cast of cosmic boldness. To presume so much was to "make himself equal with God"; to presume less was to be false to his own genius.

INDEX

Absolute, 33, 313, 354, 374, 378, 391, 434.

Acquisition, instinct of, 67, 79, 119, 272.

Activity, general instinct to, 70 f., 468.

Admiration, 220.

Adolescence, 272 ff., 320, 321.

Æschylus, 291 f.

Æsthetic experience (see also Art), 66, 83, 217, 327, 329 f., 338, 377 f., 392.

After-image, mental, 184 f., 195, 199, 339.

Alternation, chs. XXXIV, XXXV, esp. p. 312, and pp. 353 f., 392 f.

Altruism, 113, 211, 213, 253 f., 481.

Ambition, ch. XLIII and pp. 167, 202, 302, 304, 345, 404, 414.

Anger (v. Pugnacity), 58, 59, 66, 141, 143, 442.

Animism, 268.

Anxiety-neurosis, 27, 165 f.

Appetence, Appetite, 29, 53, 56, 454.

A priori, 58, 328, 332, 338.

Aquinas, Thomas, 486 ff.

Aristotle, 111 f., 135, 163, 211, 212, 218, 256, 300, 308, 422, 489.

Art (v. Æsthetic experience), ch. XXXVIII, p. 339, and also pp. 5, 8, 97, 104, 132, 217, 256, 315, 354.

Asceticism (v. Saintly ideal), 241, 350, 352 ff., 379 ff.

Atonement, 405, 419, 438 f.

Augustine, 163, 357.

Authority (v. Recommenders), 121, 154 f., 220, 273.

Babbitt, I., 35 n.

Bagehot, W., 224 n., 337 n.

Balance of instincts, 65, 71, 207.

Beautiful, The, 343.

Behavior-ism, 50 f., 103, 365, 444, 447, 461.

Belief, 264.

Bergson, H., 7, 43, 63, 99 n., 193, 239 n., 342, 436, 452.

Blame (v. Justice), 164, 165 n.

Body and Mind, ch. XII, p. 102, and also p. 453.

Bohemia, 132 f., 263.

Bosanquet, B., 22.

Brahmanism, ch. XXXVII passim, and also pp. 356, 418 ff.

Buddha, Buddhism, 23, 98, 135, 357, 397 ff., 418 ff.

Burke, Edm., 34 f., 154, 209.

Cabot, R. C., 353 n.

Calvinism, 127.

Carpenter, J. E., 419 n.

Carver, T. N., 27 n.

Catholicism (v. Church), 402.

Causality, 182 ff.

Central instincts, ch. X, p. 80, and also pp. 66, 73, 91 f., 139, 466 ff.

Chadbourne, P. A., 63, 75.

Character, 125, 162, 172, 172 n., 347.

PRINTED IN THE UNITED STATES OF AMERICA